Stephen Bull

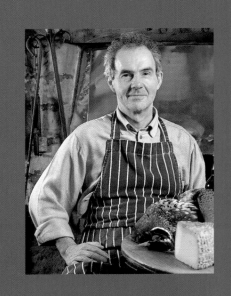

Classic Bull

An Accidental Restaurateur's Cookbook

MACMILLAN

First published 2001 by Macmillan
an imprint of Pan Macmillan Ltd
Pan Macmillan, 20 New Wharf Road, London N1 9RR
Basingstoke and Oxford
Associated companies throughout the world
www.panmacmillan.com

ISBN 0 333 76650 4

1 3 5 7 9 8 6 4 2

A CIP catalogue record for this book is available from
the British Library.

Printed and bound by New Interlitho, Spa, Milan

Contents

Foreword vi

Introduction 1

Sauces, Salsas, Dressings and Stocks 21

Cold Starters 41

Soups 57

Salads 69

Hot Starters 77

Chicken Livers 93

Fish 101

Meat 133

Vegetables 169

Puddings, Ice Creams and Cakes 181

Chocolate, Tarts and Fruit 193

To Start, Finish or Go With . . . 213

Recipe Index 224

General Index 232

Foreword

This is not a book designed for restaurant chefs, to act as a manual or to embellish coffee tables. There are recipes here, yes, but the book is also a distillation of my life as both a restaurant chef and a restaurant operator; one who has always remained fundamentally an amateur and who also – let's face it – has a bit of a love-hate relationship with the business. Still, there must have been something special to persuade me to leave the well-paid world of advertising and do something which couldn't be more different and which I knew nothing about.

The love part: I love the process of transforming inert raw materials into objects of desire and reward. I love the importunate nature of good food, the urgent demands it makes on both producer and consumer – the shine on the sauce that fades and dies so quickly, the leaves of a salad, the cells tight with water, that have to be dressed at the last minute, the soufflé that can't wait. I love the way the skill and imagination of great chefs can always extend the boundaries of the possible; I love the ready sacrifices more humble chefs (much maligned as they are) make in pursuit of an ideal even if imperfectly realized.

The hate part: hate is probably a bit strong, but I do resent the obstacles that have to be negotiated before an apparently simple aim – putting good food and wine before the public – can be realized. Producing restaurant meals is a bit like putting on a live TV show twice a day. Cues can't be missed or lines muffed, the cables all have to be hidden away, and there's no safety net – one mistake with a main course, or all the customers arriving at once can sabotage the best-drilled crew. Ever-increasing bureaucracy, the expensive support structures of consultants, contractors, solicitors, surveyors, engineers for this and that, the steady decay and occasional hostility of machines, all these go with the territory, but sometimes the wish surfaces that it were all a bit less complicated.

This book, I hope, offers glimpses into the restaurateur's life, which is trying, exhausting, ridiculous and farcical but also exhilarating, fun, and never, ever dull.

The recipe part of the book – the important bit – has been written for the home cook who knows the basics, likes to cook for the buzz of achievement but is also looking for simple, interesting, no-fuss dishes; who has a decent range of equipment (you'll need a food processor but not a mandoline), and limited time but can occasionally push the boat out; who has a budget to keep to and a store cupboard smaller than Selfridges' food hall. Some of the recipes have been with me a long time, some of them, the chocolate soufflés, for example, can't be bettered I think for their effort-flavour ratio; some of them I have brought out of the retirement that fashion has forced on them. I hope they give you the pleasure they give me.

Introduction

In Abergavenny, the small town on the Welsh border where I grew up, there were two places to buy home-made ice cream – Toni's Café and Barney's, which was a sweet shop. Toni's had one of those enormous chrome boilers which hissed and bellowed and eventually produced a cup of coffee the colour of a day-old corpse. Its ice cream was much better, pale yellow and creamy textured, but somehow it didn't have the hard, crystalline edge that Barney's pure white version produced. Barney's, too, had a little lacy room behind the shop where you could, if you were a grown up, take the weight off your feet after a hard morning's shopping (well, perhaps I exaggerate – this was Abergavenny, Mon. not Knightsbridge) and tuck into what rosy retrospection insists was the nonpareil of banana splits. Were Aber and I specially blessed in having *two* places making their own ice cream? I think we probably were. I'm sure it was because I knew how good real ice cream was that I recoiled in horror one day when I was about eight, walking down King Street past Sergeant's the printers and taking a bite out of a Wall's wafer. That was the last time I ever had an 'ice cream' made out of non-dairy fat, the memory of that oily, chemical flavour staying with me to this day.

I don't think this rather precocious reaction was due to some sort of juvenile food snobbery, as I didn't grow up in a family where there was a history of good cooking. However, we did live in a house with a garden full of old apple trees and my parents planted potatoes, raspberries, strawberries, redcurrants and blackcurrants, more out of the need for cheap food than any gastronomic imperative, so although my mother was not at all an accomplished cook there was plenty to enjoy. As with most people, I imagine, certain memories remain on the mind's palate. Apart from stewing the most delicious apples and making endless pots of blackcurrant jam, my mother cooked a wonderful rice pudding using Golden Syrup and a very low oven. This had an irresistible brown membrane on the top which I now know was nothing but a sheet of coagulated proteins, but then represented a deliciously textural preamble to the syrupy creaminess beneath.

Other memories: potatoes, and the mint to go with them, straight out of the earth for Sunday lunch with *Ray's a Laugh* on the radio; hot corned beef before going off to hospital in Pontypool to have my tonsils out, aged six; my landlady's chocolate cake when I was a weekly boarder at school, aged ten; the custard slices sold by Pinch the baker in Frogmore Street (still there!). And then a couple I would rather forget. My first attempt at eating an artichoke took place over my first advertising lunch when I took a client to San Frediano – the San Lorenzo of the day – and boldly ordered this unfriendly vegetable. I don't think I even knew what one looked like.

I certainly didn't realize until too late one used the knife and fork to eat the middle bit and not the leaves. This shaky start in the lounge lizard school of advertising wasn't improved upon with my next lunch, where I dropped my gin and tonic on the stone floor and took such a large mouthful of horseradish sauce that I couldn't see or speak for five minutes.

These inglorious moments at the lunch table were left behind when I started to work for a small creative ad agency which handled the Olivetti account. My boss was Peter Mayle, a master of the succinct, resonant headline who went down better with the Italians than he did later with the French. Olivetti then had a rather grandly named Cultural Relations Department which, dedicated as it was to exploring the philosophy of design in the workplace, had considerable respect for the value of lunch in encouraging debate. However interested I tried to be in the metaphysics of information technology, or the visionary designs of Ettore Sottsass, I was really more interested in the food we ate on our visits to Turin and Milan than in listening to dronings about abstract ideas of industrial virtue. My first revelation was a risotto milanese with white truffles shaved over it, which I swooned over on the first floor of a crumbling palazzo with refectory tables and a painted ceiling. Eating this in such atmospheric surroundings was like being hit by a truck, with lesser jolts coming from dishes of hare, venison, wild mushrooms and unintelligible kinds of pasta which still beguile in retrospect, eaten in small wood-and-gingham trattorie in the Milan canal district, and in the silver, starch and mahogany glow of Savini in the Galleria Vittorio Emanuele. Just saying those three words still gets me going.

Although that risotto was my very own Damascus road, to my regret I haven't eaten white truffles very often since. At £500 a pound even I – a restaurateur! – can't afford to eat them more than once a year. Everyone should try them once in a lifetime, and I wouldn't even say that about Château Lafite 1945. Inevitably, the first dish I ever cooked, once I had made some chicken stock, was risotto milanese, including the beef marrow but not the truffles. Even without them it's a great dish.

Suddenly a new world opened before me, and I wanted to run away and join the circus. This is it, I thought – to hell with office life, the world of business machines and fast-moving consumer perishables, I'm going to dive, carefree, into the world of food and restaurants and clasp it to my bosom.

Sustained by this novel, consuming and rather overwrought enthusiasm, I soaked up the behind-the-scenes ethos of restaurants and hotels evoked in Nicholas Freeling's *Kitchen Book* (the first half anyway); Ludwig Bemelmans' (yes, he of the Madeline books) stories of life behind the green baize door in the Plaza, New York; George Orwell's *Down and Out in Paris and London*; and books of Richard Condon's like *Mile High* and *The Ecstasy Business* which featured a majestically talented Basque chef called Juan Francohogar, modelled I imagine on Armanatégui, one of Nico Ladenis's heroes. Condon was obviously obsessed with food and wrote about it with helpless reverence, trying vainly to weave gastronomy into his surreal and preposterous plots, but along the way succeeding in making it an object of fascination for me. All together these stories of bizarre characters in circumstances at once exotic and sordid, enjoying a vicarious and imagined glamour, discharging their strange and complicated duties under ludicrous pressures, and underlying everything the idea that food could take over your life, fed my enthusiasm because by now I understood what they meant.

It wasn't too difficult resigning from my promising job and abandoning my privileges, even if I was eventually to replace one set of clients with another. At least in my own restaurant I would be able to throw out the objectionable ones. In advertising it always seemed to me that with rare exceptions the best ideas were thrown out by clients. In their desperation to avoid controversy or offence and thereby taint their product, most advertising at the time was bland, puerile and patronizing. Even though I worked in agencies which produced the best work, I could see no further than the frustration of banging one's head against the pedestrian obduracy of the average client. If your brilliant idea for Dewdrop shampoo was rejected because the pack didn't hog the limelight there wasn't much you could do except kick the cat or (as one of my bosses did) throw the telephone out of the window seven floors up. In my restaurant I would cook what I wanted, eat it if I wanted and maybe even serve it to whom I wanted. That was the theory, at any rate.

An unusual burst of common sense made me get a job in a restaurant to see how things worked, just in case there was more to it than finding premises, hiring a chef and waiting for the rush. I answered an ad for a waiter in a restaurant where until recently I had been a customer, Odin's in Devonshire Street, just around the corner from Harley Street where I lived. Odin's was owned by a large, charismatic and at times intimidating Irishman called Peter Langan who later went on to open his mould-breaking Brasserie off Piccadilly, the blueprint for today's large where-to-be-seen restaurants, and to acquire notoriety for various kinds of outrageous behaviour. I started as a commis waiter, cleaning the loos, hoovering the floors and carrying trays, disguised with a beard in case any of my former clients came in, or worse, people who had worked under me and who might enjoy some Schadenfreude at seeing their old boss working as a skivvy.

Working there was certainly not dull, although I didn't pick up many of the waiter's arts and wished I had been able to watch the cooks more. Peter wasn't really a very good role model either. After a few 'cold beers', always Löwenbrau (these were his pre-champagne days), when he had finished his stint at the stoves, he would tour the restaurant looking for people to startle or insult, usually good-looking women to whom he would make the most lubricious propositions, particularly if they looked as if they might be offended. If they took it in good part Peter would amble on happily enough, but he would be more delighted at the displays of injured dignity he provoked. I was disappointed never to see him challenged by an offended husband, but I was there for only six months.

Peter's way was not management by example. It was not uncommon for us waiters to turn up for the morning shift and find the patron face down on the floor, snoring loudly, broken glasses, puke, and even blood on the tablecloth near his chair. Philip Norman in a (largely) affectionate memoir recalls the atmosphere generated by Peter a bit later when his proprietorial skills had become a bit more polished: 'You would see people scanning the Brasserie's soft-lit horizon like tail-gunners watching for kamikaze; dreading the approach of that tousled figure in its trademark white suit, that pudgy Irish face like a younger Brendan Behan – fixed in a look of woozy belligerence or even more dangerous goodwill. For the unwary their first inkling that the restaurateur had joined them might be Langan's approach on all fours to ram his chin into a soup plate, or the sudden crack of his forehead striking the table.'

Peter had a big personality and a big physical presence too. My chief recollection of him was our crossing Marylebone High Street together to visit a shop selling chandeliers and chandelier parts, some of which he was thinking of putting in his new bistro next door, where I was going to be manager (my second career was obviously taking off). Always happy to indulge in a bit of craic, Peter sat down to talk on a raised dais at the front of the shop. The chair's back legs were close to the edge and as his sixteen-stone bulk leant back, the chair toppled over, propelling Peter backwards into – yes – a glass-fronted cabinet full of pieces of chandelier. Over it went in a ghastly domino effect, colliding with tables covered in more glass. The noise of thousands of brittle crystals, rigid with glassy tension, snapping and shattering, was colossal and quite shocking, as if a shell had burst in the shop, the waves of concussion going on it seemed for minutes, until there was a diminuendo to a series of tinkles which gradually slowed down to be replaced by a terrible silence. This was the only time I saw Peter discomfited. Ashen-faced, he and the proprietors exchanged a few words, only one of which was 'insurance', and we left. Ears still ringing, chastened, we walked back to Odin's. I was thinking that the old saw about bulls in china shops badly needed updating. But I didn't say it.

Did I learn much about the business during my short stay with Peter? I must have thought so. At least the way Peter did it, it seemed pretty straightforward, although I wasn't sure how good I would be at importuning female customers or eating cockroaches in public. Certainly it would help to keep one's wits about one – over a no doubt very good dinner in France Peter signed an order for a quantity of wine to be delivered to the restaurant, but somehow an extra zero appeared on the consignment note, an oversight discovered only when an entire lorry load of cases arrived and was unloaded on the pavement outside Odin's. It was a long time before we could move around behind the scenes without walking sideways.

After six months of making Melba toast, clearing tables and pouring wine, I thought I knew enough to embark on my voyage to fulfilment, and I did – just enough. If I had been more aware of the pitfalls ahead, I would probably have carried on regardless, but it would have been with a burden of apprehension that would have put a dangerous brake on my enthusiasm. I wanted a place in the country to add the 'rural' part to my idyll, and maybe to make a complete separation from my previous life, but funds were short so I had to look in North Wales or East Anglia where property was cheap. The likely scarcity of customers too didn't occur to me.

On a beautiful day in June 1973, the last fine day of the year as it turned out, I found what I was looking for in the valley of the River Conwy in Gwynedd, a small town called Llanrwst far from everyone except the retired Mancunians of Llandudno and Colwyn Bay. Obviously, an ideal place to start. Here I thought I would teach myself to cook in obscurity and, if my enterprise crashed, I could slink back into the advertising world without anyone except my bank manager noticing. The house I bought was a large, granite-ribbed building looking west over the Conwy to Snowdonia, perfectly placed to catch the sun setting over the mountains at three in the afternoon, and to receive the unhindered force of the winds that came barrelling down off the peaks, usually driving torrents of North Welsh rain before them. It blew so hard sometimes that this three-storey slab-sided building literally shook and the fitted carpets I had put in mysteriously rose about four inches off the floor in the middle of the rooms. When some time after I moved in I discovered the place had been condemned by the local council some ten years before, but never demolished, I did rather wonder if the council were waiting for the Snowdonia winds to do the job for them. As the building is still standing I can only assume it was built like the Eiffel Tower and designed to bend in a high wind.

While the builders were trying to make what were three flats into a workable restaurant, and acting as a reluctant tasting panel for some of my messy early efforts, I was learning to cook on an electric three-ring stove, opening *Mastering the Art of French Cooking* at p. 13 ('this is a book for the servantless cook'), and ploughing doggedly through. *MAFC* is a great book to learn from. Idiots are taken by the hand and led carefully from step to step with absolutely nothing left to chance. Almost completely ignorant as I was, although in the Melba toast premier league,

I must admit to having found the process totally absorbing. Not having cooked anything but breakfast before, and that not including scrambled eggs, I was gripped. I was astonished at how indispensable was the onion, at the incredible versatility of the egg, at the weird behaviour of sugar and chocolate, at how easy I found it to make a soufflé, at how difficult I found it to use gelatine properly. This learning curve was a bit like playing a game of emotional snakes and ladders – shin up twelve rungs for successfully clarifying a stock, slide down a python for tasting the sugar to see how the caramel was getting on. Start again when you leave a pan of sauce reducing and go off to the pub for two hours, wondering on your return why the house – a big, eight-bedroomed house – is full of tiny bits of sooty gossamer from top to bottom; you suddenly realize they must have come from a saucepan that has melted into a pool of gently flaming aluminium.

In some ways, going to North Wales wasn't such a bad idea. I was fairly sure that if business wasn't brisk for much of the year, the summer months would see me through. So it turned out, although I had some beginner's luck in the proximity of two accountancy training colleges whose students (with nothing else to spend their allowances on) were a big help in getting me started (thanks, John Anderson and Mike George). As I had low overheads and no family to support, eventually I used to open only three days a week, out of season, the rest of the time either looking out at the rain or getting soaked by it up in the mountains.

There was also the best produce you could wish for, bar a few exotica like mangoes or red peppers (really!): teal, widgeon and mallard from the Denbigh Moors; wild salmon from the river, into my kitchen five minutes after being landed; huge juicy mussels, always laceratingly barnacled, scallops and lobsters from the quay in Conwy; cream from the Jersey herd up the road; and Emrys Roberts the butcher's lamb and beef (Welsh, of course, and as sweet as you like), some of it raised in his own fields, hung as long as you wanted. (I nearly forgot – butter from Kwik-save in town. I had to buy something from there as its MD was one of my best customers. His divorce was financially damaging for me as well, as I lost 5 per cent of my turnover. I bet he didn't think about *that*.)

When I opened for business I could cook about forty dishes well, but hadn't got around to really tricky things like deep frying or making puff pastry, so I certainly couldn't offer my customers (when they eventually turned up) anything as commercially sensible as a chip. Indeed, come to think of it, I've never served chips in any of my restaurants, although I have absolutely nothing against them. And I've still not fried any myself either, for some reason.

Eventually I made entries in the guidebooks and even, at the end of three years, received a Red M (now it's a Bib Gourmand) from those nice but inscrutable Michelin people. At least I think I did. I could never be absolutely certain – unless one asked, and I was too much in awe – and I have a strong feeling that the Red M was aimed at me during my last year in Llanrwst, but had been printed alongside the wrong entry, the one next to me in the guide. This was a hotel which emphasized its Welshness, particularly on its menu. I ate there only once, a pork steak with cockle sauce which ranks high on my list of what I never wish to meet again. What Michelin-toting enthusiasts from France and Belgium would have made of their menu written in Welsh with sub-titles I can't imagine. As I left Llanrwst in February and missed the summer rush I was spared the agony of watching all those foreign cars go whizzing past my door towards their rendezvous with disappointment just up the road. I presume the hotel's owners would have had to develop a damage-limitation strategy to cope with the dashed expectations. And I did wonder what the Michelin men would say when they removed the Red M at the end of the year.

I decided I should move on to somewhere drier, with a few more customers per square mile. I aimed at Guildford, but couldn't find premises so fetched up in Richmond. Here I bought a cafe that was a bit of an institution, having for many years fed the old dears of Richmond getting by on their pensions with meat and two veg for not very much money. Queues formed at lunchtime, sometimes right down the street, and I wondered if I should really be the cause of bringing this useful social service to an end. I soon found out that the owners were retiring and hadn't found another buyer, so I could go ahead with a clear conscience. After a while I opened up as Lichfield's, named not after the noble lord but the building which contained the restaurant.

At first my confidence faltered. I thought, to be on the safe side, if business was very good I should hire a head chef to get me out of trouble and I hoped teach me some professional tricks. Actually, business was terrible. For an ex-ad man my marketing efforts were lamentable, as there weren't any. Unlike Llanrwst, where I wasn't really surprised when nobody turned up at all for the first two days, I thought Richmond's citizens would be a bit more curious. Wrong. The combination of poor trade and feeling that I could do better persuaded me to take over the cooking and for the first time I felt I could wear proper chefs' clothes and not feel an impostor.

After a shaky first year I was in the guidebooks, the *Good Food Guide* being very nice about me, and in 1980 I was given a grown-up gong by Michelin. Its significance was rather lost on me, but I gradually realized in chefs' terms I had done quite well. Michelin stars have rather lost their lustre recently but then it seemed everybody wanted one. To give them their due, the Michelin men have never presented themselves as arbiters, they merely have an award for what they consider is good. It's not their fault if wishful thinkers start reading some almost mystical significance into those pretty little stars. Anyway, it was a good confidence booster and business did improve. One unexpected consequence was the many bookings from Americans, quite a lot of whom clearly got lost on the way to Richmond. If they did manage to find me they would eat at six thirty with black coffee and iced water to go with their meal. I wondered why they bothered. And there were a few people who came 'just to see how good you are'.

Perhaps over-impressed by an 'official' seal of approval, I started to write my menus completely in French (how bizarre this seems now – but at least the time I'd spent in a Brussels ad agency was coming in useful), and not just the odd word like crudité, mousseline or tapénade. (On my very first menu at Lichfield's I had a starter of raw vegetables with hummus, bagna cauda and tapénade. This was in 1978. It amazes me how tapénade became one of the great clichés of 90s cooking and is still going strong. It doesn't deserve it.) This period of rampant Francophilia lasted about five years. It had been whispered to me that a second star might be on the way if I kept on improving, but it never materialized. Maybe I had hit my peak. Whatever the reason I started to grow a bit tired of doing so much mise en place: amuse-bouches and petits fours seemed to multiply uncontrollably, and the cost of employing the staff to make them was becoming difficult to justify so I gradually detuned the menu and went back to writing it in English. Lest you think this was a bit fickle, it was over a period of altogether nine years, the heyday of nouvelle cuisine. At least I can truly say I have never tied up a bundle of French beans with a chive.

By now I wanted to move away from a sort of updated French style, broaden my horizons a bit, and loosen my culinary stays. This meant becoming cheaper, which in turn meant more seats, so I found premises in Marylebone and opened up there in 1989 hoping to bring really good, but not so elaborate, cooking to a wider audience. It also meant I could hire more help. I had found that running the business and doing most of the cooking were a very taxing combination indeed. Eighteen months after selling Lichfield's my legs still ached painfully.

This freer style seemed to find favour with the public and the restaurant took off straight away. We had however lost favour with Michelin who thereafter only gave me a couple of crossed knives and forks. I couldn't get very excited about that. Was it because of the courgette mousse taken out of the fridge too late? I suspect it was, in 1990 at any rate. Does Michelin have records of these things? Perhaps they could go and check.

I thought at the time we were cooking some of the most exciting food in London, a mixture of updated classical French (lobster consommé with orange peel and star anise) with updated bourgeois French (pressed terrine of duck confit and cabbage), German (beef olives with mustard and pickled cucumbers), British (omelette Arnold Bennett, boiled leg of lamb) and Italian (semolina gnocchi with porcini cream, carpaccio with capers and almonds). Were we the first to offer rocket and Parmesan salad with olive oil and balsamico? If we were, I'm sorry. I think we also did something with rice noodles, ginger and soy, but that didn't last long.

Recession affected us a bit, but even so I hubristically thought London needed another Stephen Bull. I found a site in Clerkenwell, not at all fashionable at the time, but it was right on the edge of the City, four minutes from Islington by car, parking was easy, and there was little competition – three other restaurants of any quality within a five hundred yard radius. There were exciting redevelopment plans for Smithfield, the Barbican was nearby, and we would be only a short taxi ride from banks and legal and accountancy firms – although my bank at the time wouldn't lend me a penny. I went ahead anyway. The premises I found were awkwardly shaped, housing a restaurant that had overspent on a redesign and gone bust. Then it was much more difficult to get planning permission for restaurant use, so even though these premises were difficult – narrow entrance, little natural light, the pastry kitchen literally on top of the hot kitchen – these were the only ones available. Ironically, one of the recession's effects was the relaxation of planning laws to allow buildings previously occupied by banks, estate agents, post offices and so on to find other uses. The fact that this would lead to an oversupply of restaurants in London was far from my mind in those days. Now, nine years later, there are forty-five restaurants and bars in that five hundred yards, which is more than pushing it.

SB Smithfield was bigger, cheaper, more colourful and more relaxed than its Marylebone parent. There were no tablecloths, so it felt casual, an open-necked sort of place, although plenty of people in pinstripes turned up. A few of the men wore suits too. An article in the *Independent* wrote about how successful it was going to be, but how apprehensive I seemed to be about things going wrong. At the same time there was a piece in the *Western Mail* (published in Cardiff, fortunately) about how miserable I was. Well, I wasn't. I was just worrying about the rising cost of bin liners. (There is a famously tight-fisted chef – one of the very best – who used to recycle his binbags. You try doing that.) Actually, I don't know which to worry about more – binbags or clingfilm. I know each year we get through enough clingfilm to wrap an entire Valley of the Kings.

In 1994 I opened a more expensive place in Chelsea called Fulham Road, which was a very good restaurant but a crushingly awful experience, so I sold it after a couple of years. Unfortunately, the proceeds started to burn a hole in my pocket rather quickly so I invested them in premises in Covent Garden, two doors up from Peter Stringfellow's nightclub. This site had seen a succession of operators come and go and there wasn't a queue of would-be buyers. However, I was keen to have a foothold in the West End. So far I had always opened in 'secondary' locations where rents were lower, and if there wasn't a river of people flowing past the door, my reputation for 'gastronomic integrity' (thank you, Jonathan Meades) would pull enough people in. Anyway, going to a restaurant where you have to spend between £35 and £40 each is a considered decision, not something done on a whim, as you pass by and spy a menu. 'Oh, this looks nice, let's go in and spend £80.' I don't think so. St Martin's Lane certainly is the West End; theatreland even, so there was the prospect of helping revenue with early and late evening menus, and filling the tables twice over (a bit of a novelty for me).

Although we did good business from theatregoers, the part of St Martin's Lane where I was – the top – seemed to be something of a secondary location too, even if I was only a hundred and fifty yards from Leicester Square. It was impossible to park; although a car park was only twenty yards away, it always had a queue and was ferociously expensive. The arrival of good restaurants in the inner suburbs also meant fewer people needed to travel to the centre of town for a good meal. That was what we offered: good food, an interesting wine list, polished service and fair prices. It wasn't enough. Not only that, Covent Garden is an area where it is rare to spot anyone over forty after 7 p.m. As most of my faithful customers seemed to be keeping pace with me birthday for birthday, the temptation to eat locally or go to bed with a good book kept them away. My designers Virgile and Stone had done a brilliant job with the space, but the only windows were at the front, and sitting in it was still rather like being in a jumbo jet with a bend in the middle. Eventually, the gap between income and expenses became too wide. How could I get it wrong? London's restaurant economy was booming, more people were eating out than ever, some restaurants had week-long waiting lists. But the fact was, eighty yards from that river of people, Long Acre, we were dying of dehydration. There's no getting away from it – it's bums on seats that counts.

Eventually I managed to sell the damn thing, having lost rather a packet, and although it wasn't a fire sale, when a good offer came along for my place in Clerkenwell I was in the mood to take it. This left me with Blandford Street and a consultancy with the Wallace Collection, that small but brilliant jewel among London's museums, just around the corner in Manchester Square. The Wallace is a wonderful place, full of gorgeous paintings, furniture, porcelain, and arms, and now had a restaurant in a central courtyard. True to the usual form, the contractors were late in allowing us access, so there was no time to train the staff properly, or give the equipment in the kitchen any time to prove itself. On opening night it was inevitable that the food hoists would refuse to go up or down and that the heat in the underventilated kitchen would set off the museum's fire alarms, causing the evacuation of the building. It was nice to be able to feel calm about this, as for once it didn't seem to be personal.

The charms of running restaurants in London were now wearing thin;

those of living in London had disappeared long before. With only one restaurant left it seemed a good time to sell up, release my long-suffering shareholders, and realize a long-held vision of moving work and home back to the countryside. Herefordshire isn't quite South Wales but the Wye's a good substitute for the Usk (salmon from the one, brown trout from the other), and the vernacular architecture is more interesting. More important, the border country is heaving with excellent things to eat and drink. The pub I have bought, the Lough Pool Inn near Ross-on-Wye, is deep among the apple and pear orchards that produce delicious food-friendly ciders and perries; I can buy rare breeds of pork and lamb that live in five-star luxury; pedigree Herefords and Welsh Blacks provide my beef, which the butchers are please to hang for a month for me, and whose milk goes into some of the UK's best cheeses. The woods and fields of this bumpy country between the Malvern Hills to the east and the Black Mountains to the west (a great view of them on a clear day from Marcle Ridge) are stuffed with pheasant, partridge, and all kinds of wild duck.

None of this was on the menu when I took over the pub. I did, however, have seven large freezers packed to the brim. I am now down to one, for bread and ice cream. Somehow, I had to improve the pub's food drastically while not increasing the prices very much. My raw materials were going to be more expensive and labour intensive, and the pub urgently needed various kinds of improvement after years of benign neglect. But this was Herefordshire, where burly sons of the soil expected plates groaning under the weight of overcooked roasts, mountains of chips, and vegetables cooked two days in advance. I was amazed at what people were not just tolerating but actually enjoying – and this was in a pub with a decent reputation for its food. Main courses were so large that few people ate either starters or puddings, so the notion of the three-course meal was one which would have to be broached with some delicacy.

Somehow finesse had to be introduced without offence, which meant reducing waste as well as portion sizes, and being ingenious and creative in making our pricey chickens, long-hung beef, and the twice-weekly seafish from Brixham go further. At the time I'm writing this I am about to introduce a new menu and wine list. Poor Herefordshire. Does it need these shocks? Will I lose the baby of regular if modest cashflow with the bathwater of a freezer full of herrings marinated in Madeira? Will the two Johns, Gunther, the two Kevins, Gary, Roy and David decide that although I haven't put in a fruit machine, piped music, a pool table or a dart board, I'm still a City slicker who is bound to corrode the charm of their beloved pub? I've had such a generous and accepting welcome from them so far, and feel so at home there, that I rather doubt it. Of course, you could always come to see if I'm telling the truth.

My Cooking 'Philosophy'

I suppose if you learn to cook out of *Mastering the Art of French Cooking*, Elizabeth David (French and Italian), Jane Grigson and a bit of Margaret Costa, it's not surprising that you'll end up with a Franco-Italo-British style, although it was probably more Franco than Italo, and I guess still is. I've always found enough excitement, challenge and diversion in our own or our neighbours' cooking to make me happy to stay within European boundaries. In addition to the extreme range and sophistication of French cooking, and the breadth of diversity in Italian, it's hard to ignore the achievements of other European countries in elevating some of their own produce to equivalent levels – one thinks of the German ways with pork butchery, mustard, dill, and caraway; the Hungarian with paprika, dumplings and sour cream, the Scandinavian with pickled fish, the Spanish with sweet peppers, pulses, ham and blood sausage. And then there are Poland, Russia, Greece, Turkey, the Lebanon, Morocco . . . all with a lot to offer and all using materials on the whole well within the ken of the British cook. I have to confess, too, to a liking for the American way with baking and salads, but then so much American cooking is European inspired that this seems a natural extension of one's curiosity.

The regional nature of European cookery is for me what gives it its strength, although it's not at all difficult to imagine these different strands becoming, over time, subsumed into a kind of pan-European style, which may well be led by ourselves. We have no powerful native tradition to which we can bend the knee, even though we have had the makings in the last couple of hundred years. Our fine baking and preserving traditions are still alive and well but they represent our strongest claims to a culinary nationhood, the 'John Bull' spirit of the eighteenth and nineteenth centuries having rejected the elaborations of the foreigner – effete and inimical by turns – as a threat to the manly, no-nonsense British diet of bleeding chunks, boiled fowl and fish fried plain.

Thank goodness there was India to inject a little excitement into the dreary upper-middle-class culinary landscape, much as Elizabeth David did somewhat later with her persuasive accounts of the cooking of France and Italy. Another period of change is taking place now, this time on a broader scale. Geographically we may be perched at the top of Europe, but our cultural connections are wider. The evolving modern cooking of Australia, New Zealand and North America, which itself refracts the cooking of south-east Asia, 'the Pacific Rim', and conspicuously emphasizes the worth of native ingredients, in turn influences our cooks through travel and the press, and all far faster than in the days of Colonel Kenny-Herbert.

Indeed, everything is changing so quickly that it isn't surprising if the senses of proportion and balance are sacrificed to the demand for novelty and the approval of fashion. The new, large restaurant-going public that has emerged over the last few years and the corresponding increase in media activity have placed a premium on innovation and variety for their own sake, to divert a population with a shrinking attention span and a cultural weightlessness that embraces each new sensation briefly, turns it into a cliché and rushes on to the next. Last week's sun-dried tomato is yesterday's panna cotta, today's verjus and tomorrow's dried dolphin flakes.

With all this going on it is easy to forget the intimate relationship good food has always had with the earth that produced it, and the economic factors that allowed it to flourish. It is a salutary aspect of human history that the European peasant farmer with his pig, his ducks, his olive oil, garlic and grapes, with mushrooms in the woods nearby, could eat and drink almost as well as the most pampered monarch. In cooking no amount of ingenious saucing, dressing or modifying will improve the nature of the raw material; disguise it, yes, provide impressive and delicious diversions, yes, but turn a badly hung, chemically treated and unhappily raised piece of meat, badly farmed fish or hothouse vegetable into something of real value – no. Even for us, in the midst of the plenty of the 'developed' world, a potato, apple or runner bean from our own garden is going to taste better than something from a cold store or the featureless acres of East Anglian agribusiness. However, as we don't all have gardens, let alone pigs or olive trees, we have to buy what is available, even though the bounty in our shops can be illusory.

My feeling is that, as long as you have access to a good butcher and a decent fish counter, if you know roughly what to look for your most important raw material is likely to be satisfactory: you just may have to go that extra mile (or ten). With a supply of onions, carrots, celery and garlic, some good bread and olive oil, and some red and white wine, your meat and fish can be transformed into meals that would find favour with both the Calabrian farmer and the captain of industry. To me these things and maybe a few others – butter, cream, a green herb or two – are the sine qua nons of good cooking. To these basics add eggs, capers, anchovies, bay, mustard, ginger, nutmeg, cumin, wine vinegar and a bit of ham or bacon in one form or another and I wouldn't feel unduly deprived or circumscribed. As I am still getting to grips with what Europe has to offer, twenty-five years after I began, and don't know enough about many other kinds of cooking, I don't need bottles of nam pla, oyster sauce or sesame oil in my store cupboard. I do have them – it's just that I don't really feel comfortable using them, any more than I like using stock cubes, as there's too much of the artificial, the factory-made, about them. Soy sauce is to me like a stock cube, to be used as a seasoning agent, as an incidental, rather than as a central ingredient, and then only as a short cut. There's nothing wrong with short cuts; it just depends on the effect you are striving for and the effort-reward factor.

I'm happy therefore to leave fusion recipes to others, even though I'm well aware of the sort of dialectical, evolutionary path all cooking has taken over the centuries. I just prefer to work within the European tradition where the influences of other cultures are absorbed more gently than they are in Australian, New Zealand or some modern British cooking, and where lemongrass has its place in the order of things but is not at the head of the queue, and Thai green curry is part of a Thai restaurant menu rather than an English one.

Away from the bigger picture, I feel there is a rightness and wrongness about certain things which is more an emotional reaction than anything else, but is also based on the view that living things that flourish in one set of geological or climatic circumstances aren't automatically going to harmonize with their distant neighbours. The cooking of a region or a country develops gradually as affinities between local ingredients are discovered, and the sudden expansion of the 'ingredient horizon' isn't likely to change this. There has to be some kind of symbiotic relationship between the different kinds of produce that flourish in areas where climate and geology are similar, some underlying sympathy known only to the great god Pan but surely evident to us mere mortals in the completeness of dishes like bouillabaisse, cassoulet, sauerkraut, risotto milanese, cocido madrileña, goulash and so on. This is only a broad principle, of course, because over the centuries even the English have absorbed the tomato, the lemon, nutmeg, saffron, and cinnamon in particular, but it was a gradual process, and dishes evolved around them. It seems distinctly unwise to me to make arranged marriages, just because they are all so widely available, of the flavours of the north – mustard, horseradish, vinegar, sour cream and smoke – with those of the south – garlic, basil, olives, chilli, sweet peppers. Goulash, made on the cusp of both latitudes, is the proof of this principle, the pimento of the south in bed happily with the sour cream of the north.

As a rule of thumb this has kept me out of trouble, away from the outlandish and contrived, but it can't be followed slavishly. Venison, in or out of red wine, just doesn't go with chickpeas, or smoked haddock with olives (although it does with curry spices), or turbot with chilli, or wild duck with basil (although it does with orange) and even I put olive oil with mustard in my all-purpose salad dressing. The lesson to be drawn from this is not to be dogmatic but not to be over-optimistic either, and to give some thought to which ingredients are still likely, after brief acquaintance, to be on friendly terms with each other.

One of the interesting things about cooking is its infinite variety, its opportunities for diversity of outlook and execution, for exploring different ways of doing things; in short, for embracing all the opinions of men. Like everyone else, I have my own views about how things should be done, and my own likes and dislikes. Orange peel, capers, and hazelnuts are among my preferences, as I'm sure will be apparent, but I make no apology for that (indeed, my liking for orange as a flavour is about the only thing I have in common with Raymond Blanc – apart from our saturnine good looks). I think walnut and hazelnut oils, white truffle oil, black truffle juice, foie gras, clotted cream and acorn-fed ham are all made in heaven. They don't really feature in this book because they are complete in themselves, but everyone should try these sensational examples of cooperation between man and nature at least once in his life.

There are, fortunately, other great flavour sensations to be had from more homespun materials. One of my more memorable experiences was eating a dish of snails, ceps, and garlic/nettle butter all in an airy, buttery pastry case in Les Eyzies (Le Centenaire, chef Roland Mazère). Another, a parfait of crayfish tails in La Marée, Paris. Freshwater crayfish (écrevisses), as opposed to crawfish, or spiny lobster (langouste), although much liked by Scandinavians, I think are only worth eating for their shells, another of nature's great flavours. These tails, pounded in a mortar until perfectly smooth, were what gave this parfait its flavour. These dishes were great cooking – devastating combinations of nature's marvellous raw materials and the effort, technique and judgement of man.

This book very much reflects my preoccupations – I've always liked well-defined, distinct flavours, which I suppose draws into service words like 'strong' and 'robust' as there seems little point in eating things which leave no mark, which don't attract attention to themselves in the nicest possible way.

Cooking by the Seat of the Pants

Cooking is an inexact science, although in its higher reaches in its ability to transform the everyday I'm not sure that 'art' doesn't describe it better. Great cooking doesn't make us see the world in a different way nor, perhaps, can it reveal 'truth' in a terrine of foie gras, but it has the power to transform the ordinary into the wonderful, and who's to say the sensory pleasure it can deliver is of less account than the intellectual pleasure provided by, say, Beethoven's Late Quartets? Certainly if 'art' is the process of using technique and vision to make the ordinary transcendent, cooking is right up there; a dish where disparate elements are combined into unexpected harmony, where the whole is infinitely greater than the sum of its parts, is as much a reflection of the originator's view of the culinary world and its objects as that of Cézanne and his apples.

Mazère, he of the ceps and snails, wouldn't have needed to measure out the quantities for his nettle butter, nor his pastry chef the butter for the puff pastry; experience would teach them 'about' how much of everything to use. Most of us don't have that sort of experience, but the majority of the cooking we are likely to do, which is outside the realms of haute cuisine, doesn't demand tremendous precision, because on the whole cooking is generous with its tolerances. It doesn't really matter if you don't measure out your tablespoons completely accurately, or if you haven't quite enough butter to go in the shortcrust, because you will very likely arrive at a perfectly good version of your dish anyway. Nearly all recipes give what look like ironclad instructions – 50 g of this, 250 of that: well, the fact of rounding up or down in moving from Imperial to metric is all we need to know to realize that this rigidity isn't necessarily so. A long time ago, when recipes were written in both measures, 4 oz was never 112½ g, and yet using either measure would have been successful. Of course, care has to be taken with strong spices like clove or chilli, with those little flavour bombs the anchovy and the caper, with handling gelatine, with seasoning, but even garlic and mustard, truculent at first, will yield quietly if heated for a while.

There are, of course, some exceptions: eggs, for example, can sometimes be a bit difficult. Broken egg yolks must never meet egg whites if the whites are for beating; they froth, but too feebly to be useful. Never apply too much heat to the egg base of your hollandaise or Béarnaise, or it will scramble (this doesn't mean you can't cook them over direct heat – just make sure you move the whisk or beaters constantly all over the bottom of the pan). Add the oil gently at the start of mayonnaise. Apart from these instabilities, even the egg is an easygoing chap.

Otherwise, as far as this book is concerned, there's not a lot to worry about. You *can* make a stable emulsion with butter, cream and oil, unlikely as it seems (for bagna cauda); you *can* thicken a hot sauce with mayonnaise (in a bourride, for example), if you have made it yourself. You *can* make a beurre blanc without whisking endless cubes of cold butter into the base; just put the butter in one rectangular piece on to the reduction, and boil hard. And you can certainly open the oven door to inspect a soufflé, as long as you close it again.

You can't, on the other hand, sauté or sear something without it sticking if the fat in the pan isn't hot enough, so make sure it is. And you must, always, let salt dissolve for a few seconds while you stir it around before you taste and add any more.

Produce

Restaurants are fortunate in the range and quality of supplies available to them – our fish goes from boat to table far quicker than is the case for the home cook; as we buy meat from butchers not supermarkets ours is *always* properly hung. We can buy unusual varieties of fruit, salads and vegetables from small specialist growers like Frances Smith of Appledore, Kent, who delivers nettle tops, yellow raspberries and tomatoes, white aubergines, the apples of old England, wet walnuts, elderflowers, geranium leaves, purslane, claytonia, even medlars (although I'm ashamed to say I can never decide what to do with them apart from making jelly, which is a bit feeble).

We can get four different sizes of scallop, five of langoustine, eight of oysters, soft-shell crabs, clams and sea urchins. We can get keta (salmon eggs), bottarga (dried mullet or tuna roe, sturgeon sometimes) and mojama (dried tuna flakes). We can get more ham, cured meats and blood sausages than you can shake a salami at. We can get suckling pigs and red mullet livers (delicious), cod's cheeks and pigs' cheeks, calves' feet and pigs' trotters, bladders and stomach membranes (caul fat – very useful stuff). We can get powder made from dried wild mushrooms. We can get French and Italian flours to make our bread and pasta, and vinegar made from old Cabernet Sauvignon. We buy sea kale, salsify, and scorzonera. All nature's bounty, and some of man's!

Now, in some large supermarkets, Cabernet Sauvignon vinegar is creeping in. Puy lentils already have, along with truffle oil, baby capers and dried morels. The gap is closing, but is still not close enough. Not so much in terms of range but in quality. Supermarkets ought to worry less about having eight different varieties of something and more about the quality of what they offer, especially meat and fish. Do try to buy these from the specialists if you can find one: fishmongers are so few and far between and, horrors, butchers are slowly going the same way – out.

If you have to buy meat from the supermarket, buy from the dispense counter if you can, as the meat there will certainly have been hung for longer, and will always be worth the extra cost. If you're lucky the servers might even know something. Far better to buy an expensive organic chicken once a fortnight than an anaemic softie once a week, full of antibiotics, growth hormones and worms.

If you buy fish, ask to look at the gills which should be pink, and the skin and eyes bright. Smell it if you can, especially fillets. Curiously, sometimes the prepackaged fish will be better. If it's a white fish, check that it is white: dazzling, if possible.

On the other hand, there's not much a supermarket can do to ruin offal or game, but beware of pork. Quick-cooking cuts will nearly always be intractable (pork fillet/tenderloin excepted) and only a weeklong bath of pineapple juice will render the average loin chop edible. Roasting joints will also benefit from a dip in the marinade.

A few suggestions:

- If you aren't going to use prepackaged fish or meat straightaway, remove from the plastic box and wrap closely with Clingfilm to exclude all the air – this will keep them fresh for three times as long.

- When you buy oranges or lemons, buy them with hard, very slightly knobbly skins, in case you want to grate the rind. With limes, look for the reverse: the juicy ones are larger and have thin skins.

- Buy cabbages that feel heavy for their size, and heavy, white cauliflowers that feel hard as a brick. Cauliflowers that aren't bouncing fresh aren't worth having.

- Frozen peas, broad beans, and spinach are much better than nothing.

- Open mushrooms taste better than closed ones, for some reason – evaporation of moisture, I suppose.

- If you can't find ripe tomatoes, and haven't time to let them ripen, used tinned, or the equivalent weight of passata.

- Don't buy any vegetable that's soft, especially roots.

- Don't buy anything wrinkly, except passion fruit, when you mustn't buy anything else.

- On the other hand, do buy misshapen and particoloured aubergines, curvy cucumbers, and spotty grapefruit.

- You'll get more or better spinach, coriander and spices at ethnic shops or markets. Use the spices quickly – they've really had it after about three months – or put them in the freezer if you don't use them very often.

- Occasionally check the sell-by date on your baking powder as it loses its power gradually.

- Don't underestimate the swede, or be frightened of scorzonera.

- Avoid kohl-rabi at all costs.

Notes

- A teaspoon is always a level teaspoon.

- A tablespoon is always a level tablespoon.

- Some of the recipes, notably in the puddings section, are indicated gluten free. At home we have a particular interest in cooking with non-gluten flours (rice, chickpea, maize, potato) as our daughter is a coeliac, and therefore has an intolerance to gluten. In practice we have found that many of the recipes which indicate wheatflour can quite successfully work with an alternative; I have given recipes which either work better with the alternative, or where there is no discernible difference in result should you wish to use a flour other than wheat.

- All recipes are for four, unless otherwise stated.

- All eggs are medium, unless otherwise stated.

Sauces, salsas, dressings and stocks

Sauce-making is another branch of cooking that's out of favour in restaurants, apart from (the necessary exception) Béarnaise with, usually, rib-eye steak and chips. Suddenly, sauces were kicked aside by jus, salsas and flavoured oils. Great to have these newcomers, but let's not suddenly bin the idea of sauce – a more complex and versatile liquid than the 'jus', which is for the most part just a reduced stock. I can understand the relief felt by cooks when something came along (nouvelle cuisine) to break the shackles that bound them to the béchamel and velouté, but the baby was rather thrown out with the bathwater. Sauces, I suppose, were seen as emblematic of a corrupt ancien régime of cooking and had to be ruthlessly suppressed by the commissars of the revolution (not so much the great chefs who started the subversion as the commentators who didn't really understand it, and the plodding imitators who then bowdlerized it). Perhaps at home you haven't noticed this curious exile: but how long is it since you saw hollandaise sauce or beurre blanc on a menu, not to mention their variations? I don't think it's due to health preoccupations: it's mere fashion.

I readily admit to liking the ease, speed and zingy flavours of salsas, and appreciate the lightness and directness of purées, but it seems an unnecessary impoverishment to banish anything made with a thickening agent or a few tablespoons of cream. At home we don't have to worry too much about these shibboleths. Many's the time I've thickened a sauce with cornflour, rice flour or potato flour and even once or twice with bits of bread. These sauces have their place, just as modern flourless or liquidizer-based sauces do. It takes only a few seconds to blend the juices and buttery onions from around a roast chicken into a gorgeous gravy, only a bit longer to chop a shallot and add it to the pan some meat has cooked in – roast or fried – and scrape the brown bits into a ladleful of stock, a splash of red wine, a blob of tomato paste, a pinch of sugar and a knob of butter to finish it off. As quick to do, almost, as reading this sentence.

Salsas offer plenty of scope for improvisation, too. If you have mint or coriander leaves, a tomato or two and a shallot or red onion you have the basis for several. Cucumber, avocado, papaya, mango, chargrilled corn kernels, apples, sweet peppers, capers, oranges, limes and chillies – all these can be roped into various permutations, according to what you have in the fridge or fruit bowl. Prepare the ingredients by hand, rather than in the food processor, which will not only not produce pleasingly regular shapes but will swiftly produce a sludgy texture.

Salad dressings are similar, in that you need some basic elements but then can add extra ingredients according to what you need dressed. I would say you can't do without two kinds of oil – olive and another good quality vegetable oil like sunflower or grapeseed; an acidulating element – wine, cider or balsamic vinegar; lime or lemon juice; and, for me, mustard, shallots, and a sweetening agent. You will always be able to make a respectable dressing with these, but there's no reason why you shouldn't use your imagination and call other things into play. It would be a shame to be without walnut or hazelnut oil, both of which benefit from more dilution than the other oils, and garlic and orange rind come into the picture too. Then yogurt, cream and the soft herbs, dill, chervil, and chives. Use tarragon and mint too, but remember how strong they are.

It's not orthodox to use sugar or honey in a salad dressing, but (and allowing for my sweet tooth) they are useful in moderating the acidity of a dressing where otherwise you might have to use more oil. I even use sweet wine successfully, hoping it might have a certain logical connection with grapeseed oil.

As the nut oils sometimes need slaking, with water, wine or orange juice, so it pays to be aware of the strength of your wine vinegar, particularly the smart Cabernet Sauvignon, and also of your balsamico, which loses considerable acidity as it ages in cask, and thickens at the same time.

Olive oil of course also varies in strength. It's not worth using your best cold-pressed, extra-virgin single estate for a salad dressing – best on its own – so choose one that's not going to be too aromatic or expensive.

Béarnaise Sauce

This is similar to the recipe ingredients in Michel Guérard's *Cuisine Gourmande* (not as iconoclastic as *Cuisine Minceur*, but as intelligent). The method, though, is mine.

> 7 tbsp red wine vinegar
> 50g shallots, finely chopped
> 6 crushed black peppercorns (optional)
> 2 tbsp chopped tarragon
> 225g butter
> 4 egg yolks
> 1 tsp chopped chervil (this is optional, really)
> salt

Put the vinegar, shallots, peppercorns if using and half the tarragon into a heavy-bottomed stainless-steel or enamel saucepan and bring to the boil. Reduce rapidly for 4 minutes. Pass through a sieve into a bowl and return to the saucepan. Allow to cool.

Melt the butter in a small saucepan. Add the egg yolks to the vinegar reduction and beat with a spiral whisk. (A balloon whisk is likely to be too big to agitate the mixture enough to aerate it.) Place the pan over gentle heat and whisk the mixture slowly at first then more quickly as the pan heats up.

When the egg mixture has thickened to the consistency of double cream, gradually pour on the melted butter, whisking as you go. When all the butter is incorporated, add the rest of the tarragon, and the chervil if using, and check the seasoning. If you have used unsalted butter you'll need to add salt, but with salted butter you may not.

This sauce is best used straightaway, but it can be kept hot for about 45 minutes in a bain-marie of very hot water.

Hollandaise

One needn't be aware of the subtle chemistry of the multiphase colloid system – oil-in-water emulsions – to be impressed by the transformation of melted butter and egg yolks into some of the most delicious things known to man. I know that there are more hollandaise recipes than there are days in the week, but my humble contribution to the great recipe continuum might save you some time and effort. Being of an impatient turn of mind, I thought there must be a quicker, and accordingly less effortful, way of thickening the egg yolks than whisking them in a bowl over hot water. This is of course to do it over direct heat. As long as you have the right sort of pan, it can be really fast, but the heat has to be monitored closely lest the eggs suddenly scramble. The best pan to use is undoubtedly an enamelled cast-iron type, which heats up slowly and holds heat well; almost as important, its shallow corners allow the whisk to cover the whole of the pan bottom, so keeping the eggs moving all the time. A stainless-steel pan will do, as long as the base is thick, but it is more likely to cook the eggs before you spot the danger as the heat conduction is better and faster. A bowl of iced water nearby into which you can immerse the pan bottom would be useful insurance.

I like my hollandaise also to be simple, well differentiated from Béarnaise and its extended family, so I don't start off with an infusion of shallots, wine or vinegar, and herbs. I prefer to use lemon juice only as the acidulator, and water to dilute the egg yolks enough to enable them to absorb the butter. The butter must be the best. I prefer salted, from a Welsh farmhouse if I can get it, otherwise one from Charente in France, but whatever it is it must be good. Because this sauce is really just two elements, the other important one should also be the best, so try to use organic free-range egg yolks if you can. It's just too horrible to think your gleaming, luscious, tongue-clinging symbol of saucely purity could contain anything remotely pathogenic.

These quantities will make plenty for four people, to accompany steamed or poached fish (baked too – why not?) or vegetables. Using less butter and 2 egg yolks would be enough for four, but the smaller quantity of egg is slightly trickier to handle.

> 225g butter
> 3 egg yolks
> 1 tbsp water
> lemon juice
> salt

Melt the butter over low heat in a pan with a rim (so when you pour, slowly, the melted butter won't just run down the side). Put the egg yolks in the pan you've chosen as above, and add the water. Place the pan over moderate heat and start whisking, slowly. As the pan heats up increase your whisking speed (after about 3 minutes, or 2 if using stainless steel).

The eggs will form a thickish foam. As they do this turn the heat right down and keep whisking, covering the whole of the pan bottom, lifting the pan away from the heat two or three times, just in case. When you feel your egg yolks are quite thick and still smooth (well done so far) take the pan off the heat and start pouring the butter in slowly, whisking all the time. Mercifully you can do this much faster than if you were making mayonnaise, something to do with the colloids (or is it phospholipids?). Not too fast, though. When all the butter has been absorbed, add a good squeeze of lemon juice and taste to see if the sauce needs more salt. If you ever make this sauce with any frequency you'll find 3 egg yolks will absorb quite a lot more butter, depending on the thickness of your sabayon, but the amount given here gives less risk of separation.

With this behind you, or even under your belt, it's the merest step to add embellishments if you wish, although the sauce doesn't demand anything extra. A few tablespoons of double cream will add, well, creaminess; lightly whipped cream will turn it into the haute cuisine sauce mousseline; blood orange juice into sauce maltaise, the classical gopher of asparagus, but not as good, I think, as the grated rind and juice from an ordinary orange. Other ideas are mustard, green herbs, ground toasted hazelnuts, walnuts or almonds, small dice of tomato pulp, pounded anchovies, capers, or crushed green peppercorns.

Sauce Nivernaise

This is a sauce described by Elizabeth David in *French Provincial Cooking*; incidentally she suggests hollandaise as a sauce for œufs mollets (very soft-boiled eggs) – imagine. I once employed a waiter from Nevers, who had never heard of sauce niver-naise. Perhaps I should have asked a chef from Nevers. (I once asked a waiter from Bandol what tapénade was. I've really got it in for tapenade. He didn't know either.) Anyway, its origin doesn't matter. It's an absolutely wonderful sauce with lamb and grilled fish of the snapper or mullet variety, and is up there with bagna cauda as a dipping sauce for veg. This is a Béarnaise made with garlic and parsley butter – snail butter. A much better sauce than paloise – a Béarnaise made with mint.

My method is slightly different (lazier, actually).

1 glass dry white wine
2–3 shallots, finely sliced
2 cloves of garlic, bashed
2–3 sprigs thyme
½ a bay leaf
6 black peppercorns
2 or 3 parsley stalks

3 egg yolks
200g butter
2 cloves of garlic, peeled and finely chopped
2 heaped tbsp chopped parsley
salt
lemon juice

Pour the wine into a small saucepan with the shallots, bashed garlic, thyme, bay, peppercorns and parsley stalks. Bring slowly to a simmer, turn down the heat, and let the flavours infuse for 10 minutes. Boil down until about 2 tbsp are left. Strain this off, pressing on the solids, into another pan, ideally enamelled cast iron. Whisk together the infusion and the egg yolks, and thicken as described in the hollandaise recipe (page 23). Melt the butter while you are doing this, and when the eggs have thickened satisfactorily, slowly whisk in the melted butter. Stir in the chopped garlic and parsley and season with salt and a drop of lemon juice if you think it necessary (the wine may not have enough acidity). This sauce is better if it's slightly thicker than hollandaise, although it would really be at its best if one could chew it. Even Harold McGee (*On Food and Cooking*) can't explain how we could do that.

Beurre Blanc

Although Escoffier (d. 1935) lists thirty-three flavoured butters in his *Complete Guide to the Art of Modern Cooking* (published 1907; my edition 1939), beurre blanc isn't one of them, nor is it to be found in the sauce section. This is a bit off, because this butter sauce occupies (or did) a resonant corner of the French psyche. Maybe he thought it was too closely associated with the freshwater pike and the River Loire to be admitted to the sacred halls of haute cuisine. But even if its finest pairing is with pike (and I've not tried the two together), it's another excellent, simple and versatile sauce that everyone should know, especially as my method of production is another short cut. It might possibly betray the heroic ideals of the dish: that you whisk the butter in cube by cube, and you don't use cream. I can understand the latter, as it does alter the sauce a tiny bit, but to insist on whisking the butter into a teaspoonful of liquid (a shallot/vinegar reduction) seems a bit perverse, as the end result isn't at all different from doing it the short way.

I feel this is simply an aspect of the mystique with which the French like to surround their favourite dishes, the effect of which, consciously or unconsciously, is to move them out of reach of ordinary mortals. Thus develop the legendary skills attributed to the masters (and mistresses) of the past: the omelette of La Mère Poulard, the Mère Brazier's way with sole meunière, the seven years Fernard Point spent developing his gratin of crayfish tails. Seven years! Modern masters contribute to the idea that French cooking is so refined and delicate that to carry it off well almost means being admitted to the priesthood.

Even Roger Vergé is guilty of this: 'You can keep the sauce [beurre blanc] hot by putting a folded newspaper in the bottom of a large saucepan, placing the pan containing the beurre blanc on top of the paper, and putting the whole thing on the edge of the hot-plate where it will keep warm without overheating.' With all this and the curdling to worry about it's a wonder anyone would ever screw up the courage. And hollandaise sauce has eggs in it too! This is all a bit of nonsense, really. As long as the butter is emulsified well with the liquid, it will be stable enough to keep for hours. Certainly fierce heat will make it separate, but keeping it hotter than tepid is danger-free.

1 shallot, finely chopped
50 ml white wine vinegar
125 ml dry white wine
2 tbsp double cream
175 g butter, cold, cut into three pieces

Put the shallot, vinegar and wine into a small saucepan and over moderate heat let the liquid reduce gradually to about 4 tbsp. Pour in the cream, let it bubble for a moment, and add the butter. Turn up the heat so the butter melts into the boiling liquid. The only thing you need to watch is that all the moisture might evaporate before the butter has emulsified. If this seems likely, add a tablespoon or so of water and carry on. As soon as the sauce is finished, remove from the heat and season. If you've used an iron pan it may go on cooking, so pour the sauce through a sieve (or not, as you like) into a warmed sauce boat or jug. (If you make a large amount, say using a whole block of butter, you can boil it in one piece.)

There you have beurre blanc, plain and simple, great with asparagus, artichokes, shellfish, turbot, smoked haddock (and pike). I add ginger root and orange peel to the reduction in the recipe for seafood nage, but there are several variations which I think are very good and which the French never seem to have thought about. One-third of a vanilla pod, split in half lengthways, added to the liquid, will give a fugitive, haunting vanilla flavour which is delicious with lobster, scallops, or any firm-fleshed fish, baked, poached or steamed. A couple of heaped teaspoons of Dijon-style mustard and one of chopped tarragon or marjoram will give an excellent sauce for kidneys (horrors), liver, steak or hamburgers. Two tablespoons of chopped chives or basil, or 3 of dill or chervil, will give a wonderfully light and fresh-tasting sauce for poached eggs, sole and plaice fillets, or salmon. Finally, 2 firm tomatoes, peeled and deseeded, cut into 1cm dice and added at the end will make it look pretty, particularly if you have included a pinch of saffron stamens in the reduction. Use as for most of the above plus grilled fish.

Beurre Rouge

This uses the same method as beurre blanc (page 26) but the white wine and vinegar are replaced by red, and the cream is replaced by 1 tbsp of tomato purée and several good pinches of sugar. As this has a more robust flavour I like to include a sprig or two of fresh thyme and a crushed clove of garlic in the reduction. Use a wine which has body but is not acidic – a Merlot, a Syrah/Mourvèdre or a Cabernet Sauvignon would be fine. Use with poached eggs on toast or something like skate, John Dory or bass – fish with relatively strong flavours.

Tomato Sauce

Everyone needs a good tomato sauce. This one is full of flavour and works pretty well with tinned tomatoes. It's good with hamburgers, steak, good sausages, and hot or cold starters, and makes a great omelette filling with some grated Swiss cheese.

25g butter
1 medium Spanish onion, finely chopped
1kg firm ripe tomatoes, chopped, or 2 × 450g tins
2 cloves of garlic, crushed
4 parsley stalks
1 small bay leaf
2 sprigs fresh thyme or ¼ tsp dried
6 black peppercorns
½ tsp fennel seeds

4cm piece orange peel
a pinch of sugar or two
salt

Melt the butter in a medium saucepan and soften the onion over medium heat for about 10 minutes, without browning. Add all the other ingredients except the sugar and salt and cook slowly, covered, for 15 minutes. Uncover and cook over low heat for at least half an hour. The longer you cook it the better. At the end of cooking add sugar if necessary – unless the tomatoes are ripe, you'll need it, and maybe more than a pinch – and salt. Press everything though a sieve into another pan and reduce gently if the flavour and consistency need concentrating.

If serving this hot 25g or so of cold butter will give it a rich, velvety texture.

Romesco Sauce

This suggested the skate stuffing on page 120. It's one of the best sauces I've come across for grilled or fried fish or chicken, but it's great with stuffed squid, stirred into fish soup or spread on fried bread with eggs, and I've even eaten it with fried potatoes. Very good too. It comes from around Tarragona in Spain, where they particularly enjoy it with prawns.

There are many versions of this sauce but the central principle is the pungency of garlic, chilli and vinegar offset by the sweetness of the nuts. It's worth giving two very different recipes, both terrific. Sometimes I like one better, sometimes the other. If pushed I'd just favour the one with the hazelnuts (boring!). It's quite important to use the dried peppers; version 2 uses dried pepper flakes instead of dried chilli. Serve both versions at room temperature.

Version 1

4 dried nori peppers (or pastilla dried peppers)
1 small dried red chilli
1 slice white bread, 2 cm thick
150 ml olive oil
3 cloves of garlic, roughly chopped
10 blanched toasted almonds
10 toasted hazelnuts
350 g firm ripe tomatoes
3 tbsp sherry vinegar or red wine vinegar
salt and freshly ground black pepper

Remove the seeds from the dried peppers and chilli and soak for 30 minutes in cold water. Drain and dry. Fry the bread in 1 tbsp of the oil until golden brown on both sides. Remove to the food-processor bowl. Fry the peppers a second or two in a drop more oil and transfer to the bowl with the chilli, garlic and nuts. Cut a cross in the top of the tomatoes and drop into boiling water for 20 seconds. Remove to a bowl of cold water and peel off the skins. Cut into quarters, remove and discard the seeds and stalky bits and add the flesh to the processor. Blend at top speed adding the remainder of the olive oil slowly at first then faster. When all the oil is incorporated scrape the mixture into a bowl and stir enough vinegar in to give a pleasing sharpness. Season with salt and a few turns of the pepper mill.

Version 2

large ripe tomato
5 cloves of garlic, peeled
1 dried sweet red pepper
125 ml water
3 tbsp plus 1 tsp red wine vinegar
1 tbsp plus 125 ml olive oil
1 cm slice white bread from a baguette or
    similar
10 blanched almonds
¼ tsp hot red pepper flakes
salt and freshly ground black pepper

Preheat the oven to 375°F/190°C/Gas 5.

Roast the tomato and garlic in a dry roasting pan for 30 minutes. Put the dried red pepper in a small saucepan with the water and 3 tbsp of the vinegar. Bring to the boil, cover, and simmer for 5 minutes. Heat 1 tbsp of the oil in a pan and fry the bread until golden brown on both sides. Transfer to the food-processor bowl or to a liquidizer jar. In the same oil fry the almonds until golden and transfer to the bowl with the drained, boiled red pepper, the pepper flakes, garlic and tomato. With the motor running slowly pour in the remaining olive oil, gradually increasing speed, until incorporated. Add the remaining vinegar and salt and pepper and scrape into a bowl.

Turnip Cream Sauce

I quite like turnips but rate them more for what they can contribute to other things (like ham stock or to a venison stew) than as objects to enjoy on their own. This is a surprisingly delicious sauce to go with cold chicken or with vegetable terrines – perhaps the one with Jerusalem artichokes on page 52.

2 medium turnips, peeled and chopped
4 tbsp mayonnaise
4 tbsp single cream
4 tbsp well-flavoured chicken stock, cold
salt

Cook the turnips in water until tender, about 5 minutes. Cool and place in the liquidizer jar with the mayonnaise (home-made is best, of course, but a decent brand will do), the cream and stock. Blitz for a couple of minutes at high speed, add a little salt, blitz again, and check seasoning. Add more salt if necessary, and a few drops more stock if the sauce is too thick. Serve at room temperature.

Bagna cauda

I put this on my very first menu at my restaurant in Richmond, Lichfield's, in 1978, as one of three things to eat with raw vegetables. Bagna cauda is a rich and pungent sauce which can be made thick, with cream, as a dipping sauce, or thinned with olive oil or white wine as a sauce for fish. I admit to going the whole hog and adding cream to it. Even with all the fat, if you mash the anchovies and garlic to a paste you can make it emulsify. I can't imagine what it would be like with shaved white truffles added to it, as apparently happens in Piedmont where it originates. Dynamite, I should think. Here is a thick version for coating bits of cauliflower, broccoli, fennel, and sweet peppers with their skins blistered and removed.

100 ml good olive oil
75g unsalted butter
75g anchovy fillets (10–12)
1 head of garlic
4 tbsp double cream

Melt together the oil and butter in a stainless-steel or enamelled saucepan over low to moderate heat. Chop the anchovy fillets finely with the garlic, mash to a paste with your largest knife blade and add to the pan. Add the cream and whisk together for a couple of minutes until an emulsion forms. The longer you cook it, the milder the garlic. That's up to you. After eating this you may well want to live on a diet of grass and wild berries for a time.

Mango Salsa

Look for a mango that smells sweet and feels firmish, not hard or soft, to the touch.

> ¼ a large ripe mango, or 1 small
> 1 sweet red pepper
> 2 firm ripe tomatoes
> 3 shallots, finely chopped
> 1 tbsp balsamic vinegar
> 1 tbsp lime juice
> 1 tbsp olive oil
> 2 tbsp chopped coriander
> salt
> pepper (optional)

Preheat the grill to very hot.

Peel the mango (a swivel-bladed peeler is best, but a very sharp small knife will do). Cut wedges along the long axis (i.e. from top to bottom), rather like removing the segments of an orange from between their membranes. Cut into 5 mm dice. Remove the stalk from the top of the pepper and cut into 4 pieces, going from top to bottom. Remove the ribs and seeds. Place the pepper on a sheet of foil close to the heat and grill until the skin blackens and blisters. Remove as much of the skin as you can and cut into 5 mm dice. Cut a cross in the top of the tomatoes and plunge into boiling water for 20 seconds. Remove to a bowl of cold water and take off the skins. Quarter, remove the stalky bits and seeds, and cut into 1 cm dice. Transfer the pepper to a bowl and mix in the mango, tomato and shallots. Shake together the vinegar, lime juice and oil in a small screw-topped jar (or whisk in a small bowl) and stir into the mixture along with the coriander, salt and some ground black pepper if you like it. Mint can substitute very well for the coriander.

Serve this with escabèche or ceviche, or grilled oily fish. It's very good with mackerel.

For a papaya salsa, replace the mango with papaya and the red pepper with an orange or yellow one. Increase the lime juice slightly, decrease the balsamic, and add a good pinch of sugar.

Pineapple Salsa

Another salsa to serve with densely textured or oily fish.

> 150g fresh pineapple, cut into very small dice
> 1 small red pepper, skinned and cut into 1 cm dice
> ½ a red chilli and ½ a green chilli, both very finely chopped
> 2 shallots, very finely chopped
> 2 tbsp finely chopped coriander
> 1 tbsp balsamic vinegar
> 1 tbsp red wine vinegar
> 2 good pinches of sugar
> salt

Mix all the ingredients together in a bowl. Let stand in the fridge for an hour or so.

Tomato Salsa

This is a simple salsa which forms the basis of several variations, such as suggested previously (page 30).

4 firm ripe tomatoes
1 shallot or ½ a small red onion, very finely chopped
½ a mild green chilli, finely chopped
¼ tsp red wine vinegar
a large pinch of sugar
1 heaped tsp mint or basil, finely chopped
1 tbsp olive oil
salt and freshly ground black pepper

Cut a cross in the top of the tomatoes and plunge into boiling water for 20 seconds. Remove to a bowl of cold water and take off the skins. Quarter, remove the stalky bits and seeds, and cut into 1 cm dice. In another bowl mix all the other ingredients, seasoning to taste, and stir in the tomatoes. Use quickly, as the salt will draw water out of the tomatoes.

Dressings

There are so many different oils and vinegars available now that if one ate a salad every day for a month it would be easy to dress it differently every time. The usual starting point would be to combine oil and vinegar in whatever proportion and move on from there, but a moment's thought suggests plenty of other possibilities. Oil of one kind or another is pretty much essential, but different kinds of vinegar can be employed – cider, balsamic, sherry, single grape varieties – or replaced by citrus juices, verjus, dry white wine, even passion fruit juice. Or in the case of hazelnut or walnut oil, no acid element at all, although unless you are an addict a bit of dilution is in order. The short-term emulsion of a conventional vinaigrette can be stabilized, and the complexion of the dressing transformed, by introducing raw or hard-boiled egg yolks, made mustard, pounded anchovies or nuts, plain or sun-dried tomato purée or ketchup, cream and so on. Add another dimension with different herbs – use lavishly – and yet another with shallots and garlic – and there's tons of scope for the imagination.

Don't worry too much about exactitudes – play around with quantities if you don't like mine; these just happen to suit me. Remember that the dressing will effectively have to season the whole salad; you can of course season it separately, but do it after you've dressed it.

Remember, too, in the case of leaf salads, or salads with croutons, to toss them at the last minute.

Store nut oils in the fridge, and nuts in the fridge or freezer.

All-purpose dressing

This is the one I use most often because it's as suited to leaf salads as to those mixed-up salads using odds and ends from the fridge that can be so good – quartered small potatoes, broccoli or cauliflower florets, black olives, capers, bits of cooked pasta, sliced cos lettuce, chunky granary bread croutons, chopped toasted nuts, and so on.

  2 tbsp Dijon mustard
  2 tbsp white wine vinegar
  4 tbsp sunflower oil
  3 tbsp olive oil
  1 tbsp runny honey

Try to find a screw-top jar with a tight-fitting lid and shake them all together vigorously. This doesn't need any extra seasoning.

This basic dressing can be varied by adding 1 tsp grated orange rind and 1 tbsp orange juice, or 1 tsp very finely chopped shallots or red onions for more pungency, or a strong herb like tarragon, sage or very finely chopped rosemary. Let it stand for a while for the flavours to develop.

Sesame Seed and Coriander Dressing

For mixed leaves or cold egg noodles.

  1 tbsp sesame oil
  1 tbsp olive oil
  2 tbsp sunflower or groundnut oil
  3 tbsp orange juice
  a squeeze of lemon juice

  2 tbsp toasted sesame seeds (toasted in a frying pan until popping)
  2 heaped tbsp chopped coriander leaves
  salt and freshly ground black pepper

Shake all the ingredients together in a screw-top jar, seasoning to taste.

Green Herb Dressing

This is for a salad of mildly flavoured leaves – cos or Romaine, Webb's, lamb's lettuce, baby spinach – given a bit of oomph with some rocket or red trevise.

  4 tbsp olive oil
  1 finely chopped shallot

  1–2 tbsp finely chopped mixed sweet herbs (e.g. chives, chervil, basil, tarragon, marjoram)
  1–2 tsp lemon juice
  salt

Liquidize together. Add salt to taste.

A Creamy Mustard Dressing

For all kinds of salads – with an old-fashioned sort of flavour, but nice.

1 hard-boiled egg yolk
½ tsp dry mustard
1 tsp Dijon or German-type mustard
2 tbsp olive oil
½ tbsp Worcestershire sauce
1 tsp red wine vinegar
1 shallot, very finely chopped
3 tbsp single cream
salt and freshly ground black pepper

Mash together the egg yolk with the mustards and gradually incorporate the oil. Whisk in the sauce, the vinegar, the shallot and the cream. Season to taste.

Anchoïade

This is rather like the dressing for haricot bean salad (page 75), but is a stiffer consistency, and as such is just the job for spreading thickly on croutes of toasted bread brushed with olive oil.

16 anchovy fillets, drained
1 egg yolk
1 tbsp olive oil
cream
parsley

Put the anchovies and egg yolk in the liquidizer and add the olive oil gradually, or mash them with the yolk and gradually whisk in the oil.

Dilute with several tablespoons of cream and add 2 tbsp of finely chopped parsley for a runnier dressing.

Green Peppercorn Vinaigrette

A hottish dressing for potato salad.

125 ml olive oil
2 tbsp red wine vinegar
2 tbsp green peppercorns
2 tsp runny honey
2 tbsp single or double cream
2 tbsp finely chopped shallots
1 tsp lemon juice
salt (optional)

Put all the ingredients into the blender and whizz until smooth, or into a screw-top jar and shake until emulsified. You may well not have to add any salt if the peppercorns are packed in brine.

Caper Vinaigrette

This is absolutely simple, but all you need for a salad of lentils cooked with some finely diced carrot and onion with a clove of garlic. Enough for about 250g lentils.

4 tbsp groundnut or sunflower oil
4 tbsp white or red wine vinegar

1 tbsp finely chopped shallots
1 tbsp finely chopped capers
2 tbsp finely chopped parsley
salt and freshly ground black pepper

Whisk all the ingredients together in a bowl, seasoning to taste.

Ginger Vinaigrette

This is delicious with fish – hot or cold (the fish, that is).

10g piece of fresh ginger
125 ml olive oil
juice of ½ a lime
1 tbsp sherry vinegar
salt and freshly ground black pepper

Peel and grate the ginger to give about a coffee-spoonful. Blanch in boiling water for a few seconds, drain, and press out the water.

Put the oil, lime juice, sherry vinegar, and ginger in the liquidizer, and season with salt and pepper. Whizz for 1 minute, and add 50ml of boiling water. Whizz for another 20 seconds. Check the seasoning.

Orange Caraway Vinaigrette

This is very good with salads containing apple, beetroot, chicory, watercress or cauliflower (or all five together).

Makes about 150 ml

2 tsp caraway seeds, pulverized in a mortar or
    spice mill
rind of ½ a large orange, grated
50 ml orange juice
½ tsp Dijon mustard

1 tsp chopped shallot or red onion
4 tbsp sunflower or groundnut oil
½ tbsp white wine vinegar
2 tbsp water
2 pinches of salt

Put all the ingredients in the blender and whizz for 1 minute. If you replace the caraway with crushed fennel seeds you have a good dressing for a salad of thinly sliced fennel bulb, oranges and black olives.

Stocks, and a small rant

I try to have some sort of stock, usually chicken, always in the fridge, mainly for making quick dishes likes risottos or soups, but also to make simple sauces. Even a good steak usually benefits from a tablespoon or two of liquid that dissolves the sticky bits in the bottom of the pan. This liquid could be water or wine, but some stock will give it strength of character.

There are no secrets to stock making. It's a very flexible and forgiving procedure, as long as a few basic rules are followed. The first is that water should be kept to a minimum, so break up bones and carcasses so they occupy the smallest saucepan and cover with the minimum of water. The ingredients must be submerged. (This may be self-evident, but it is surprising how many good cooks leave their bay leaves just floating on the top.) This is partly to save time but chiefly to give the stock enough flavour without it having to be reduced by boiling (see below). The second is to try to include the essential aromatic vegetables, the triumvirate of onion, carrot and celery. The third is to do the same with another trio – bay leaves, parsley stalks and thyme. Omitting one or two of these isn't the end of the world, but the stock will be a bit unbalanced. A clove of garlic, crushed, and a few black peppercorns would also be helpful.

Neither fish nor meat stocks should be boiled hard, or they will become cloudy as whatever fat there is emulsifies with the liquid. The odd bubble on the surface is enough to let the heat of the liquid leach the flavours out of the ingredients.

Strain meat stock into tall, narrow receptacles. When the stock is cold it will be easier to remove the fat from the surface.

Stock will keep for 3–4 days in the fridge, but should be boiled for a few minutes after that time. It will keep a few more days, but then you had better use it.

Finally, a word on stock cubes or bouillon paste. It can't be denied that they can be mightily convenient, but there is a price to pay for this, and that price is the chemical artifice that makes the stuff possible at all. The main ingredient is salt, and I would like to know why – apart from the obvious answer that salt exaggerates flavour, in the mouth of a food technologist, anyway. In chicken stock cubes one would expect chicken to feature fairly well down the list, which it does: behind various flavour enhancers, including MSG, 'flavourings' (what they?), and the dreaded (in my house anyway) hydrogenated vegetable oil. One of our children persistently suffered from a mild lethargy, a coated tongue and bad breath, which we at first put down to a lactose intolerance. Several other guesses further on, a homeopath diagnosed HVO as the centre of the problems, and he was right. HVO is found in all sorts of things and although my wife and I are fiercely anti-junk food, it is virtually impossible to deny the modern child the occasional 'treat' (for which, read junk). Even healthy-seeming vegetable-based spreads are stuffed with it. HVO is simply poor quality oil – usually coconut or palm, extremely high in saturated fat – which when processed retains remnants of nickel and aluminium, which we eat, and almost certainly shouldn't.

So no more crisps or popcorn, unless we make them at home. En route the homeopath had a go at MSG, which it seems literally eats away at brain cells, and which he bluntly called 'brain rot'. Thanks to the experiences of my children I'm far more careful of and interested in what we all eat, without I think becoming neurotic about it. But seeing what HVOs were doing to my son I reckon those little tubs, jars and packets of stock would literally be bad medicine.

Chicken Stock

The carcass of a 1.5 kg chicken, broken into pieces (raw or cooked: raw will obviously give up more flavour, but a cooked bird will still make a worthwhile stock)
1 smallish onion, peeled and quartered
1 medium leek, washed and sliced
1 medium carrot, sliced
1 bay leaf
3–4 parsley stalks
1 clove of garlic, crushed

8–10 black peppercorns
water, just to cover
⅓ tsp dried thyme or 2 sprigs fresh

Put all the ingredients except the dried thyme into a saucepan and bring to a simmer. Skim off any scum that rises, add the dried thyme and simmer very gently for about an hour (more won't hurt). Strain, cool and refrigerate until needed.

Meat stocks

The above ingredients would be fine for a meat stock, but substitute meat bones and trimmings for the chicken. Reduce the flavourings accordingly if your quantities of meat are smaller. I prefer to brown the trimmings, bones and vegetables to produce more flavour (and colour; I can't think of any occasion when you might need a pale meat stock). Roast the bones in a hot oven in an oiled tin, and the trimmings and veg, chopped and sliced, in a lightly oiled pan. Don't forget to rinse out the tin and pan with a little water or wine, scraping up any tasty brown residues.

Variations

For lamb stock, add some bashed rosemary sprigs and an extra garlic clove or two. For ham, add a couple of turnips and cloves. For pigeon, venison, duck or game, add a few crushed juniper berries, a couple of cinnamon sticks, a couple of strips of orange peel and maybe three or four bits of star anise.

Celeriac peelings can be used instead of celery, and mushroom stalks or two or three dried porcini mushrooms won't do any harm.

Fish stock

Fish stock is slightly different, as it should not be cooked for much longer than 25 minutes or it starts to taste gluey. Therefore slice your vegetables thinly. You also need a pale colour, so use either no carrot or very little. Use flat fish – sole, brill, bream, turbot, halibut – if possible. Monkfish trimmings or whiting would do at a pinch, but not cod, haddock, bass or mullet.

For about 1 litre

about 400g fish bones and heads (and skin from
    sole, turbot or halibut)
1 small onion, peeled and thinly sliced
1 medium leek, white part only, thinly sliced
a 10cm piece of celery stalk, thinly sliced

fennel bulb trimmings if you have any
8 fennel seeds (optional)
4 parsley stalks
¼ tsp dried thyme or 2 sprigs fresh
6 black peppercorns
a piece of pared lemon peel, 3cm × 1cm
6 white mushrooms, thinly sliced, or
    mushroom peelings (optional)
water, just to cover

First wash the bones under cold running water for about 15 minutes to remove any blood. Put all the ingredients in a large wide pan and just cover with water. Simmer very gently – poach, really – for 20–25 minutes and strain through a fine sieve. Cool and refrigerate until needed.

Water on the Brain

Some people have a difficult relationship with machines, their hostility seeming to choose victims at random. Although I've had the occasional rebuff from liquidizers – which make you pay dearly for inattention with the lid – and electric sockets (I must stop cleaning them with a wet cloth), it's water that really seems to have it in for me. It's not that water is an element with any inherent malignance, as like its chums it can also be benign, but there's an unpredictable, mischief-making quality about it, an ability stealthily to insinuate and destabilize, that has earned it a regular place at the back of my mind. I had various skirmishes with it in North Wales.

When the River Conwy rose after torrential rain, the water table under my wine cellar, which had an earth floor, rose in sympathy. The first time this happened I found a large quantity of wine bottles bobbing merrily about, having thoughtlessly shed their labels. Apart from differentiating Bordeaux from Burgundy and white from red, little could be done to mitigate the damage, except to bin-end them as 'decent burgundy – I think Lebegue's Nuits-St-George 1970, but it could be 1969 Volnay'. At that stage of my career I couldn't tell the difference and, I shall whisper this, neither could my customers. And the first time I tried out a new bathroom the water ran out of the plughole straight into the entrance lobby below, the plumber having forgotten to fit the waste, much to the alarm of the plasterer working underneath.

Hostilities escalated a bit after that. I turned up early for work one day in Richmond to be met with the sight of the entire basement floor (kitchen, loos, office) shimmering under 10cm of water. The feedpipe to my icemaker had sprung a leak, and a high-pressure spray had been gushing all night. As I paddled through the water to turn off the main I noticed a rather a pleasant tingling sensation around my ankles; the water level must have risen above the electricity sockets. The tingling remained just that – I presume the volume of water was enough to dilute the current sufficiently to save me from an abrupt end – but it wasn't enough for the Fire Brigade's 12cm hoses, so we shoved the water out over the doorstep with trays and brooms.

Altogether water and I have boxed the compass. I've had water come in from above, below and sideways. On my opening day at Blandford Street the kitchen flooded with evil-smelling water from the drains. I had clearly been targeted for a while because the timing of this invasion was spot on. After that I bought myself a set of drain rods . . .

I was anxious to avoid anything similar at when I opened my Chelsea place, so in a cunning outflanking movement I had the drains professionally cleared and a video made of the result (I thought of submitting the film as an entry for the Turner prize but decided it was a bit too creative). The drains still flooded later, of course, but not on opening night.

Two of my restaurants had flat roofs as part of the premises, both surrounded by a cill of several inches. Each had a drain in the middle. It was remarkable how quickly rain accumulated when these were blocked and how accurately most of the plastic bags that blow about Marylebone would home in on that little dome of chicken wire crouched protectively over the drainhole. Or in the case of Chelsea, how awesome was the downward force of rain on the fragile branches of the Fulham Road's trees. In no time at all a thick pile of plane tree leaves would cover the chicken wire, an accidental triumph of insulation. The water would then cascade into the bar, and down to the main switchgear, fusing all the lights and knocking out the kitchen extraction. This happened once at nine in the evening when the restaurant was full. There were candles, of course, in the kitchen, too, but without extraction there was nowhere for the heat and smoke of the kitchen to go – so the candles were shrouded in fog and the heat rapidly became unbearable. My manager at the time, Marion Scrutton, had to ask everyone to leave in mid-meal; nearly all did with a very good grace.

Cold Starters

Aubergine with Garlic and Anchovies
(and bread soldiers)

I guess this is another variation on the theme of baba ganoush and muttabbul, but to my mind this has the virtue of being uncompromisingly robust – strong flavours delivered with no nonsense. This could be part of an hors d'oeuvres including bagna cauda (page 29) and hummus (page 43), eaten with an eclectic mix of raw vegetables or (better, I think) with good granary bread cut into thick soldiers, toasted in the oven until brown and crisp, and sprinkled with olive oil, salt and black pepper. Given the difficulty of finding the really tasty, small, misshapen and particoloured aubergines we would all prefer, this is a satisfactory way to take advantage of the glossy and blemish-free 'Class 1' objects we're used to.

2 large aubergines
salt
olive oil
4 anchovy fillets
2 medium cloves of garlic, peeled
1 large onion, peeled
25g or more coarse breadcrumbs

Cut the aubergines into slices 5 mm thick, salt them lightly, and put them in a large colander or a couple of sieves, under a weight, to give up some of their moisture. Leave for an hour, and pat dry with kitchen paper. If you feel you've salted a bit heavily, wash and dry them – there are anchovies to come.

Preheat the oven to 350°F/180°C/Gas 4.

Brush oil over the bottom of a roasting tin or baking dish and fill with the aubergines. Brush the visible ones with more oil and bake for about 25 minutes, until they are soft. Purée in the food processor, scrape into a sieve and push through with the back of a ladle to remove bits of skin. This isn't essential, but improves the appearance and takes away any possible bitterness.

Remove the oil from the anchovies then chop the garlic and anchovies together very finely indeed. Grate the onion on the fine grater and mix into the aubergines with the garlic mixture and the bread-crumbs. Leave in the fridge for an hour and beat in some olive oil with a wooden spoon – 4 tbsp should be about right. Finally, check the seasoning. Serve with bread soldiers, as above.

Cream Cheese and Black Olive Pâté

A light and delicious first course, particularly for a hot day. Cut into slices and drizzle with olive oil, with a dollop of tomato salsa (page 31). Without the gelatine, it makes a good creamy dip for raw vegetables.

Serves 10–12

1 large clove of garlic
1 kg low-fat cream cheese
35 black olives, pitted (90–100g)
50g anchovy fillets, chopped
2 generous tbsp Dijon mustard
a large pinch of cayenne pepper
2 egg yolks
2 tbsp lemon juice
2 sachets gelatine
350ml whipping cream

Lightly oil and line a 1kg loaf in with clingfilm, following the shape of the tin as closely as possible; half the above quantities just fills an 800ml soufflé dish.

Finely chop the garlic and mash to a paste with the blade of a large knife. Put the cream cheese, olives, anchovies, mustard, cayenne, egg yolks, lemon juice and garlic in a food-processor bowl and run the motor for 30 seconds. Meanwhile sprinkle the gelatine over 6 tbsp warm water in a small saucepan, and stir over low heat until dissolved. In a large bowl whip the cream until it holds soft peaks. Scrape the cheese mixture on to the cream and fold together alternately with the gelatine.

Pour the mixture into the tin, level off and refrigerate for at least 3 hours. Unmould when set.

Hummus

When I was perspiring over my schoolboy Latin, I wish I had known that the orator Cicero was actually Mr Chickpea. This wouldn't have made the wretched subject any easier, but would have eased the pain a bit. Was it just a nickname? A bit irreverent if so. Thus was I first charmed by this endearing pulse. No apologies for another recipe for hummus, as I dare to say I have improved upon the standard versions, by replacing tahini with peanut butter. A bit heretical but the subtle nuttiness does good things for the chickpeas. The cumin is a bit unorthodox too.

3 tbsp olive oil
250g dried chickpeas, soaked overnight in cold water, then simmered for 45 minutes in fresh water, and drained, or 450g tin of chickpeas, plus 3 tbsp of the liquid
2 cloves of garlic, chopped
1 tsp grated lemon rind
2 tsp or more lemon juice
1 tbsp smooth peanut butter
¼ tbsp ground cumin
1 tsp salt
paprika
cumin

Blend 1 tbsp of the olive oil and the next seven ingredients in the food processor, and scrape into a small bowl, or into 4 small china dishes. Sprinkle the paprika and cumin in a criss-cross fashion and drizzle over the remaining olive oil.

Serve with thin slices of decent bread rubbed with cut garlic, sprinkled with a little salt and black pepper, and toasted lightly under the grill, or with water biscuits or Bath Olivers.

Caraway Biscuits

These are ideal served with a beetroot bavarois (page 44).

175g flour
110g butter, cold, cut into pieces
2 tsp salt (1½ tsp if using salted butter)
2 heaped tsp ground caraway seeds
1–2 tbsp cold water

Preheat the oven to 350°F/180°C/Gas 4.

Put all the ingredients except the water into a food-processor bowl and run the motor for 10 seconds. Add the water and run until a ball of dough is formed – about 10 seconds. Roll out on a floured surface to a thickness of about 1cm and cut into circles or fingers. Gather up the trimmings and roll out again until all the dough is used up. Bake for 15–20 minutes.

Beetroot Bavarois

As someone who doesn't like the unadorned flavour of beetroot, it may seem odd that I've included several recipes using it. This has only a little to do with childhood memories of the great British salad – it's just that I find its flavour, rather like that of kidneys, slightly uncongenial. However, used in combination with a limited palette of other ingredients, its moist, direct earthiness and vibrant colour can add a certain lustre to a dish. As one might expect, it marries best with its traditional, northern-latitude companions, horseradish, sour cream, mustard, vinegar, and caraway, but also with orange and garlic. But then these two dignify most things.

The beetroot bavarois is made in a similar way to the sweet pepper bavarois (page 46). Ready-cooked beetroot are fine for this.

½ a medium onion, finely chopped
20g butter
500g cooked beetroot
1 tsp grated orange rind
juice of 1 orange
2 tsp ground caraway seeds
1½ tsp salt
6 tbsp Cabernet Sauvignon vinegar or other
    red wine vinegar
1½ envelopes gelatine
3 egg whites

Sweat the onion in the butter for 5 minutes. Don't let it colour. Drain the beetroot, reserving the juice, and chop roughly. Add to the onions with the beetroot juice, orange rind and juice, caraway, and salt. Cover and simmer gently for 5 minutes. Meanwhile pour the vinegar into a small saucepan and sprinkle over the gelatine. Heat gently, swirling the pan, until the gelatine has dissolved. Pour the vinegar into the beetroot mix and scrape everything into a liquidizer jar and blitz for 30 seconds. Place a fine sieve over a bowl and pour in the purée. Leave to drain, pressing on the purée gently until about half a teacupful of liquid has collected. Do this through muslin over a coarser sieve if you like. Keep the liquid at room temperature.

Transfer the purée to a large bowl and cool. When it starts to set, whisk the egg whites to hold soft peaks and fold in the purée using a circular motion starting at the centre of the bowl, turning the bowl a little with each stroke. Place a straight-sided 20 cm or 18 cm flan ring (if it's 18 cm it must be at least 4 cm high) over a large flat plate and pour in the bavarois. Level the surface. Refrigerate for an hour or two until firm, and pour the reserved liquid gently over it. Refrigerate again until set – 20 minutes should do it. Run a hot knife blade round the inside of the ring and lift off carefully. Serve with caraway biscuits (page 43) and a big blob of sour cream.

Sweet Pepper Bavarois

Bavarois, mousses, jellies all seem to be out of fashion at the moment. Is it, perhaps, because orthodontics has strengthened the nation's teeth so much that if it isn't al dente or a bleeding chunk it has to be classed as fit only for babies? What a shame if these things were to become preserved in, well, aspic, to suffer the fate of the briar pipe or the antimacassar. The creamy unctuousness of the bavarois, which in the capricious way of fashion is still OK in puds, has much to recommend it, as long as it has plenty of flavour. I'm sure its eclipse is only temporary, like leg warmers and winkle-pickers (but not kaftans, please).

This can be made with yellow peppers too, but the stronger, sweeter flavour of red is better. The creaminess is offset by the sweet-sour notes of the vinegar.

½ a large Spanish onion, finely chopped
40g butter
4 red peppers, deseeded and chopped fairly finely
4 firm ripe tomatoes, peeled
a 5cm strip of orange peel, without pith
1 heaped tsp paprika
a few drops of Tabasco
a large pinch of sugar
1¼ tsp salt
125ml red wine vinegar
2 sachets gelatine
400ml whipping cream

Sweat the onion in the butter for 5 minutes. Add the peppers, tomatoes, orange peel, paprika, Tabasco, sugar and salt, and cook, covered, over medium heat for 20 minutes, stirring occasionally. Don't let anything catch on the pan bottom or let anything brown. In a separate pan reduce the vinegar by three-quarters, pour into a bowl and let cool. Sprinkle over the gelatine and stir over gentle heat until it dissolves.

Scrape the pepper mixture into a sieve set over a clean bowl. Let about half a cupful of liquid drain into the bowl and set aside (for the mirror topping). Liquidize the contents of the sieve and pass the liquid back through the sieve into another bowl. Pour most of the vinegar into this, and the rest into the bowl with the liquid for the mirror topping (about ⅘ and ⅕).

Let the pepper/vinegar mixture cool in the fridge until it starts to set. Whip the cream until it's semi-stiff and fold in thoroughly.

Take a straight-sided flan ring, 20cm or 18cm in diameter (if it's 18cm it must be at least 4cm high), place it on a flat plate or baking sheet and pour in the bavarois mix. Let this set in the fridge for at least an hour, then gently pour the jelly over the top (it may have to be warmed gently before you pour it on). Let the whole thing set for another hour. Run a knife warmed in hot water round the inside of the ring and lift it off carefully.

Feta, Chard, and Pine Nut Tortilla

This is great for snacking or for taking on a picnic or serving as a first course. Spinach is fine for this too but use chard if you can find it. In fact, always use chard if you can find it. More chard in the shops, please.

1 tbsp finely chopped white of leek
1 small clove of garlic, peeled and chopped
2 tbsp olive oil
750g chard leaves, or about 250g cooked, chopped and squeezed spinach
3 tbsp pine nuts
75g feta, cut into 5mm cubes
1 tbsp finely chopped of any of the following: parsley, basil, mint, oregano, chervil, thyme, chives
2 large eggs
2 tbsp crème fraiche or double cream
G tsp salt
5 turns black pepper

Soften the leek and garlic in 1 tbsp of the oil in a 30cm frying or omelette pan. Do this gently for 5 minutes. Meanwhile, cook the chard leaves, washed in cold water and shaken, in a covered pan, over medium heat for about 10 minutes, stirring twice. Cool, squeeze out the moisture, and chop fairly finely. Toast the pine nuts under the grill, shaking two or three times, until they turn a pale golden brown. Watch them carefully as they burn very easily.

In a large bowl, mix together the chard or spinach, the leek and garlic scraped from the pan, the nuts, feta and herbs. In a small separate bowl, beat the eggs together with the crème fraiche or cream and stir thoroughly into the chard mixture. Season. Be careful with the salt as feta is quite salty already. Heat the remaining oil in the same pan, brushing the oil at least halfway up the sides. When very hot, but not smoking, pour in the mixture and spread over the base of the pan, smoothing the top. Cook about 8 minutes. Heat the grill to high and, when the 8 minutes are up, place the whole pan under it. Keep the pan 15cm from the heat, and let the top of the tortilla firm up without browning. When it's firm, remove from the grill, loosen the underneath with a spatula or metal slice, and invert a large plate over it. Reverse the position of each and the tortilla should turn out neatly on to the plate. Serve, cut into wedges, with a tomato sauce (page 27).

Mousse of Broad Beans

Delicate and delicious, a bright creamy green, this is the essence of broad beans. It's a dish to make when you have time on your hands. Oh, all right then, when the *Archers* is on (not just the omnibus) or some sixteenth-century choral music, or when your three daughters are gathered cosily around you and are *begging* you to let them help . . . In other words, it's either a displacement activity or a sharing, enriching activity that unites the family . . . Is anyone still reading? You *can* use frozen broad beans (try those 'from field to freezer in 2½ hours'). If you use fresh, you'll need about 4 kg of pods. Reject any with black bits.

500g beans, podded weight
300ml whipping or double cream
1 tbsp marjoram leaves
1 tsp salt

Bring a saucepan of water to the boil and pour the beans in. Boil for 5 minutes only. Remove and plunge into a bowl of iced water. When cold slip off and discard the skins. Purée in the food-processor bowl with 6–8 tbsp of the cream, scraping down the sides of the bowl and pulsing alternately. Scrape into a medium-sized bowl, chop the marjoram leaves finely (they discolour quickly) and stir in. Whisk the rest of the cream to hold soft peaks, and fold in until the colour is homogeneous. Add salt to your liking as you go. Refrigerate for at least a couple of hours to allow the marjoram flavour to develop.

Serve by forming quenelle shapes with two spoons dipped in hot water. A mixed leaf and orange salad tossed with a walnut oil dressing would go well.

This mousse is good piled on top of artichoke hearts. The same method (but quicker, of course) can be used with peas. Flavour with mint or summer savory and serve with a sharper dressing.

Ceviche

Ceviche belongs in that category of first courses which includes escabèches, tartares and carpaccios. Mildly astringent, refreshing and healthy, you could call them a more nourishing form of aperitif – particularly if vodka, gin or aquavit is included in the 'cure'. That, however, is probably only for our younger readers. The basic principle is raw fish given acidulation by some kind of citrus juice, usually lime, although grapefruit, Seville orange, and passion fruit juices are all suitable. Thereafter it's a simple choice of serving the fish immediately, or waiting for the acids to 'cook' the fish by stiffening the fibres. In the case of an escabèche, the fish is seared briefly over a high heat and then left to cool and finish cooking in an acidulated marinade.

Ceviche originates in South America, where it usually includes some hot chilli; add some if you like. My weedy British palate finds it OK without. I also have to add a bit of sweetening, which I'm convinced makes limes taste more limey. The thing is to please yourself. You may like your limes straight. If using sugar, though, you must remember that the fish will absorb the acids gradually, so if you leave the fish long enough it will be cooked through and you will have a sickly-sweet liquid residue. This is why you must prepare a double quantity of juice for this recipe: you pour off the used marinade residue and pour over some fresh to serve.

This makes a brilliant first course if something rib-sticking is to follow.

Immersing the limes in boiling water for 5 minutes will make it easier to expel all the juice. Small limes often have very little juice.

1 firm ripe tomato
juice of 3 limes, with dark green firm skins
30g caster sugar
400g firm-bodied fish fillet that you can cut
     into thin slices: tuna, swordfish, shark,
     monkfish, salmon or large sea bass.
     Try to buy before they have been cut into
     steaks. If you have no razor-sharp slicing
     knife, cut thin chunks and flatten with a
     heavy knife blade or a rolling pin.
1 shallot or ½ a small red onion, very finely
     chopped
1 heaped tbsp finely chopped coriander leaves
sea salt crystals

Cut a cross in the top of the tomato and plunge into boiling water while you count to 20, then remove the skin and seeds and cut neatly into 1 cm dice.

Mix together the lime juice and sugar and let stand for a few minutes, to make sure the sugar has dissolved.

Slice the fish as thinly as possible and arrange it in a circular shape on 4 plates. Pour over half the juice and leave in the fridge for 2–6 hours. Pour away the liquid residue and pour on the fresh juice. Scatter over the tomato dice, the shallot or onion, and the coriander leaves. Sprinkle over some sea salt to finish.

Ceviche of Salmon or Sea Trout with Passion Fruit

450g middle cut of salmon or sea trout
juice of 8 wrinkly passion fruit, rubbed
    through a sieve
10g sugar
1 tbsp olive oil
30ml good dry white wine, preferably with
    some body, e.g. Aligoté or Mâcon
salt
1 tbsp chopped dill

Bone and skin the fish and cut into batons 1cm wide, then across at 5cm intervals. Mix together the other ingredients except the dill. Gently turn the fish in half the liquid. Leave for 30 minutes, pour off the liquid and mix the reserved liquid in. Divide between 4 plates and sprinkle with dill.

Tartare of Tuna

Such a nineties thing, the fish tartare. That's rather like saying that tarragon chicken was a sixties thing, steak au poivre a seventies, viennoise of cod an eighties. A bit of a recurring theme in this book is the foolishness of the fashion-conscious, who seize upon a dish and put it on a pedestal so everyone of lesser talent feels bound to imitate it; the dish becomes devalued and bowdlerized and is consigned to outer darkness. This has happened to squid ink risotto, and it's happened to the fish tartare, which like those other dishes above should have become part of the repertory. A tartare is like a salsa, in that you can put in lots of different things and, as long as they are carefully chosen, the thing will work. The difference with tartare is that the flavour of the fish must be protected. This recipe I think pays its correct respects to the tuna. The fish must be as fresh as possible.

1 egg yolk
2 tbsp olive oil
2 tbsp lime juice
grated rind of 1 lime
2 tsp dill, finely chopped
2 tsp chives, finely chopped
1 tsp Dijon mustard
2 anchovy fillets, mashed to a paste
2 tbsp red onion, very finely chopped
2 tsp drained, finely chopped capers
350g fresh tuna, free of membranes, cut into
    1cm dice

Mix together in a bowl all the ingredients except the tuna, then add the fish and let stand in the fridge for half an hour or more. Don't serve it fridge cold – bring it out about 15 minutes before serving and stir it a couple of times. This is one occasion when serving in a small ring is desirable, perhaps with a thin layer of sour cream on top, and a few salmon eggs (keta) to make it look (and taste) pretty.

Terrine of Jerusalem Artichokes

If I had to compile a list of the top ten vegetable flavours, the Jerusalem artichoke would be pretty close to number one, running the globe artichoke to a short head, and with only asparagus possibly to come between them and get up on the line. I guess in terms of all-round allure the asparagus would shade it, if only because preparation is pretty simple, if you have a swivel-bladed peeler, and in this respect the artichoke is pretty much left at the start.

The Jerusalem artichoke has the curious property of a random cooking time – some will be well cooked and completely soft in 10 minutes, where others will need 20, and there's no way of telling which. Try to find tubers without too many limbs or there will be too much waste. Supermarkets sell them ready-scrubbed, and it's tempting to slice them without peeling. The skins don't soften much with cooking, though, so if you don't mind that, leave them on.

Serves 10–12

1 kg Jerusalem artichokes
juice of 1 lemon
150g thinly sliced Parma or Serrano
    ham
250g (or slightly more) butter
3–4 lemons with very firm skins, grated
4 heaped tbsp chopped mixed green herbs
    – any combination of parsley, tarragon,
    chervil, chives and marjoram

Wash the artichokes, peel and wash again, cut into chunks roughly the size of the smallest, placing them as you go in a large bowl of water with the lemon juice. Remove to a saucepan, cover with salted boiling water and cook for 10 minutes. Refresh in cold water, and after a few minutes remove and cut into 5 mm slices.

While they are cooking, line a 1 kg loaf tin with clingfilm, leaving enough to overlap the top on each side, and line the clingfilm with slices of ham, trying to ensure there aren't any gaps. Cut them to fit the ends and the corners. Leave enough overlap to cover the top when the tin is full.

Melt the butter gently in a small pan and add the grated lemon rind and herbs. Pour a thin layer in the bottom of the tin and put in a layer of artichokes, cutting them to fit so the gaps are small. Cover with more herbs and butter and add another layer of artichokes. Continue like this until the terrine is full, trying to keep enough butter to anoint the top layer. Fold over the ham and the clingfilm. You will now need a piece of thick card or wood or even a long thin book to place inside the top of the tin, and upon which you must place as heavy a weight as you can find. This pressure should compress the artichokes and distribute the butter. Put in the fridge for several hours then unmould carefully. Slice with the clingfilm in place, removing it as you go.

Serve this with a simple refreshing tomato sauce (page 27) or the turnip cream sauce (page 29), or a hazelnut oil and orange juice dressing with a little water, salt, and chervil.

Jellied Ham

One of the few decent cuts of meat you can buy from a supermarket is a joint of gammon, as it will be little different from the equivalent sold in the average butcher's shop. And although it will probably have been injected with water and cured with too much salt, it can still be turned into a dish well worth eating. However, you must be prepared to remove as much salt as possible. This is, of course, a version of the rustic French classic jambon persillé, which if traditionally done involves an enormous amount of work, starting with curing your own ham, then cooking it in white wine with pigs' feet. Indeed, the first time I made this, I bought a Victorian oval iron cauldron in Welshpool market and did it from scratch. It took me two *whole* days. Here, we have to make do with gammon, but it's still pretty good.

Serves 6–8

1 unsmoked gammon joint, approx. 1.2 kg
½ bottle good dry white wine
bouquet garni of 3 thyme sprigs (or ½ tsp
    dried), 1 tbsp chopped tarragon, 2 allspice
    berries, 1 bay leaf and 1 clove of garlic,
    all tied in a muslin bag (no muslin?
    – then remove the herbs later)
1 medium leek, sliced
1 medium onion, roughly chopped
1 small carrot, roughly chopped
1 small celery stalk
1 small turnip, quartered (optional – I happen
    to like the flavour of turnip in ham stock)
2 egg whites (or 1 large)
2 sachets gelatine
1 tsp white wine vinegar
1 tbsp finely chopped parsley, flat if possible
½ tbsp chopped tarragon
½ tbsp chopped chervil
1 medium clove of garlic, very finely chopped

Put the gammon in a large saucepan and cover it with cold water. Bring to a simmer, taste the water for saltiness, and pour it away. Do this once or twice more, depending on how much salt is coming out of the gammon. Now pour in the wine and enough fresh water to cover by 2 cm and add the bouquet garni and all the vegetables. Bring to simmering point, skimming, and simmer gently until the meat is tender – an hour and a half, maybe more. Fish the gammon out and set aside until cold.

Strain the cooking liquid into another saucepan and leave to get quite cold. Remove all bits of congealed fat. Whisk in the egg whites very thoroughly and heat the liquid slowly, moving it to the side of the heat as it comes to simmering point. Leave it until you can see clear liquid under the crust. Remove most of this crust with a large spoon. Line a sieve with muslin or a clean tea towel, and ladle the liquid through it into a clean pan. Boil this down until you have about 700 ml. Pour about 100 ml into a smaller pan, cool, sprinkle over the gelatine and stir gently until dissolved. Add back to the rest of the liquid with the vinegar.

Cut the gammon into 2 cm pieces, trimmed of all fat and gristle. Pour a little of the liquid, to a depth of 5 mm, into a 1 kg loaf tin and set in the freezer for 10 minutes. Put a layer of meat on top, mix the parsley, tarragon, chervil and garlic, and sprinkle the ham with about one third of the mixture. Cover with liquid. Do the same with two more layers of meat and liquid, which should just about fill the tin. Make sure no chunks of meat are poking out of the top of the liquid. Refrigerate for at least a couple of hours. Unmould by dipping into a large bowl of hot water and turning out on to a flat dish. Slice with a very sharp knife, and serve as is.

Nasty Moments: 1

Very rarely have I had to ask any customer to leave, which I like to think is more to do with civilized clients than my having a diffident personality, but one Tuesday evening at Blandford Street a troublesome type – I'll call him Mr Stone – suffered the ultimate sanction.

He and his two womenfolk didn't like their table, but we were full and couldn't give him another one. He clearly knew some other people there and was probably put out because he had, he thought, an inferior table. Disgruntled, he complained about the length of time his first courses took to arrive (only sixteen minutes – we knew because all our orders are timed) and then sent back two of his main courses. These were replaced, and then one of the replacements was sent back.

Having to splice an extra main course into a busy service is difficult enough, but having to do it twice is a nightmare. I couldn't find anything wrong with the food anyway (I was front of house that evening) so decided enough was enough and asked him to leave. After puffing and blowing for a while he did. I also said I didn't want his money (although I was crying inside while I said it). This was supposed to be insulting but I think it made him feel better.

On his way out he stopped at a table near the door and talked for a minute to a crony, leaning over him and speaking closely into his ear. After Mr Stone's baleful exit, this chap called me over, pointing to something on his plate. Oh hell, I thought, now what? The two of them are out to get me! I carried the plate over to the bar and looked at it under a bright light. Yes, there was something in the sauce around his wild duck, something small, black and with spiky bits sticking out. Uh oh, they've planted a bug and they are going to sue me after they've called the Environmental Health Officer, the Health and Safety Executive, the Trading Standards Officer, old Uncle Tom Cobley and all. Visions of men in white coats and gauzy trilbies holding 'notice of closure' papers flashed before my eyes. But hold on – what looked very much like a dead beast with frondy bits turns out to be – after all – a feather!

Relieved, I explain that a piece of shot had pushed a feather into the meat, and he had simply dislodged it. Poor man – what fuss could he make now? Deflated, that particular table passed the rest of the evening quietly. Mr Stone had obviously just been arranging a wife-swapping party in Penge after all. Unfortunately, history doesn't record whether the piece of shot ended in one of his mate's fillings, but in the absence of any letters to me in green ink, I suppose it didn't.

How to Borrow from the Bank

One of the more bizarre episodes of my restaurant career was trying to raise a small loan from a new bank in Bond Street whose assistant manager had been recommended as a good bet by my mortgage broker ('I'm the slickest bastard in the business'). I rang this chap who suggested, rather to my surprise, that we meet at Crockfords, the casino in Curzon Street. I arrived before time and was offered a drink and some canapés. The drink was champagne from the bottle kept for him and the canapés were smoked salmon and more caviar than I had eaten in the last ten years. Lunch was taken in the Crockfords dining room – a vast barrel-vaulted chamber which somehow gave the impression, thanks to its furnishings, of a gigantic bedouin tent rather than an exercise in neoclassical overkill. The enormous buffet that was being eyed by the only other customers, a couple of Arabs in flowing robes, did little to dispel this feeling.

After lunch the Crockfords limousine, a magenta Daimler, took me all the way to the nearest tube station – about three hundred yards. I couldn't help wondering what my 'fixer' had said about me and my prospects, and what my treatment might have been if I'd been asking for £4,000,000 instead of a paltry £4,000. Not that I was complaining, but it's sadly true that my subsequent dealings with bank managers have been conducted at a less rarefied level. Anyway, I got the loan. When I called my benefactor to thank him, I found he had just been moved to the branch at Billericay. No bedouin tents there.

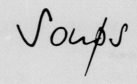 *Soups*

Watercress and Almond Soup

Years ago, before I didn't know any better, I used to make a celery and almond soup. Good, but not great. Trying to develop a really good watercress soup, I thought I would try the same method. The ingredients turn out to be sympathetic, and the sour cream picks up the slight pepperiness of the watercress. The result is quite distinguished (I think).

Serves 8

2 bunches watercress
75g butter
50g flaked almonds
110g ground almonds
1 litre chicken stock
2 large egg yolks
300ml soured cream, 4 tbsp reserved
salt

Wash, drain, and chop the watercress, removing the coarser stalks. Melt the butter in a large saucepan and cook the flaked almonds over a medium to high heat until they take on a medium brown colour. Lift them out with a slotted spoon and reserve for garnish. Turn the watercress in the butter until it's shiny and cook over a low heat for 5 minutes. Add the ground almonds and stock and bring to the boil. Cool a little then liquidize. In a bowl whisk together the egg yolks and sour cream and whisk in about 200ml of the soup. Transfer to a small saucepan. Pour on some more of the liquid and heat, whisking, until the soup thickens. Let this cool in a cold saucepan, pour in the rest of the soup, and check the seasoning. This stage is simply to preserve as much of the bright green colour as possible, as the more some green leaves or vegetables are heated, the more their colour will fade, darken, or turn yellow. This applies particularly to watercress, but also to leeks, asparagus, broccoli, lettuce and sprouts.

Although watercress does make a good cold soup, with a base of onion and potatoes, this soup is better hot. Swirl the reserved sour cream into the soup and sprinkle with the flaked almonds.

Sweet Pepper and Ginger Soup

This works well either hot or iced. I made it once when I had a cold, not realizing that my taste buds had been nuked and I could taste *nothing*. I added more and more ginger, more and more salt – my supper guests were restrained in their enthusiasm. My wife told me later it was almost inedible. So make this when you're healthy.

4 large red peppers, seeded and roughly chopped
2 large leeks, white parts only, finely sliced
75g butter
4cm cube of fresh ginger, peeled and grated
1 tbsp paprika
1 tbsp caster sugar
1 tsp salt
juice and grated rind of 1 large orange
600 ml chicken stock
600 ml buttermilk or yogurt
crème fraiche
fresh coriander
grated lemon rind

Cook the peppers and leeks in the butter in a large saucepan for about 15 minutes, over moderate heat. Stir now and again. Add the next 6 ingredients and simmer for 20 minutes. Cool a little. Liquidize and pour though a sieve into a bowl, pressing on the debris in the sieve. Mix in the buttermilk or yogurt.

Float blobs of crème fraiche with lots of chopped fresh coriander and grated lemon rind on the top.

Cold Tomato Soup with Basil Mayonnaise

A quick, refreshing cold soup for a hot day and when decent tomatoes are available. Don't try this as a hot soup. You can cut down on the cream if you're in denial. If you want something crunchy to go with this, try the garlic croutes (page 216). If you like the texture of the avgolemono that follows (page 60), this also takes well to a bit of jellification. Use 1 sachet of gelatine.

800g firm, ripe tomatoes
1 tbsp grated onion
grated rind and juice of 1 lemon
1 tbsp caster sugar
200 ml single cream
salt
4 heaped tbsp mayonnaise (preferably home-made)
2 tbsp finely chopped basil

Roughly chop the tomatoes and purée in the liquidizer for a few seconds. Press through a sieve into a bowl. Stir in the onion, lemon rind and juice, sugar and cream. Season with salt.

In a small bowl mix together the mayonnaise and basil. Divide the soup between 4 cold bowls and float a big spoonful of basil mayonnaise on each one.

Jerusalem Artichoke Soup

This is an unashamed lift from Escoffier. His feet, size 6 on their built-up soles, may have been made of clay (he had some twentieth-century fin-de-siècle counterparts in Paris) but the breadth and depth of his knowledge are astonishing. Surrounded as we restaurant chefs are today by labour-saving gadgets, plentiful hot water and (fairly) sophisticated ventilation, Escoffier's energy and accomplishments, and those of his lieutenants, are awe-inspiring. His books are so packed with instruction, so stuffed with recipes from the domestic (in *Ma Cuisine*) to the most elevated of haute cuisine, that one can't imagine him having a life outside his kitchen, whether at the London Carlton Hotel, the Ritz, or on board the Holland-Amerika line. It's instructive to read his recipe for fish stock in successive editions of *L'Art Culinaire*, as the amounts of caviar added to the mix and then thrown away reduce gradually until, after the end of the Great War, they disappear altogether. The discipline of haute cuisine was an unforgiving one, based as it was on several centuries of evolution, evolution which by Escoffier's time had become tradition, and which he, the greatest chef of the epoch, codified for the flame-bearers of the future. There are many recipes of his which are worth cooking today at home, particularly for soup.

This one is based on a 'cream of rice', which acts as the bland (but delicious) support structure for other flavours. As I'm so keen on Jerusalem artichokes I think that one is best, but this soup base works very well, as le Maître says, for celeriac, lettuce, asparagus and mushroom. I haven't tried the curry and paprika versions.

1.2 litres full-cream milk
4 tbsp ground rice
1 small onion, stuck with 2 cloves
8 black peppercorns
1 sprig thyme (or ½ tsp dried thyme)
½ a bay leaf
2 sprigs parsley
350g Jerusalem artichokes
12g butter
salt
freshly grated nutmeg
2 tbsp single cream

Reserve a few tablespoons of the milk and mix it with the ground rice to make a smooth paste. Put the rest of the milk into a saucepan with the onion, peppercorns, thyme, bay leaf and parsley, and bring slowly to the boil. Stir the rice paste in thoroughly and simmer to 20 minutes over low heat. Strain into a fresh pan through a fine sieve. Meanwhile peel and slice the artichokes roughly. Simmer them in a pan of enough salted water just to cover them until tender – about 10 minutes – and drain. Melt the butter in the hot pan and turn the artichokes in it for 10 minutes, covered, over moderate heat. Mash to a rough purée with a potato masher or fork and push through a sieve with the back of a ladle into the cream of rice, and season with salt and nutmeg. Stir in the cream. If you want something else in this soup to alleviate the pale colour, add some fried bread croutons or a sprinkling of chives.

For the other variants listed above, the quantities required are 350g celeriac, 250g lettuce, 450g asparagus, 225g mushrooms.

Jellied Avgolemono with Dill

This is a variant of the classic Greek egg and lemon soup, which I thought would be welcome on a hot day. The chicken stock will jellify itself when cold, but only if made with the whole carcass. If you're in doubt about this, simply sprinkle some gelatine over some of the stock, leave it a few minutes, and warm it, stirring, until it dissolves. As a thickening medium, egg yolks and cream on their own add a velvety delicacy without any of the flavour-masking offered by most thickening agents – rice flour, I would say, is an exception, as in the Jerusalem artichoke soup (page 59). Although, strictly speaking, you don't need the thickening element, it gives a pleasing colour and body, I think. The dill isn't there just for the pretty colour – it goes well with the lemon.

Perhaps needless to say, you need firm- and thick-skinned lemons.

800 ml strong chicken stock
3 egg yolks
80 ml double cream
grated rind of 1 large lemon
up to 3 tbsp lemon juice
6 tbsp finely chopped dill
salt

Heat some of the stock until it simmers. In a stainless-steel or enamelled pan, beat together the egg yolks and cream and pour in the hot stock in a stream, whisking the while. Place the pan over moderate heat and whisk until it thickens, making sure the whisk covers all the base and corners of the pan. If you're not sure you can do this without scrambling the yolks on the pan bottom, have a bowl of iced water ready, and at the first sign of any danger put the base of the pan in the water and whisk furiously. By then the mixture should have thickened enough. A teaspoon of cornflour whisked into the egg yolks would prevent this happening, but that would be cheating, wouldn't it?

Add the rest of the stock, the lemon rind and enough of the lemon juice to give the flavour you like. Let the soup cool, add the dill (heat tends to discolour it), and season. Ideally the consistency should be lightly jellied when the soup is completely cold, although it's better fridge-cold on a hot day. Anyway, a few stirs will loosen it up if it comes straight from the fridge.

Chestnut Soup

A winter rib-sticker. Not everyone, it seems, likes chestnuts. Perhaps it's their rich stickiness (or sticky richness) or their annual arranged marriage with Brussels sprouts that gives them a marginal position, but most likely it's just their distinct flavour. As often as not they will be pushed aside by my restaurant customers. This even extends to the glacé versions, which – drained of syrup, of course – make great partners with a decently hung pheasant (the syrup can be used to make an interesting butterscotch sauce). I can understand that their rather mealy texture might be discouraging, but their flavour is so good this shouldn't be an issue. The French get round this neatly by puréeing and canning them.

One aspect though is definitely a minus – preparing the fresh variety. I don't think there's a best way; every one is laborious and awkward. Probably the least troublesome is to cut a nick in each one and plunge into very hot oil for 2 minutes. The skin and the membrane will come off fairly easily, with some lost to your fingernails. Much the best approach is to use dried chestnuts, which are fairly widely available. They'll need to be soaked at least 12 hours.

12g duck fat (or mixture of bacon fat and butter)
1 large Spanish onion, chopped
1 large carrot, chopped
1 stick of celery, chopped
500 ml well-flavoured chicken stock
3 blades of mace
250g dried, soaked chestnuts
salt

To serve
cream
streaky bacon (optional)

Melt the fat in a large saucepan and cook the onion over low heat for 10 minutes. Add the carrot and celery, cover the pan, and cook a further 10 minutes without browning. Add the stock, mace and chestnuts and simmer for half an hour. Cool, liquidize and season. Serve with a swirl of cream and, if you like, some miniature thin-cut streaky bacon rolls crisped in the oven.

Cannellini Bean Soup

Although they look like haricot beans, only a bit larger, cannellini beans have a slight edge on flavour. Creamier, slightly less earthy, these beans are only available in their dried form, unfortunately, although I'm sure we could perfectly well grow them here. This is one of those soups that you could eat more or less as a vegetable, in the way the Italians seem to, with a small amount of liquid, some of which is olive oil. To me this kind of soup seems better suited to being a main course – just to look at all those beans, probably with some rude chunks of bread and more than drop of the oily stuff, is enough to make me feel I've eaten already (this may just be a function of not really having eaten lunch, at lunchtime anyway, for about twenty-five years). So this soup is a bit less rustic, although serving it with some big croutons and a slick of olive oil floating on the top won't compromise my principles.

The only real problem with this soup is the colour, which can look a bit like dishwater, so there's some cream to improve matters in that respect.

125g cannellini beans, soaked overnight
800ml light chicken stock or water
1 stalk of celery
1 clove
1 small onion, sliced
1 large clove of garlic, peeled and crushed
1 bay leaf
1 small turnip, quartered
4 tbsp double cream
salt
olive oil
a few chunks of granary bread fried in mixed
    butter and olive oil
freshly ground black pepper
marjoram or oregano leaves

Drain and rinse the beans. Put them in a large pan and pour on the stock or water. Boil for 10 minutes, skimming off any white scum. Add the next six ingredients, and simmer until the beans are soft – about an hour. Discard the clove, bay leaf and turnip. Cool a little and liquidize the beans with the cream. Season with salt. When ready to serve divide between 4 bowls and, pouring from a spoon, zig-zag olive oil over the top. Put the croutons in the centre and turn the pepper mill a few times over the olive oil. Marjoram or oregano leaves, chopped at the last minute to prevent them discolouring, would be nice scattered over the top.

Turnip and Brown Bread Soup

This has always been one of my favourite soups. It's a recipe from Michael Smith's *Fine English Cooking*, which has some excellent things in it. There is a completeness about this soup that belies its simple components – the humble turnip, onion, bread, stock and nutmeg. A bit like potage bonne femme, in fact, in that the result of mixing these things together is quite surprising. Michael Smith uses a small quantity of olive oil, presumably to stop the butter scorching. I think we can allow him that liberty. Turnips and cinnamon are good, but nutmeg is better – at least in this soup.

50g butter
35g chopped onion
500g firm turnips
75g good brown bread, crusts removed
1 tbsp olive oil
750ml chicken stock
½ tsp grated nutmeg
salt and freshly ground black pepper
single or double cream

Melt two-thirds of the butter in a large saucepan and cook the onion in it over moderate heat until it starts to brown at the edges. Peel the green thinly from the turnips, and top and tail them. Cut into 3cm chunks and add to the onions. Stir about thoroughly, cover, and cook over low heat for about 25 minutes, until the turnips are tender.

Meanwhile cut the bread into 2cm cubes. Heat the remaining butter with the olive oil in a frying pan. A few seconds after the foam has disappeared, throw in the croutons and sauté them until well browned on all sides. Add half to the turnip pan and pour in the stock. Add the nutmeg. Simmer the soup gently for 20 minutes. Add salt and a few turns of the pepper mill. Liquidize.

Serve with a swirl of cream and the rest of the croutons floating on top.

Feta, Almond and Fennel Soup

I've always liked the juxtaposition of feta cheese and almonds, so they seemed a natural pairing for this soup. The fennel gives it a mildly interesting undertone as well as providing the thickening. I can't decide if this is better hot or cold, which isn't really very much help.

25g butter
100g Spanish onion, chopped
50g feta cheese

50g flaked almonds, lightly toasted
2 cloves of garlic, chopped roughly
75g finely sliced fennel
1 small stalk of celery, sliced
500ml light chicken stock

Melt the butter in a medium saucepan and soften the onion in it over gentle heat for 10 minutes. Add the other ingredients and cook over moderate heat for 20 minutes. Cool a little and liquidize.

Cauliflower and Gorgonzola Soup

A good cauli is a fine thing – hard, creamy-white and heavy, it's rather a beautiful object with a distinct and interesting flavour, neither coarse nor delicate. It's a good base for a veg salad, mixed with brown bread croutons, black olives, capers, toasted almonds and bits of orange, and makes a lovely purée when mixed with reduced double cream and nutmeg.

This is an intriguingly delicate soup with the creamy Gorgonzola flavour playing a polite and restrained supporting role. You must use a 'morning fresh' cauli.

400g cauliflower
500ml chicken stock
25g butter
½ a Spanish onion, finely sliced
75g potato, cut into 2cm pieces
50g mild Gorgonzola
½ tsp salt
a big pinch of nutmeg

To serve
chives, croutons, or almonds

Trim the cauliflower of leaves and central stalk. Cut into 3cm pieces, trimming off the stalky bits. Bring the stock to the boil, plunge the cauli florets in, and simmer for 7 minutes. Pour the stock into another pan through a strainer and refresh the cauli in cold water. Melt the butter in a saucepan and cook the onion over moderate heat for 10 minutes. Add the potato and put the stock back in. Simmer until the potato is soft. Drain the cauli and put in the liquidizer jar with the Gorgonzola. Pour on the contents of the potato saucepan and add the salt and nutmeg. Whizz until smooth. Serve with a scattering of chopped chives, croutons, or toasted almonds.

Take with a Bucket of Salt

I've always maintained to my chefs that there is a difference between the way a finished dish seems to them before it is sent from the kitchen and the way it is 'experienced' by a customer. Leaving aside the obvious difference between levels of critical attention (the customer making a booking presumably in order to enjoy himself), the customer's senses should have been beguiled before he eats by the pleasing decoration of the restaurant and the spotless symmetry of the table he sits at, with linen crisp, glasses and cutlery sparkling, the plate in front of him alluring with its shining colours and stimulating the most bashful appetite.

But even with his senses a little heightened his palate would be neutral, not having spent the previous three hours tasting a dozen different preparations, as the chef would have done, under harsh neon lights with the kitchen cacophony in his ears. In a decent restaurant, where the pleasures of the table, the quality of the food and wine, are accorded their proper importance, and not subordinated to some transitory notion of peer group approval, every element deployed is ultimately at the service of the moment when the first course arrives. So although the first mouthful will be the powerful focus for attention, it ought also to be received with a measure of enthusiastic optimism. There is, however, one more element that must be added to this thought process, and this is the predisposition to enjoy oneself that comes from having eaten well before at the place in question.

This must have been the reason why two long-familiar customers of mine ploughed through a gratin dauphinois which was so salty as to be truly horrible. I had discovered this while they were eating and tried to limit the damage by going to their table. Too late, every scrap had gone, and apparently not into someone's handbag. I asked if they had noticed anything about the gratin. 'Well, now you mention it, it did seem a bit salty, but we thought that as Stephen had cooked it, it must be all right.' So favourably disposed were they to enjoy themselves, to immerse themselves in the theatre that a restaurant provides, that such a gross solecism could be reduced to a minor hiccup.

Of course, the reverse can, unfortunately, be true, all too often. But how marvellous to have such devoted admirers, even if there are only two of them.

Eating on One's Own Doorstep

I may be wrong, but one of the attractions, to the uninformed, of owning a restaurant must be the idea of eating in one's own place, being fussed over by one's staff as the restaurant fills up with people buying bottles of Montrachet '79 and Lafite '82, airkissing Joan Collins/Lord Bragg/Johnny Depp/Tara Palmer Tomkinson, and thinking complacently of those extra zeros appearing on your bank statement. A number of things could be further from the truth than this, but the restaurant owner soon realizes he is at the mercy of forces which gnaw at the edge of this rosy vision. Gradually the knowledge will grow that he is in the inescapable grip of the repetitive, twice-daily imperatives that compel restaurants to try to greet, seat, feed and water their customers with skill, charm and efficiency, and which will, as sure as eggplant is aubergine, turn him into a victim of obsessive-compulsive disorder.

To bring this vision into being presupposes a restaurant infrastructure that completes its routines with unfailing reliability despite having to do them over and over again, and which never has a weak component or if it did could instantly grow a replacement. Unfortunately, this totally ignores the annoying randomness of life which can introduce spanners into the best-lubricated machines. Nature, however, has taken this into account by allotting mankind (even people in 'the catering trade') the ability to adapt to and learn from experience. So after quite a short time it becomes automatic for the restaurateur to run through a mental checklist. Have all the chefs arrived, is the pavement clean outside, particularly where the rubbish was collected, has the floor been swept/mopped/vacuumed properly, the windows cleaned, the menu spelled correctly, the flower water changed, are the lavatories clean, sweet-smelling and well-towelled, do the tables wobble, are all the right lights on, and are the knives, forks and glasses without blemish?

The habit of mind thus developed – of unceasing appraisal – can't be switched off just because, for whatever reason, one is transforming oneself into a customer. Lunches with the bank manager, lunches with journalists, meals to test the speed and flair of a new head chef or the cut of a new manager's jib, even on a quiet day dinner just to fill an empty table and improve the waiters' tronc; in their various degrees these events represent part of one's working life. Even Peter Langan would have agreed with the last bit.

But. There is something about the boss being a customer that seems to disturb the restaurant ether – at least, so it seems to me. Most of the time I don't actually enjoy the experience, partly because I can't suspend my forensic interest so I can't surrender to it, and partly because I'm wary that something untoward might happen. Very often my presence will paralyse an otherwise competent waiter who will serve me before my female guests, or exaggerate his discretion so much that apart from having to deliver the plates sent from the kitchen there will be no service at all. The kitchen isn't free of this either. I'll have much more on my plate than anyone else and quite often my table will have to wait longer than anyone else to be served. Indeed once, when I hosted a lunch for the editor of the main trade journal and other weighty figures, my table was served last even though it had arrived first. My sous chef had not cooked for me before and I think subconsciously kept putting off the moment when the bullet would have to be bitten. Bitten it was, but not until twenty past two.

Other hazards can appear too. I once sat next to a table of four who went through the menu and thought it all sounded dreadful and there was nothing they wanted to eat. I couldn't remain silent at these slurs upon my character – as I saw it – so asked them what they didn't like. 'There's too much fish, my guests can't eat scallops, my wife doesn't eat rabbit, and most of this has garlic anyway, doesn't it?' Other more star-spangled egos than mine would have contumaciously thrown them out, but I was depressed by this dogged philistine ignorance, wondering how these representatives of Middle England's indifference to good food had got lost on the way to one of the branded pub chains. It's probably silly, but one does take these things personally.

The Food Critic and the Flying Saucer

About a year after I had started in Richmond I was struggling a bit, so was very pleased to find out that the *Good Food Guide* had made me their London newcomer of the year. A Sunday paper got hold of this and had a little brainwave – publish a piece about me by both the *GFG* and their main competitor, which didn't seem to know I was there (even thought I had told them twice). The first I knew about this was when I opened the paper and saw myself – enthusiastically reviewed by the *GFG*, harshly by the other guide. Indeed, it was the worst review I've ever received. That was a bit unnecessary, I thought – was this anything to do with professional pique? This certainly wasn't the sort of review a business struggling to establish itself needed, particularly as I thought there hadn't been much wrong with the food – I'd cooked it, after all.

Over the years the rankle quotient faded, even though I never did find favour with that particular guide. Anyway, what did they know?

One lunchtime at Smithfield this old score was nearly settled for me. Nearly. There were only two tables left, one of which was occupied by Egon Ronay. Sitting at the other one about twenty feet away was a man fiddling with his coffee saucer, turning it over and over in his fingers. Suddenly it flew from his hand towards Egon, smashing into the wall by his head. Naturally one's astonished manageress asked the thrower why he had done it. 'I didn't do anything,' came the bizarre reply, and, although April was determined to get an explanation for this weird behaviour, he beat a retreat, pursued valiantly but in vain.

I knew, of course: at some time or another this unfortunate had been on the receiving end of a Ronay diatribe and finding himself unexpectedly near his tormentor had taken the chance to get his own back.

Egon was probably used to this sort of thing as he said calmly that he had thought it wasn't me, 'As I don't suppose he'd have missed.'

Salads

Asparagus, Artichoke and Broad Bean Salad

May and June are my favourite months. The flat-racing season really gets into gear, there's a chance of a bit of sunshine, smells of fresh-cut grass arrive – oh, and it's asparagus and broad bean time again; English asparagus, that is, which has only a few miles and a few hours to travel from bed to table, and my favourite bean of the year. Combining them in a salad with that other delicacy, the globe artichoke, and some fresh marjoram and a hazelnut oil dressing is a perfect proof of the whole being greater than the sum of its parts. There are no doubt some diehards who won't have their asparagus other than plain, with melted butter. Well, that's fine: leave it out, and substitute a cooked pasta of a similar size to the artichokes – penne would be fine.

water to cover the artichokes when prepared
    as below
¾ tsp salt per 575 ml water
2 large globe artichokes
½ a lemon
1 bunch of asparagus
1 kg broad beans, in their pods
4 tbsp hazelnut oil
juice of 1 orange
salt
leaves from a few sprigs of fresh marjoram
    (basil, tarragon or oregano would do as
    a substitute, but not parsley)

Bring a large saucepan of water to the boil. To prepare the artichokes, cut off the stem at the base, break off the small leaves at the bottom and rub the base with the cut side of the lemon. Place the artichoke on its side and with a bread knife slice about 2 cm off the top of the leaves. Squeeze the lemon juice from the cut lemon into the water and add the artichokes – there should be just enough water to cover – and the salt, and simmer the artichokes for about 35 minutes. They are cooked when a knife-point goes in easily – but don't overcook. Remove and refresh in cold water for 5 minutes, then take out and place upside down to drain. Remove the outside leaves, scraping off the bases with your teeth as you go – cook's privilege – and then carefully lift out the central core of tender leaves. After this you should be able to lift out the hairy choke or use a spoon to scrape it off. Trim the edge of the heart and cut it in 8 segments.

Cut the asparagus on the bias into three or four pieces, discarding the woody base, and cook for about 4 minutes in simmering salted water. Remove and refresh in cold water. Pod the beans (there won't be that many) and boil and cool likewise, but for 1 minute longer. Slip the bright green centres from their jackets (worth the effort).

Gently mix the artichokes, asparagus, and broad beans together, pour over the mixed oil and orange juice to which you have added a large pinch of salt, and sprinkle over the marjoram leaves.

Crab and Cardamom Salad

I love the slight menthol quality of cardamom, apart from the delicacy of its flavour. It has a great affinity with orange (try it to flavour ice cream), as orange has with crab. This simple logic led to this salad, which is expensive, but worth it. I prefer crab to lobster, so if you compare prices crab doesn't seem so expensive. You *could* mix white and dark meat, but it's better with all white. If fresh cooked crab is hard to get, frozen is next best, but make sure you pick through it thoroughly for bits of shell.

Serves 6

25g butter
1 medium carrot, finely diced
1 medium stick celery, finely diced
3 shallots, finely diced
450g white crab meat
grated rind and juice of 1 orange
seeds from 10 fresh cardamom pods (if yours
    are a bit old you'll need a few more),
    crushed fine in a mortar
salt and freshly ground black pepper
2 tbsp olive oil
1 tsp lemon juice
mixed salad leaves

Melt the butter and sweat the carrot and celery in it for 2 minutes, then add the shallots and cook another 2 minutes. Cool. In a bowl stir together this mixture with the crab meat, some of the orange rind and juice, and the cardamom – the orange flavour should be just detectable. Season lightly with salt and black pepper, and press gently into lightly oiled ramekins or small dariole moulds.

Make a light dressing from the olive oil, the rest of the orange juice and the lemon juice, and season. Toss the salad leaves in the dressing, and arrange around the rim of each plate. Unmould the crab into the middle and serve.

Duck Skin, Walnut and Orange Salad

Over the years I've noticed the following as perennially unpopular on my menus: glacé chestnuts (with pheasant or guinea fowl); spinach; broccoli; morels; caramelized cloves of garlic; prunes, except in ice cream; the skin on red mullet, unless it's crisp; red mullet livers; foie gras (as a garnish). And worst of all, duck skin.

Here's a recipe which gives duck skin another chance. It's a decent salad on its own, with the duck skin giving it distinction. You may well have to wait until you have two ducks' worth of skin trimmings before you have enough, but it freezes well. Any large, fresh duck will have some loose skin at the vent and neck ends, which doesn't cover any meat. Remove this with a sharp knife, trimming off any extraneous bits. Otherwise, you could use the skin from two magrets, which cook perfectly well without it. When you have cooked the trimmings, they are best eaten on the same day.

duck skin trimmings
salt
1 large orange
3 tbsp walnut or hazelnut oil
4 large handfuls of mixed salad leaves
about 16 walnuts, chopped, roasted in
    a medium oven for about 20 minutes
    (or grilled – watch them carefully),
    rubbed in a clean tea towel
freshly ground black pepper

Preheat the oven to 350°F/180°C/Gas 4. Cook the skin trimmings in the oven until crisp, pouring off the fat from time to time (keep this for roasting or frying potatoes). This will take anything up to an hour. Sprinkle lightly with salt and drain on kitchen paper. Cut into bite-sized pieces.

Slice the top and bottom off the orange and with a very sharp knife remove all the skin and pith by slicing down the orange, the knife following its shape. Holding the orange over a small bowl or saucer, cut the orange segments out from between the membranes, and cut each segment into 3. Squeeze the juice out of what remains and whisk together with the oil.

Place the salad leaves, walnuts, orange pieces and skin in a large bowl, season lightly with salt and black pepper, and dress with the oil and orange juice.

Chickpea, Walnut and Cumin Salad

The fastest of food – a bit of a standby at home. Dried chickpeas would be better, but I feel no shame in using the fat canned version if I haven't planned ahead. Anyway, the point of this dish is that it's just about instant.

Serves 2–3

50g broken walnuts, roughly chopped
a 450g tin of chickpeas, drained
¾ shallot or 6 spring onions, or ½ a red onion,
    finely sliced or chopped

lemon juice
½ tsp ground cumin (or more if you like)
salt and freshly ground black pepper
2–3 tbsp good olive oil

Toast the walnuts until their colour darkens a little, and then rub them in a tea towel to remove some of the skins. Add to the chickpeas, along with the shallot or spring onions, lemon juice, the seasonings and enough olive oil to moisten the mixture well.

Avocado, Cucumber and Tomato Salad with Mustard and Chervil

This is a delicate salad with rather understated flavours, but moreish for all that. It goes very well with crab, lobster or prawns, but is fine on its own too.

1 cucumber
salt
2 ripe, firm tomatoes
2 ripe, firm avocados
4 heaped tbsp crème fraiche
2 tsp Dijon mustard
2 tbsp lemon juice
½ tsp sugar
2 tbsp chervil, finely chopped, or 3 tbsp dill

Peel the cucumber (a swivel-bladed peeler is best for this), cut it in half lengthways and scrape out the watery centre with a teaspoon. Cut the cucumber into 5 mm dice and place in a sieve over a bowl. Sprinkle with salt, mixing in well, place a saucer on top and a weight on top of that. Leave for an hour. Rinse away the salt under running cold water, and pat dry with kitchen paper. Place in a salad bowl. Cut crosses in the tops of the tomatoes with a sharp knife and plunge into boiling water for 20 seconds. Remove with a slotted spoon and lift off the skin. Cut into eighths, take out the seeds and cut into 5 mm dice. Cut the avocados in half and twist apart. Poke out the stone, pushing a sharp knife through the flesh underneath, and cut each half in two lengthways. Cut into 5 mm dice. Add the tomatoes and avocados to the cucumber.

Mix together all the other ingredients in a bowl and carefully fold the dressing into the cucumber mixture. Taste to see if there's enough salt. Depending how well you have rinsed the cucumber, you may need a bit more. Use black pepper if you like it, but it's a bit brutal for this salad.

This looks good served piled into a ring, and the ring then removed, on individual plates.

Bulgur Salad

This nutty-flavoured and pleasingly textured grain is another of those culinary staples where other more attention-seeking ingredients can show themselves off. Although we're more familiar with it as a salad, in the Eastern Med it's used as a pilaff, and I think it works well as hot ballast for fish, chicken or lamb dishes. You can use the same method of preparation: simply soften the shallots in some olive oil first, then add the swollen bulgur and whatever other things you care to put in. If you have any leftover cappon magro sauce (page 124), this is where to use it.

This is my version of tabbouleh, which is probably stretching the description a bit.

Serves 6

200g bulgur
400ml boiling water or light stock
    (stock is better if it's going to be used hot),
    plus some more boiling water for the
    tomatoes
4 firm ripe tomatoes
¼ cucumber, peeled, centre removed, cut into
    small dice
1 tsp salt, and more for the cucumber
1 large orange, rind grated and all skin and pith
    removed
2 tbsp walnut oil
2 tbsp finely chopped shallots
3 tbsp chopped curly parsley
2 tbsp chopped mint
3 tbsp chopped coriander
1 heaped tsp ground cinnamon
25g almonds, blanched, roasted and chopped
    fairly finely (the same size as the bulgur)
1½ tbsp lemon juice

In a large bowl mix together the bulgur and water or stock. Leave to stand for half an hour while you prepare the other ingredients. Cut a cross in the tops of the tomatoes and plunge them into the boiling water for 20 seconds. Place in a bowl of cold water, remove the skin and pips, and cut into smallish (1cm) dice. Put the cucumber in a sieve over a pan or bowl and sprinkle well with salt. Put a small plate or saucer on top and weight it down. Leave for 30 minutes, rinse under the cold tap and dry with kitchen paper or in a clean tea towel. Remove the orange segments by cutting down on either side of the membranes holding them. Do this over a bowl. You should have about 2 tbsp juice when you have squeezed out the orange skeleton. Add the juice to the walnut oil and reserve. Chop each orange segment into three.

Mix the tomatoes, cucumber, orange pieces and rind, shallots, herbs, cinnamon, and almonds into the bulgur, then add 1 tsp salt and the lemon juice. Finally stir in the walnut oil and orange juice. Check that there's enough salt.

Red Cabbage Salad

The humble (which means cheap) red or white cabbage hasn't a lot of flavour in its raw state, but rather like pasta is a great facilitator. It does, however, have an inimitable texture when sliced very thin – crunchy and chewy at once, unlike the brittle celery or crunchy onion and carrot. The salads made with them are pretty easygoing – you can play around with ingredients (especially nuts and oils) and dressings, but they work best when restricted to, on the whole, northern-latitude ingredients like mustard and horseradish. Having said that, most oils go extremely well. Fennel has a similar texture and elusive flavour and could be used instead.

This is really a slaw but that's not a word I can get used to. Anyway 'salad' covers it perfectly well. This is all crunchy texture with a sweet-sour background.

Serves 6–8

Dressing

2 tbsp Dijon-type mustard
3 tsp runny honey
3 tbsp cider vinegar
1 tbsp ground caraway seeds (optional)
a pinch of salt
100 ml vegetable oil
75 ml hazelnut or walnut oil

In a jam jar with the lid on tight, shake together the first four or five ingredients (the salt needs to be added before the oils). Now add the oils and shake well again.

Salad

1 small red cabbage, quartered, core removed, and finely sliced
200g carrots, grated coarsely
3 stalks of celery, very finely sliced
4 shallots or 2 medium red onions, peeled, finely sliced and soaked in iced water for 20 minutes, then drained and patted dry
100g roasted chopped hazelnuts or walnuts
freshly ground black pepper and salt

Mix together the vegetables, nuts and dressing in a large bowl. Grind over black pepper, and mix in up to ½ tsp of salt.

Haricot Bean and Sweet Pepper Salad
with Anchovy Cream

This is a substantial and colourful salad to eat as a first course or to accompany some grilled fish. Not for people on a diet (unless it's all you eat all day).

250g haricot beans, soaked overnight and
  drained
1 large clove of garlic, crushed
1 bay leaf
1 small carrot
1 small stick of celery
2–3 sprigs fresh thyme, or ½ tsp dried
1 red pepper
1 yellow pepper
10 anchovy fillets
150ml double cream
3 shallots, finely chopped
3 tbsp olive oil
freshly ground black pepper
flat-leaf parsley (optional)

Put the beans in a saucepan with the garlic, bay leaf, carrot, celery and thyme, and pour on enough water to cover with 3cm over. Boil for 10 minutes, skimming if necessary. Turn down the heat and simmer gently for an hour or so, until the beans are cooked but still al dente, topping up the water if you need to. Drain well, keeping the liquid for a soup base, and remove the bay leaf, garlic, thyme twigs, and vegetables. Cool.

Heat the grill to very hot. Stand the peppers up and cut down the sides to give yourself rectangular pieces free of seeds. Trim off any white ribs. Put all these pieces as flat as you can on a sheet of tinfoil and grill until the skins have blackened and blistered. Let them cool for a few minutes and remove as much of the skin as you can. Most should come away easily. Cut the peppers into 2cm squares.

Drain the anchovy fillets of oil, put in the liquidizer with the cream and whizz until smooth. If your liquidizer isn't happy with this small quantity, mash the anchovies to a paste on your chopping board and then mix with the cream.

When the beans are cold put them in a salad bowl with the shallots and peppers and stir in the anchovy cream. Drizzle with the olive oil, grind over some black pepper and scatter with some flat parsley leaves if you like.

Nasty Moments: 2

Not long after I opened my place in Llanrwst, I became aware of a customer who seemed to be spending a long time in the gents' loo when he should have been eating his main course. One of the people on his table and I decided to see if anything was wrong so we knocked on the door. Ghastly groaning sounds emerged. The man inside managed to open the door and collapsed, ghostly white, on the floor. Oh God, I've killed him, was my instant reaction, and indeed he looked like Henry Wallis's painting of the *Death of Chatterton*. The poor man couldn't stand and was clearly in need of some sort of emergency help, so I called the ambulance from Llandudno and he was carried out on a stretcher.

I knew his first course had been snails, and no one else so far had eaten them. What had I done to them and him? I knew very little about food poisoning and food allergies then (it won't be long now before restaurateurs have to take degrees in these things) so I spent the next twelve hours in tortured anxiety. The following day some news: he was better and, yes, it had been the snails – after all, hadn't the same thing happened to him the first time he'd eaten them? I wonder how many times one has to suffer the agonies of the damned before putting two and two together . . . and isn't there something called FMD?

Leek and Mushroom Custards

Savoury custards ('flans' or 'royales' as the French quaintly call them) are nothing but quiche mixtures without the pastry. There are endless variations on this theme, of which the recipes that follow are only two examples. This is a simpler version of one using artichokes I used to serve in the restaurants, where four artichoke hearts replaced the leeks. It is also less rich, so we can serve it with a hollandaise sauce let down with a little water and flavoured with ground toasted walnuts (page 23).

25g butter
4 leeks, mainly the white part, finely sliced
(to weigh about 110g)
220g mushrooms, roughly chopped
salt
150ml chicken stock
⅓ glass dry white vermouth or 1 glass dry
white wine
150ml double cream
2 eggs
2 tsp chopped tarragon
freshly ground black pepper

Preheat the oven to 350°F/180°C/Gas 4. Butter well 4 ramekins about 9cm diameter, and place a circle of buttered greaseproof paper, butter side up, in the bottom of each.

Melt the butter in a saucepan and cook the leeks, covered, over a low heat, for about 5 minutes. Don't let them brown. Add the mushrooms, cover again, and cook for 10 minutes. Season lightly with salt. Add the stock and simmer the mixture until the liquid has almost evaporated. Do the same with the vermouth or wine, add the cream and reduce by half. Cool for a few minutes. Remove to a food processor and blitz the mixture with the eggs and tarragon for 20 seconds. Season with more salt and pepper and divide the mixture between the 4 buttered ramekins. Put in a bain marie and cook in the oven for 30 minutes.

Turn out by holding the ramekin with a cloth and running a knife blade vertically inside the rim of the ramekin, then, holding the ramekin in one hand and covering the top with the other, shake the custard firmly into the covering hand. Peel off the buttered paper. They are easier to turn out once cold and can of course be reheated on a buttered baking sheet for 10 minutes in a moderate oven. Serve each one on a smallish plate, pour over some hollandaise sauce let down with a little water, and serve as is or brown lightly under a hot grill.

Porcini Custards, Chervil Sauce

In the restaurant porcini mushrooms, or dried ceps, those pungent, autumnal-smelling goodies, arrive in half-kilo bags, tempting one to use them in immoderate quantities, despite their price. But, like their fabled cousin, the white truffle, a little goes a long way, so one's natural urge to be profligate needs to be curbed. To those of us who pay retail prices, the need to extract the most from them is pretty important, so it's gratifying to know how effective just a few can be added to a meat stew, a duxelles (equal weights of cooked finely chopped shallot and mushroom) or a creamy sauce (see page 82 for porcini cream). Here is another recipe for a custard which makes an impressive first course: it's not something you would wish to cook every day. These can be made well in advance and easily reheated.

Custards
20g dried porcini
1 tbsp plus 25g butter
4 shallots, finely chopped
25g flour
150 ml milk
150 ml strong chicken stock
1 tbsp Madeira, medium sherry, or brandy
2 eggs
1 tbsp chopped chervil
3 good pinches of salt

Sauce
1 glass dry white wine
100 ml stock
6 tbsp double cream
3 tbsp chopped chervil
salt

Preheat the oven to 375°F/190°C/Gas 5. Butter well 4 ramekins about 9cm diameter, and place a circle of buttered greaseproof paper, butter side up, in the bottom of each.

Hold the porcini under running water for a few moments to get rid of any sand. Put them in a small bowl and pour about 80ml of boiling water over them, and leave for 5 minutes.

In a small saucepan over low to medium heat, melt 1 tbsp butter and soften but don't brown the shallots for about 8 minutes. Scrape out and reserve. In the same pan melt the remaining butter, add the flour, and stir for 3–4 minutes. Gradually add the milk, beating with a wooden spoon to avoid forming any lumps, and incorporate the stock, stirring to form a smooth sauce. Transfer this to a liquidizer bowl and pour in the porcini with their soaking water. Let cool for a few minutes, then add half the shallot-butter mixture, and the alcohol, eggs, chervil and salt. Blitz for half a minute. Divide the liquidizer mixture between the ramekins and place in a roasting tin. Pour in enough boiling water to come halfway up their sides and bake for 40–45 minutes, until risen slightly and firm to the touch. Turn out as for the Leek and Mushroom Custards (page 77).

For the sauce, put the rest of the reserved shallot-butter mixture in a small saucepan, add the white wine and let it evaporate over medium heat. Add the stock and reduce by about half. Add the cream and reduce by half again. Stir in the chervil, season lightly and pour over the custards. If you wish to make the custards and sauce in advance, they both reheat perfectly, but reserve the chervil until later.

To reheat them, let them get cold before turning out. Place them on a buttered baking sheet in a moderately hot oven 10 minutes before you want to serve them. Prepare 4 small round plates, stir the chervil into the reheated sauce and pour over.

Porcini Dumplings

If you like the flavour of dried porcini, which I admit I prefer to the fresh variety, this delivers plenty of rustic punch. You can serve it either as a first course, with a light, buttery sauce, or as a sort of ballast/vegetable adjunct to roast chicken or pork. A large portion would make a main course on its own, perhaps with some more open mushrooms quartered and cooked in butter, and a salad alongside.

Serves 8

50g dried porcini mushrooms
25g butter
2 tbsp finely chopped shallots
2 large open mushrooms, finely chopped
a small clove of garlic, crushed
2 tsp finely chopped rosemary
80g coarse breadcrumbs, brown or white,
  from slightly stale bread
2 tbsp chopped parsley
2 large eggs
40ml milk
salt and ground black pepper

Place the porcini in a sieve and wash under running water to remove any sand. Place in a small bowl and just cover with hot water, leave for 10 minutes, drain – reserving the water – and chop finely.

In a medium saucepan melt the butter and cook the shallots and open mushrooms gently for 10 minutes. Add the porcini and their soaking water, strained through a tea strainer, the garlic and the rosemary. Cook until all the water has evaporated. Remove the garlic, and cool. In a bowl mix together the mushroom mixture, the breadcrumbs and the parsley with your hands. Beat the eggs and milk together in another bowl and add to the mushrooms, blending well. Season to your liking, making sure the salt has time to dissolve.

Place the mixture on a double layer of clingfilm and work into a thick sausage shape – about 5 cm diameter and 20 cm long. Wrap it fairly tightly and tie with string at 5 cm intervals. Twist the ends together well, and tie with string. Place the roll in a large saucepan and cover with salted water. Bring to a simmer and poach for about 30 minutes. Remove from the pan and let it cool a little before unwrapping carefully.

Cut into 8 slices, and serve with this sauce.

Sauce

150 ml chicken stock
1 tbsp double cream
50g butter, cold, in pieces
salt
1 tbsp chervil, chopped (optional)
1 tsp tarragon, chopped (optional)

Boil the stock in a small saucepan until about 6 tbsp is left. Add the cream. Bubble up again and swirl or whisk in the butter. Add a pinch of salt. Add the herbs if you wish.

Vegetables in Parmesan Pastry

This is a rich buttery pastry that's good enough to eat on its own, but better filled with diced vegetables, or fish and shellfish (cooked prawns and/or chunks of sole and salmon), and a Béarnaise sauce – a thick hollandaise with tarragon (page 23).

Pastry
75g butter, cold
100g plain flour
25g grated Parmesan
1 egg yolk
cold water
lemon juice
salt

Cut the butter into small pieces and put into the food-processor bowl with the flour and the Parmesan. Run the motor for 3–4 seconds and add the egg yolk, 2 tbsp of cold water, a good squeeze of lemon juice and a big pinch of salt. Run again for 3 seconds and remove everything to a bowl. Add enough cold water, mixing well with a wooden spoon and then your hands, to gather the dough into a ball. Transfer to a floured surface and knead with the heel of your hand five or six times. Form into a thick sausage shape, wrap in clingfilm and refrigerate for half an hour.

Preheat the oven to 375°F/190°C/Gas 5.

Cut one-sixth of the pastry across the grain and roll out to a thickness of 3mm. Line fluted brioche moulds or 10cm fluted flan tins, taking care to ensure the pastry walls are thick enough if using fluted moulds. The pastry is very buttery so there's no need to butter the moulds. Line with foil and dried beans or rice and bake for 20 minutes. Remove the beans and foil and bake another 10 minutes.

Any mixture of vegetables with contrasting textures and colours would be suitable to fill the cases: carrots in short, thick batons – likewise green beans and celery; broccoli and cauliflower florets; baby onions; cubed swede, courgettes, celeriac, and parsnip; peas, runner beans, and broad beans; and small fennel chunks. Make sure they are cooked al dente and refreshed in iced water. Drain them well and dry with kitchen paper – this will prevent the pastry walls collapsing. Pile up in the shells and heat through in the oven. Put a big dollop of Béarnaise sauce on top and brown quickly under a hot grill.

Semolina Gnocchi with Porcini Cream

I first tasted gnocchi in a London Italian restaurant – one of the old-fashioned grand ones with fake plaster cracks in the wallpaper, fake pillars forming vistas of Portofino and bacchic friezes. These were 'alla Romana', that is with tomato sauce – a sluggish doughy cylinder cut into slices and given a smear of lipstick with some unseasoned tomato purée. I thought these really couldn't be 'le veritabile gnocchi' so tried them again in Italy – probably ricotta and spinach. Another gnocchi cliché but, with plenty of nutmeg, not bad. Ricotta, unfortunately, hasn't much flavour and its hackneyed use in cannelloni as well as gnocchi hasn't done it any favours. Although the Italians have taken a surprisingly long time to feature others kinds of gnocchi in their UK restaurants, some gnocchi dishes make superlative eating, just as some pasta dishes stand out from the crowd. Like pasta, too, gnocchi are only vehicles for other flavours, their blandness begging for the punch of Gorgonzola, pumpkin or wild mushrooms.

On the whole I prefer polenta or semolina to potato, although potato gnocchi are really good as, well, a potato dish alongside a meaty main course. For a stand-alone dish, though, a firmer texture is needed. I've experimented with adding choux paste to polenta or semolina, instead of adding eggs and flour later, but there's not much in it in terms of texture, and the method that follows is simpler.

Serves 4 generously

Gnocchi

200g light cream cheese
90g semolina
50g softened butter
50g plain flour
2 eggs, beaten
4 tbsp grated Parmesan
¼ tsp nutmeg
½ tsp salt and 6 turns freshly ground black pepper
parsley, chopped

Mix all the ingredients together until smooth. Bring a pan of salted water to just below simmering point. Dip 2 spoons in the water, use them to make oval quenelle shapes from the paste and poach the quenelles in the water until they rise to the surface – about 5 minutes, depending on size. Drain on absorbent paper and keep warm. This quantity makes about 16.

Porcini Cream

12 slices dried porcini
25g butter
2 shallots, peeled and chopped
5 cm white of leek, sliced finely
½ glass dry white wine
300 ml fairly strong chicken stock
50 ml double cream
salt and black pepper
parsley, chopped (optional)

Wash the porcini under running water and soak them in a little hot water for 5 minutes. Drain, reserving the liquid, and chop roughly. Melt the butter in a saucepan and soften the shallots and leek in it for 8 minutes. Add the porcini liquid and the wine and reduce until evaporated. Pour in the stock, add the porcini, and cook for 10 minutes. Cool, then liquidize with the cream until smooth. Season.

Serve the gnocchi in one big dish with the sauce poured over. Scatter with chopped parsley if you want some extra colour.

Pumpkin Gnocchi

Easy to make, these gnocchi make a delicious and luxurious starter or main course if drizzled with olive oil, single cream, Parmesan and sage.

Serves 4 as a starter or 2 as a main course

750g peeled and seeded pumpkin or butternut
    squash, roughly chopped
⅓ tsp ground cinnamon
60g grated Parmesan
2 large egg yolks
90g plain flour
a large pinch of nutmeg
¼ tsp (or slightly more) salt
12 screws of freshly ground black pepper
olive oil
single cream
sage leaves

Preheat the oven to 350°F/180°C/Gas 4.

Bake the pumpkin, covered, in a baking dish for about half an hour. Purée the pumpkin in the food processor; remove to a saucepan to dry out, stirring, over medium heat for 5 minutes. Tip into a bowl. Add the cinnamon and half the cheese, and beat in the egg yolks, flour and seasonings. Bring a large saucepan of salted water to a simmer. Fill a piping bag fitted with a plain 1.3cm nozzle and, resting it on the edge of the pan, extrude 2cm lengths, cutting them with a wetted knife blade. As they rise to the surface (this will take about 45 seconds) remove with a slotted spoon and place in a sieve to drain. Keep warm. Decant into a hot dish and drizzle over some good olive oil or melted butter and a few tablespoons of cream. Sprinkle over the rest of the Parmesan and some finely chopped sage leaves.

Twice-cooked Goat's Cheese Soufflé

This has been a fixture on the menu at Blandford Street since it opened in 1989. The notion of serving a soufflé unmoulded came from Peter Kromberg, chef at Le Soufflé in the London Intercontinental Hotel, and from there it seemed logical to make it in advance and just heat it through and sauce it when it was ordered. As chefs came and went at Blandford Street they varied its presentation but the soufflé remains the same. It can perfectly well be made with soft goat's cheese, but it has more flavour with a mixture of soft and hard – that is, fresh and mature, and you can add any herbs to it that you like, although I prefer it plain. It needs a denser structure than a normal soufflé to withstand the unmoulding, but otherwise is quite conventional. This recipe involves making double the quantity of soufflé base – the thick sauce – as half of it will be used to sauce the dish.

550 ml milk
1 medium onion, thinly sliced
1 bay leaf
a large sprig of thyme
12 black peppercorns
hazelnut or olive oil
25g fine stale breadcrumbs (done in the
    food-processor bowl)
1 tbsp finely chopped toasted hazelnuts
    (done in the food-processor bowl)
50g butter
50g flour
3 eggs
100g fresh goat's cheese
50g mature goat's cheese, grated
salt and freshly ground black pepper
4 tbsp grated Parmesan, Gruyère, or
    Cheddar

Preheat the oven to 375°F/190°C/Gas 5.

Pour the milk into a medium saucepan and add the onion, bay leaf, thyme and peppercorns. Heat gently for 15 minutes, but don't let it reach sim-mering point. Remove from the heat and cool a little. Pour the infused milk though a strainer into a jug, pressing on the debris with the back of a ladle or a large spoon.

Prepare 4 large ramekins or straight-sided teacups by brushing with hazelnut or olive oil and lining with the breadcrumbs mixed with the hazelnuts.

Melt the butter in a fresh large saucepan, add the flour and cook, stirring, for 3 minutes. Add all the milk gradually, whisking constantly to prevent any lumps forming. Measure off roughly half and reserve in another small pan, covered (this half is for the sauce). Pour the remaining half into a bowl and cool for 5 minutes.

Separate the eggs one by one, stirring the yolks into the cooled sauce base and dropping the whites into a large bowl. Stir half the fresh and all the mature goat's cheese into the base. Whisk the whites until stiff and carefully fold into the sauce, seasoning well just before you have folded in all the whites. Check the flavour and add more cheese if necessary. Divide the mixture between the ramekins and place in a roasting tin filled 4cm deep with boiling water and bake for 20 minutes. Remove and cool.

Finish the accompanying sauce by adding the rest of the goat's cheese to the reserved white sauce and season well. Thin with a tablespoon or two of milk or cream if necessary.

When the soufflés are cold, or cool, upend the ramekins and shake each soufflé out into your hand. Place them in a suitably sized gratin or baking dish, or dishes, pour the sauce over and sprinkle with the Parmesan or other cheese (goat's cheese isn't good at browning). Heat through thoroughly in the oven and finish off by browning under the grill.

Split Pea Fritters

These are light but packed with flavour and lend themselves to a number of variations. Try using chickpeas, haricot beans or lentils and use whatever spices you like. They would be fine as a starter served with crème fraiche flavoured with grated lemon rind or aïoli or a tomato salsa, or used as a vegetable and/or ballast with a spicy lamb or chicken dish. They do need strong herbs or plenty of spice.

110g yellow split peas
1 clove of garlic, peeled and crushed
1 small bay leaf
a 2 cm strip of lemon peel, no pith
1 tbsp onion, chopped
a 5 cm piece of carrot, split lengthways
300 ml stock or water
2 eggs, separated
1 tsp baking powder
salt and freshly ground black pepper
1 tbsp chopped coriander or tarragon (or 1 tsp ground cumin and 2 tsp ground coriander or curry powder)

Put everything but the last 4 items into a small saucepan and simmer very gently, for 45 minutes. Remove the bay leaf and lemon peel and tip the rest into a food processor. Run the motor for 20 seconds and scrape the mixture into a bowl; if the texture is slightly grainy, so much the better. Remove to a medium-sized bowl and beat in the egg yolks and baking powder with a wooden spoon. Season with the salt and pepper. Beat the egg whites until semi-stiff and fold into the mixture along with the herbs or spices. (If the mixture is too stiff to accept the egg whites, add a little stock or water; if too sloppy, add some breadcrumbs.) Check the seasoning, now that the salt has dissolved properly and the egg whites have been added.

To make neatly circular fritters, cook in oiled blini pans; otherwise drop large tablespoons of the mixture into an oiled frying pan and cook over moderate heat until golden brown each side.

Courgette and Feta Tart with Nut Topping

A tart with an interesting and piquant flavour. The courgettes gain definition when grated and squeezed and the dill tangoes with the feta. The nut topping gives it that extra something we are always looking for, in cookery and in life. Good as a first course or an informal main course, with a leafy salad drenched with something like the hazelnut oil and orange dressing (page 69).

Serves 6

Tart shell

110g plain flour
50g butter, cold, cut into small pieces
¼ tsp salt
3–4 tbsp cold water

Place the flour, butter and salt in the food-processor bowl and run for a few seconds, until the mixture resembles coarse oatmeal. Remove to a bowl and mix in, bit by bit with your hands or a wooden spoon, enough cold water to form a firm dough. It should just hold together. Press into a thick disc shape and refrigerate for half an hour.

Preheat the oven to 350°F/180°C/Gas 4.

Roll out into a thin disc on a floured surface and line a 21cm flan ring or tin. Make sure the walls are as high as the rim. Prick the base with a fork and line with foil, pressing the foil into the corners and up against the walls. Fill with chickpeas, ceramic beans, rice or some other weighting material and bake for 15–20 minutes, to set the pastry. Remove the beans and foil and bake for another 5–10 minutes, until the tart case is very lightly browned and crisp.

Filling

500g courgettes, topped, tailed and grated
2 shallots, finely chopped
12g butter
4 tbsp finely chopped dill
100g grated feta
2 large eggs
225 ml single cream
1 tsp salt
freshly ground black pepper
1 tart shell, baked blind (see above)
75g mixed hazelnuts and walnuts, coarsely
    chopped

Increase the oven heat to 375°F/190°C/Gas 5.

You need to rid the courgettes of much of their water. You can do this either by mixing them with the salt and leaving them in a sieve for half an hour, under a weighted saucer (more likely two sieves, actually), and then squeezing hard, or, quicker but calling for some physical effort, taking fistfuls of the courgettes and squeezing hard until the water comes out. This is just as effective. Whichever way, get rid of as much water as possible. Cook the shallots in the butter over moderate heat for about 8 minutes, without letting them brown. In a large bowl mix them together with the courgettes, the dill and the cheese. In a smaller bowl beat together, with a fork or whisk, the eggs and cream. Pour this into the courgette bowl and mix together well. Add the salt, if you haven't used it for disgorging the courgettes, and a few turns of the pepper mill. Pour the whole thing into the tart case and bake for about 25 minutes, until the top has set a little. Sprinkle the nuts over the surface and cook another 10 minutes or so, until the custard feels set. Like all tarts, this cuts into wedges once cold. In which case heat through for about 10 minutes in a hottish oven.

Millefeuille of Three Cheeses

This is a four-tiered puff-pastry 'sandwich' using a very thick cheese sauce as the filling. This can be flavoured with garlic, mustard, mushrooms, bacon, green herbs and so on. It's a very good filling for cheese profiteroles or gougères. Here it's used to make an impressive first course for a posh supper, but it would easily serve as a main course for two.

Serves 6

150 ml milk
55g plain flour
25g butter
2 large eggs
salt and freshly ground black pepper
a big pinch of nutmeg
a few drops of Tabasco
55g grated Parmesan, reserving about 10g
55g grated Pecorino
55g blue cheese such as Roquefort,
    Gorgonzola, or Danish blue
2–3 tbsp double cream
a 340g piece of ready-made puff pastry
watercress

In a large bowl beat driblets of milk into the flour, gradually increasing the quantity, until you have a smoothish paste. This is a messy business, but persevere. Any lumps will almost certainly disappear later. Pour into a medium saucepan, add the butter and set over moderate heat, stirring. When almost boiling and becoming lumpy remove from the heat and beat the mixture vigorously. Beat in the eggs separately and return to the heat. Bring back to the boil, stirring then beating constantly as it thickens. It will look a bit like scrambled eggs at first but it will smooth out. Remove from the heat, cool for a few minutes, season with the salt, pepper, nutmeg and Tabasco, and stir in the cheese. It should be thick, but not solid. Stir in the cream to lighten it, more if necessary. This can be made in advance – a day or two even. Cover closely with clingfilm, if so.

Preheat the oven to 375°F / 190°C / Gas 5.

Roll the pastry out on a floured surface to form a rectangle about 40 cm × 30 cm. Cut into 12 equal rectangles. Place on a baking sheet and prick fairly thoroughly with a fork. Bake for 15 minutes, remove from the oven and turn over, and continue baking until they are golden brown – about another 20 minutes. Remove and cool. Trim each rectangle to make a regular shape, and cut across horizontally. Return to the oven for 10 minutes to become crisp. With any luck, you'll have at least 16 thin crisp pieces of pastry. The rest you can discard. Set aside the 4 flattest pieces.

With the cheese sauce warm or at room temperature, roughly divide it mentally into 12 and spread a dollop on to 12 of the pastry pieces. Place one on top of the other so you have 4 triple-deckers and top each with the flattest 4 pieces. To reheat before serving, sprinkle with the reserved Parmesan and simply heat through in a moderate oven (350°F / 180°C / Gas 4). Put a handful of watercress with all-purpose dressing (page 33) on each plate as well.

Quarts into Pint Pots

Until the fairly recent arrival of financial musclemen like Terence Conran and Mr Poon of Harvey Nicks, purpose-built restaurants in London were very unusual. Some of the twentieth century's grandest places – the Connaught, Coq d'Or (now Langan's), L'Ecu de France, Prunier, Empress, the old Caprice and Mirabelle – had plenty of money behind them and could provide large dining rooms with smaller, but sufficient, back-of-house areas. If restaurateurs wanted to introduce competition to these behemoths they had to find what premises they could, most of which would be far from ideal, particularly given that most of central London – Soho, Covent Garden and St James's, for example – was built in the eighteenth century. A great many of these properties were built as private houses so converting them to restaurants would have posed some interesting design problems, even before the days of mandatory customer lavatories, the demands of fire officers, EHOs, air conditioning and disabled access.

Close parallels with the theatre spring to mind in this respect: spacious auditoria fronting teeming anthills of stagehands/actors/cooks/waiters. The priority in space allocation has to be the seating areas, but although the fiscal imperatives may be strong, to sacrifice service areas in favour of more seats would be very dangerous. The pressure is very much there, however: back-of-house areas have lower rateable values but they still cost money and don't deliver any revenue. It's almost inevitable therefore that the majority of restaurants require tolerance and flexibility from their staff and ingenuity from their designers and operators, given the number of essential elements that have to be shoehorned in. Apart from lavatories for staff and customers, there has to be room for coats to hang (it's amazing how much space they take up, and don't mention puffa jackets); for wine and mineral water to be stored in large quantities – especially the water; bread to be sliced; air-conditioning motors, fridge compressors, the water softeners for the espresso machine and glass washers to be positioned; the dustbins and produce boxes – all that polystyrene – to be kept, ventilated, and fortified against mice; and where the hell are we going to put the photocopier and the hot-water boiler?

Quite often, space is at such a premium that there is no room for fridges which contain their own motors. These motors have to be installed wherever they can be squeezed in – as long as there is sufficient ventilation to remove the hot air they generate which would burn them out. At Smithfield I had to install two of these motors next to my high-level boiler on a gigantic bracket. The space around them was so small and the air so hot I had to introduce a dedicated extraction system (which worked beautifully, I may say). At Lichfield's I had a long thin basement kitchen with a smallish window wall at one end. The hot air from the stoves was ducted out of one side of this window and up round a bend to exhaust about three feet higher. Planning regulations meant I couldn't extend it, so a lot of this hot air came straight back into the kitchen through the only fresh air intake, which was the other side of the window. In summer the temperature where I was cooking (my staff wouldn't have put up with it) used to reach 130°F on a hot day (I know because I checked it on my sugar thermometer), and very often I had to change my clothes halfway through service. (*Je suis dur, je suis dur* . . .)

At St Martin's Lane the air-handling unit was on a flat roof behind and above the flat-roof areas and so difficult to reach that access was only through some first-floor offices in Long Acre. One climbed out of their fire exit, over a four-foot-high railing, over the air conditioning ducts of Le Palais du Jardin, past a skylight where one could look down on the competi-tion it offered (something all restaurateurs are prone to do), on round an electricity substation, until there it was. In that quite large area between St Martin's Lane and Long Acre there is hardly a level square metre and none at ground level.

At Blandford Street (another late eighteenth-century building, but in Marylebone), I have to pay the church next door almost £1,000 a year to occupy some of their 'air space' with two small air-handling units, stuck on the outside of my wall, and after ten years there I still can't find the motor that powers the extraction from the staff lavatories. It's in there somewhere – maybe near the ducting where a coal-black, charcoaled pigeon corpse turned up the first time I had the kitchen ducting cleaned (just after I moved in, in case you're wondering). God knows how it got there, as there is a slatted grille at each end of the duct.

Oddly enough at Blandford Street the space division question is reversed, as the kitchen area is larger than the restaurant. Damn! But it means that the restaurant designer, Peter Glynn Smith, had to maximize the use of space in a smallish and awkwardly shaped room to house enough tables to make it viable – which he did very well, after the predecessor's tanks of tropical fish and old photographs of Polish shtetls had been removed.

My problems of squeezing the necessary elements into unsuitable spaces are minor though compared to a restaurant I was once thinking of buying, a place called Ma Cuisine, Michelin-starred, in Knightsbridge. Because of its small size – thirty seats – the owners had to be more ingenious than usual in fitting everything in, so the seating was mainly banquettes, each of which contained some essential part of the restaurant's infrastructure – wine underneath this one, mineral water under the next, eau de vie and cognac the next. When I ate there I found I was sitting on the Hoover. I decided the place probably wasn't for me when I discovered the dry-goods store could be reached only by climbing a vertical ladder to a skylight in the kitchen and crossing the flat roof to the storeroom. If one unwisely ran out of something during service, salt, say, the penalty would be severe, especially in winter. Too severe for me, anyway.

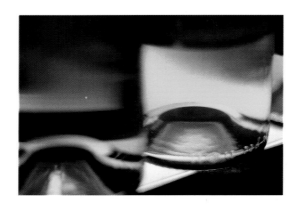

Chicken livers

Such useful things, so versatile, so delicious, and not subject to the same caveats that apply to chickens in general. They are worth a bit of extra attention. Quite often it's better to buy chicken livers frozen as they will have invariably been put through the freezing process as soon as removed and consequently be that much fresher than 'fresh'.

'Trim the livers' is a bit like those instructions 'pass through a sieve', 'remove the chine bone' or 'clean the squid' – a few questions are being begged. All livers – calf, lamb, pig, rabbit, duck – contain a network of veins and nerves which are best removed if the creamy texture of the liver is to be enjoyed properly. I find the best way to do this with chicken livers is to deal with one half at a time. First cut away any greenish bits on the surface and any small black blobs, which may be bits of gall. Press the centre of the liver down on a cutting board with the left hand and with the right hold a knife at 90° to the board. Using a back-and-forth sawing motion, pushing to the right, ease the liver away from the fibres, but not cutting through them. Then do the same with the other half. You will inevitably have some pulpy waste.

If you wish to chop the liver, as in the mixed livers with lentils and vinegar (page 141), cut them into 3–5cm pieces, avoiding the middle bit. If you are going to make a parfait or mousse you could force them through a sieve to achieve perfect smoothness but you must be prepared for some tenacious detritus in your sieve afterwards. If you wish to use a sieve, a sturdy metal one is best, with not too fine a mesh. Use the back of a soup ladle to do the pushing.

Marjolaine of Chicken Livers

And another one. I have no idea how the French word for marjoram should come to signify a sweet confection of alternate layers of pastry and buttercream, and by extension a savoury one too – perhaps it has something to do with 'Les compagnons de la marjolaine' . . . ? – but in its sweet form it can be awesomely delicious as only something with about a thousand calories a slice can be.

In its sweet form it's another of those puds – like the chocolate marquise or the fruit charlotte – that's waiting its turn for reinstatement, but I think it might have to wait a while as it's quite complicated to make and is these days seriously un-PC in its use of butter, sugar and cream. Perhaps we'll be told tomorrow that no healthy dish is complete without hefty doses of these demonized but delicious things, but I'm not holding my breath.

Anyway, this savoury version is itself a cheaper but still very good version of a marjolaine of foie gras. We make it sometimes at Blandford Street, and it involves morels as well. Here I have used ordinary mushrooms instead. The almond pastry loses its crispness if the marjolaine isn't eaten within a couple of hours, but this isn't the end of the world. The pastry itself is amazingly delicious and can be used to make savoury or, with the addition of a little sugar, sweet millefeuilles of vegetables, fruit or (gasp) buttercream.

Almond Pastry

1 egg white
25g plain flour
50g butter, softened and creamed with an
    electric beater
50g finely chopped or nibbed almonds
a pinch of salt

Preheat the oven to 375°F/190°C/Gas 5.

Butter well an oblong baking tray, 25.5 cm × 20.5 cm, and refrigerate for a few minutes before use (this prevents the mixture sliding around in the butter).

Beat the egg white with a whisk until it starts to froth, then with a wooden spoon mix in the flour, butter, almonds and salt. Using a broad-bladed or a palette knife, spread the pastry on the baking sheet into a neat oblong about 3 mm thick, making it as level as possible. Using a sharp knife, divide into 3 strips, cutting across the long axis (for use as a millefeuille, divide into smaller rectangles). Bake in the oven for 12–15 minutes, until lightly browned. Cool.

Chicken Liver Filling

175g soft butter
400–425g chicken livers (leaving 150g when
    trimmed)
2 shallots, finely chopped
2 large open mushrooms, finely chopped
100 ml decent red wine
a large pinch of sugar
2 tbsp medium sherry or 1 tbsp brandy
a large pinch of grated nutmeg
¼ tsp ground cinnamon
3 large pinches of salt
150 ml double or whipping cream

Melt 25g of the butter in a wide frying pan, and when the foam subsides throw in the livers and sauté over fairly high heat for about 4 minutes, browning on all sides. Scrape off into the bowl of a food processor. Add another 25g to the pan and cook the shallots and mushrooms over a medium heat until the latter give up their juice. Add the red wine, sugar, and sherry or brandy and cook until the liquid evaporates. Scrape this mixture into the bowl and add the spices and salt. Process for a couple of minutes and add the rest of the butter until amalgamated. Scrape everything into another large bowl. Whip the cream until it starts to hold its shape and carefully fold into the liver mixture.

Divide it in half and spread over one of the pastry layers (you may need to put the mixture into the freezer for a few minutes to make it easier to spread). Place a second pastry layer on top – don't worry if any of them break as the mixture will hold

them together – and cover with almost all the rest of the mixture and lay the third pastry layer on top. Trim the thin ends and use the last of the mixture to fill in the sides of the marjolaine so you have a neat and regular shape.

Refrigerate for at least 2 hours. When you want to serve it, cut into 1 cm slices, 2 per person. It's rich, so you don't have to eat much. Serve with slightly tart relish, like spiced oranges (page 221) or some cranberries cooked with a little sugar, grated orange rind and orange juice.

Hot Chicken Liver Mousse

Another one – but with a light, spongy texture. This is quite rich, a variation on the haute cuisine 'gâteau de foies de volailles blondes' which twenty years ago would have been served with an even richer 'sauce Nantua' – pounded crayfish shells mixed into a fish velouté. It can't be denied, though, that a thick, cloying, buttery sauce, far from taking the whole thing over the top, somehow cancels out the richness. Serving cream with something chocolatey does the same sort of thing. One of life's minor mysteries.

25g butter
1 small clove of garlic, finely chopped
1 shallot, finely chopped
225g chicken livers, prepared as on page 93,
    leaving about 150g
75g bacon, diced
a big pinch of ground cinnamon, of ginger
    and of mace
a small pinch of ground cloves
150ml single cream
2 eggs
1 tsp brandy
¼ tsp salt
6 screws of freshly ground black pepper

Preheat the oven to 350°F / 180°C / Gas 4.

Butter really well the insides of 4 ramekins or their equivalent. Cut 4 circles big enough to fit the bottoms of the ramekins out of greaseproof paper, baking parchment or tinfoil, and smear them with butter.

Melt the butter in a small saucepan and soften the garlic and shallot for 5 minutes. Place the chicken livers in the food-processor bowl with the bacon (back or streaky is immaterial). Scrape the butter, garlic and shallots into the bowl with a rubber spatula. Add all the remaining ingredients and run the motor for 2 minutes. Divide the mixture equally between the ramekins and bake in a bain marie (or roasting tin with enough boiling water to come up to at least half the height of the ramekins) for 25 minutes. Let cool a little, turn out on to individual plates and serve with hollandaise sauce (page 23). A couple of minutes under a hot grill will give the sauce an agreeable brown surface.

Cold Chicken Liver Mousse (for Canapés or Pâté)

This is a mousse with a pleasant, slightly granular texture. I used to pipe it out at room temperature on to little discs of puff pastry, but circles of toast, dried in the oven, would be fine. It makes an excellent first course if made into quenelle shapes like the chicken liver parfait (page 98). This recipe involves both trimming and passing through a sieve but the quantity isn't large so the consequences in terms of washing up won't be grave.

25g unsalted butter plus 50g cut into pieces
250g chicken livers, trimmed of all black
    and greeny-yellow bits and as many nerve
    fibres as you can (leaving about 170g)
2 shallots, finely chopped, or 2 tbsp finely
    chopped onion
3 tbsp port, or 4 tbsp red wine plus 1 tsp
    caster sugar
2 tbsp double cream
2 tbsp brandy
½ tsp salt and 8 screws of freshly ground
    black pepper
parsley or chervil

Melt 25g of the butter in a frying pan and a few seconds after the bubbles have died down sauté the livers quickly for 3–4 minutes each side – they should still be pink in the middle. Remove, using a slotted spoon, to the bowl of a food processor, letting some of the butter drain back into the pan. Briskly sauté the shallots or onion for 3–4 minutes, add the port or red wine and sugar, and reduce to 1 tbsp. Scrape into the bowl with the livers, and add the rest of the butter. Run the motor for 20 seconds and remove the mixture to a sieve. Press through into another bowl with the back of a ladle and mix in well the cream and the brandy. Season well, remembering to let the salt dissolve before you taste. Pile into a piping bag fitted with a small star or plain nozzle, cool until the consistency of softish butter, and pipe as above or into small tartlet cases. Top each with a tiny piece of parsley or chervil.

Chicken Liver Parfait

There's a bit of a dilemma to overcome with this recipe – do you take the time to trim the livers really well, and inevitably waste some, or not bother too much and pass them through a sieve later, involving more time, effort and some tough washing up? This is another recipe which has become, with or without foie gras, a bit of a restaurant standard in recent years. This is my favourite, as it should be with all the alcohol, but prettier than most with its frame of yellow-, green-, and red-flecked butter. Apart from this it has a lot less butter than some recipes. This needs to be served with oven-dried and lightly toasted bread slices – no butter! – and a pungent relish or chutney (the pear chutney on page 214 or spiced oranges, page 221, would be perfect).

Serves 10–12

about 1 kg chicken livers, untrimmed, giving
    about 650g trimmed weight
110g butter, melted
2 shallots, very finely diced
2 cloves of garlic, crushed
1 tsp thyme leaves
100 ml port
100 ml Madeira
200 ml brandy
150 ml whipping cream, semi-stiff

Orange and Parsley Butter
110g soft salted butter, mashed with the grated
    rind of 2 oranges and 2 heaped tbsp finely
    chopped parsley
salt and black pepper

With a very sharp knife cut away any discoloured parts of the livers and scrape the lobes away from the fibrous parts in the middle. Heat 25g of the butter in a frying pan and fry the livers quickly until they are brown on the outside but still pink in the middle. Transfer them to a food processor. Add the rest of the butter slowly. Brown the shallots lightly in the hot pan, add the garlic, thyme, port, Madeira and brandy. Reduce almost to a syrup and scrape everything into the processor. Purée, season, and pass through a sieve (alternatively, purée in a liquidizer; the result won't be quite as smooth). Fold in the whipped cream. Season and pour into a 1 kg loaf tin lined with clingfilm. Press the film against the sides to expel any air. Cover and refrigerate overnight.

Remove from the mould, and carefully peel off the clingfilm. Spread a thick layer of the butter on all sides but the bottom of the parfait, reserving some, refrigerate, then cover the base with the rest of the butter. Slice it straight from the fridge but leave for 10 minutes or so before serving.

As a simpler way of serving, omit the orange and parsley butter, chill the parfait in a bowl and make quenelle shapes using 2 spoons dipped in warm water. Remove from the fridge about half an hour before serving.

This will keep well for up to a week.

Black Monday

I opened up Lichfield's one Monday morning hoping for an easier day than the previous Saturday, when various increases in numbers on tables already booked and people swapping tables, Michael Winner fashion, had resulted in one party eating at the reception desk. While these complications were being sorted out, the gents' loo had started flushing uncontrollably and had covered a fair amount of the basement floor before being discovered, which meant turning off the water. This in turn meant we couldn't use the dishwasher and there was no water in the now unisex 'ladies' for washing hands. Well, I thought as we manned the bilge pumps, worse things happen at sea.

Monday morning, the plumber's here, it's a new week, let's get going! But where are my staff? By 10.00 I have just one waiter, and no cooks. At 10.30 I begin to be worried. Still no staff. Then one of the cooks arrives, but with blood all over her face and hands and her nerves in shreds. She and her boyfriend have run over a dog on their motorbike, throwing them both off and doing the dog no good at all. She's in no fit state to work so I send her home. A few minutes later I have a telephone call: another chef can't work as he's in hospital, hyperventilating for unspecified reasons. I know what he feels like. I ring my sous chef on his day off. No reply. I ring the other waiter. He's at home, sounding terminal, with food poisoning after eating out the night before. Nothing for it but for me to get stuck into the mise en place, hoping my head waiter turns up soon (he doesn't).

As neither the meat nor the fish had arrived, I rang both suppliers. Apparently no orders had been made, and there would be nothing before the afternoon. Terrific. I cobbled together a short menu, trying to turn a few Saturday night leftover sows' ears into silk purses. So two of us and the washer-up fed and served the twenty, who, considerately, all walked in at the same time. I don't think anyone noticed any deficiencies, but this was hardly a scenario that could be sustained for long in a Michelin-starred restaurant.

Eventually the fish and meat arrived, late in the afternoon – my sous chef had mixed the orders up, presumably after spending too long in the pub. But my hyperventilating chef had been kept in for observation and the sous chef was still out, so I was still jumping through hoops on my own. As it happened, Elizabeth David, the Grande Dame of British Food, was booked in that night. This was too much. I closed, for the first, and I hope the last, time ever. Considering her reaction to my cooking when she did finally visit the restaurant (see the recipe for roast duck, p. 144), I think it was just as well I did.

Is there a lesson in this? No small restaurant can afford the luxury of carrying staff to cover for illness or accident, so the answer must be – do it all yourself and close whenever it's time to go back into therapy or intensive care, or have a large restaurant, where the absence of one or two staff won't be so noticeable. Simple, isn't it?

Fish

It's impossible to write about fish without a feeling of foreboding. Fish stocks are dwindling everywhere, with catastrophic speed in the case of cod and wild salmon. Governments around the world sit on their hands to avoid losing the fishing vote, blithely ignoring the depredations of high-tech trawlers with five-mile nets hoovering the sea bare and snapping the food chain with a dogged self-interest that defies belief. Having already seen the herring virtually disappear from the North Sea twenty years ago, we now face the prospect that some of our most familiar fish will soon vanish, to be replaced, until they prove to be uneconomic, by deep-sea fish familiar to us only through photos in *National Geographic*.

The tension between increasing demand and reducing supply won't be resolved unless a miracle of international cooperation happens, so we should think ourselves truly fortunate that at the moment fish is still affordable – just – and, in the developed world, relatively plentiful. Farming has yet to provide the solution, producing large quantities of inferior and ecologically unsound salmon and not yet successfully producing viable quantities of bass, turbot or halibut.

Each one of these recipes, and each time one eats fish, is invested with the poignant understanding that some of these are pleasures which it will be difficult, and very expensive, to repeat in the nearish future. Meanwhile, that knowledge should make us appreciate the more what the sea has to offer in its amazing beauty and diversity, and even encourage us to do our individual bit to spread the message that these wonderful creatures are in deadly danger.

Having got that off my chest, I'm certainly not going to stop serving fish to my customers or argue for a boycott, because this is a problem that calls for more fundamental and economically weighty solutions. Cooking fish is also too much a part of the fabric of my life for it not to receive its due attention here, representing as it does so many opportunities for the cook to experiment in ways not possible with meat, particularly with vegetables, herbs, and sauces.

Curiously enough, although most fish have a rather bland flavour, they stand up to strong sauces extremely well, even if traditionally, in restaurants at least, we are more used to milder cream and butter ones. The recipes that follow include both kinds. I admit to a liking for fish sauces based on fish stock, but that presupposes a supply of bones, unless you fillet your own fish. This is a commonsense exercise with most fish, certainly the flat ones, and worth doing even if it's only occasionally.

Don't be scared of filleting: the only vital thing is a very sharp knife, and with one you'll end up, after a few tries, with more fish on your fillets and less on the bones than a fishmonger will.

Of all the cooking methods I rather favour baking and steaming, both gentle techniques, as fishy flesh doesn't seem to react so well to the sudden heat of frying or poaching. Poaching by starting from cold is a good method but difficult to time. Grilling is great if you have a grill that gets very hot, or an iron pan with ribs that are proud of the surface by several millimetres, but I feel grilling is best with round oily fish. I'd make an exception for a fat Dover sole, though. Whatever the cooking method, the crucial thing is not to overcook. Better by far to leave a slightly raw bit in the middle, as with fish you need never fear being ambushed by bugs. Shellfish are a bit different, but that's another story.

Monkfish with Celery à la Grècque

Although vegetables à la grècque are usually eaten cold or as a salad, I think they are just as good hot, and a pairing with a meaty fish cooked in the same court bouillon makes a light, uncloying main course. Vegetables with a pronounced flavour are best given this treatment – artichokes, mushrooms, onions, and celery. The more or less unthickened sauce (just some tomato pulp) works much better with a firm-fleshed beast like monkfish – a kind of shark, an evolutionary link between the sharks and rays – than with something friable like sole, mullet or bream, which marries better with something buttery or creamy. Tuna, swordfish, shark or John Dory would also be fine like this.

300 ml water
70 ml olive oil
juice of ½ a lemon
1 glass dry white wine
½ tsp salt
2 tbsp sliced shallots or red onions
6 good-sized parsley stalks
½ tsp fennel seeds
1 sprig fresh thyme or ¼ tsp dried
chopped leaves from a head of celery
12 peppercorns
15 coriander seeds
4 inside celery sticks, halved across
1 ripe firm tomato, skinned, seeded and roughly chopped
4 monkfish fillets, each weighing about 120g, each sliced across the grain into 4
2 tbsp chopped herbs – basil, chervil, tarragon, chives, dill, fennel

Place all the ingredients except the celery sticks, tomato, fish and chopped herbs into a saucepan and simmer for 10 minutes. Add the celery and cook for 15 minutes, then remove and slice thinly on the bias. Boil the liquid hard until reduced to about 150 ml. Strain the liquid into a wide pan, pressing down on the solids, and add the monkfish. Bring the liquid just to a simmer and poach the monkfish pieces for 5 minutes. Remove and divide between 4 hot plates. Add the tomato pulp and the celery to the liquid in the pan. Heat through, check the seasoning and pour over the fish. Scatter over whichever of the chopped herbs you fancy. Serve with new potatoes.

Chargrilled Salmon cured with Orange and Juniper

This started off as a variation on reliable but rather boring gravad lax, but one of my chefs, Danny Lewis, tried cutting the fish into thick slices and chargrilling them. Excellent fellow.

> 500g salmon fillet, centre cut if possible, from one side of the fish
> 25g sea salt
> 25g caster sugar
> 2 tbsp finely chopped dill
> grated rind of 1 large orange
> 25 juniper berries, crushed and chopped fairly finely
> 1 dsp gin

Cut the salmon in half across the grain. Mix the other ingredients together in a bowl and spread evenly over the cut sides of the fish, wrap tightly in clingfilm and leave on a plate in the fridge for 48 hours.

Rinse the fish under cold water, pat dry with kitchen paper, remove the skin, and cut into 4 thick slices. Get a ribbed cast-iron grilling pan very hot (if you haven't a grill pan, use an ordinary non-stick frying pan). Brush the fish with vegetable oil and grill for 2 minutes each side. Serve with boiled potatoes and peeled grated cucumber squeezed of water, seasoned, and quickly heated in butter.

If you would prefer the gravad lax variation, simply cut into thin slices at an angle. In either case, a big blob of sour cream or crème fraiche flavoured with grated lemon rind would go well.

Fish Pie with a Gougère Top

This is my version of a simple classic. The gougère topping, which is simply cheesy choux paste, is more interesting than the usual potato (see On Choux Paste and Piping Bags, page 106).

Apart from the quality of the fish, the important thing is the flavour of the sauce that binds, so a decent infusion is called for. Finally, try to include the herbs – I much prefer chervil's sweetness and delicacy, but then I'm not keen on parsley's rather butch flavour except in a soup or teamed up with garlic.

Serves 6

> 25g butter
> about 750g of fish, cut into 4cm chunks
>   – use any combination of 2 or 3
>   firm-bodied fish like cod, haddock, hake,
>   monkfish, John Dory, salmon (although
>   I would also use salmon on its own),
>   mussels, prawns, scallops, and (even)
>   langoustines or lobster
> 175g white mushrooms, halved, or quartered
>   if large
> salt and freshly ground black pepper

Melt half the butter in a frying pan and over medium heat cook the fish quickly until just firm, trying to prevent any moisture escaping. (If you use mussels in the shell, cook in a lidded saucepan in a little of the white wine (see below) until the shells are thoroughly open, adding the liquor to the infusion.) Transfer the fish to a large bowl. In a small saucepan, with the lid on, stew the mushrooms gently in the rest of the butter. If they release any moisture, boil to evaporate it. Add to the fish. Season lightly with salt and pepper.

Sauce

300 ml milk
a 5 cm strip lemon peel, no pith
½ a Spanish onion, finely sliced
2 blades mace or a large pinch of grated
    nutmeg
2 cloves
8 black peppercorns
6 parsley stalks
1 bay leaf
37g butter
1 medium leek, white and pale green part
    only, finely sliced
37g plain flour
1 glass dry white wine
2 tbsp double cream (optional)
salt
2 tbsp chopped chervil or dill, or 1 tbsp
    chopped parsley or tarragon

In a small saucepan, heat the milk with the next seven ingredients. Bring very slowly to a simmer and leave to cool. Strain into a jug or bowl, pressing to squeeze out all the liquid. In another saucepan melt the butter and sweat the leek, covered, for 5 minutes. Add the flour and cook gently for a further 5 minutes. Gradually add the strained milk, whisking or stirring hard to avoid lumps, and the wine. Add the cream, and salt to taste, cool, and pour over the fish mixture. Gently stir in the herbs and transfer the lot to an oblong or oval gratin dish, about 25.5 cm × 20.5 cm. Smooth the top.

Preheat the oven to 400°F/205°C/Gas 6.

Gougère Top

200 ml water
50g butter, cut into pieces
generous ½ tsp salt
a few screws of freshly ground black pepper
a pinch of nutmeg
75g plain flour, sifted
3 eggs
110g Gruyère, strong Cheddar or Parmesan,
    grated

In at least a 2 litre saucepan bring the water, butter and seasonings to a boil. When the butter has melted, shove in the flour all at once and away from the heat beat hard with a wooden spoon. Continue beating until the mixture solidifies and comes away from the sides and bottom of the pan. All the little flour lumps should have gone by now; if not, you've probably forgotten to sift the flour and will be swearing rather loudly. The only thing to do now is pass the mixture through a sieve – or you could throw it out of the window and start again.

All being well, however, you can start beating in the eggs, adding the next after the first is incorporated and so on. Lastly, fold in the cheese. Fit a piping bag with a 1 cm plain nozzle and pipe a lattice pattern over the top of the fish. If you don't want to pipe, just spread the mixture over and smooth the top.

Bake the pie for 30 minutes, by which time the top should be golden brown.

On Choux Paste and Piping Bags

Like boiling sugar or making egg and butter sauces, making choux is one of those things that seems to unman normally resourceful and well-balanced people, but it is, for pastry, very straightforward and once mastered lends itself to a multitude of useful and delicious concoctions.

The basic recipe for choux paste is given below with the fish pie. There are only two things to get right: don't use too much water and always sift the flour. Use a saucepan that's big enough to hold the flour and eggs and that will also allow you to beat the hell out of the mixture without it flying off around the kitchen.

For sweet choux paste – for profiteroles, éclairs, choux buns or dough-nuts – simply reduce the salt to a pinch and add a scant teaspoon of caster sugar.

Savoury choux can be used as above with any number of fillings or in its refined Burgundian form (it's rather like Yorkshire pudding but fancier), which is simply with diced Swiss or mountain cheese added.

Using the piping bag allows you to make the éclairs and doughnuts easily. You can, of course, just use a teaspoon to make the profiteroles or savoury puffs, but the piping bag is quicker and neater. It's also just about essential if you want to make meringue discs or baskets or want to use whipped cream as a cake or pudding decoration. The main thing to remember, apart from making sure you put the nozzle in before you fill the bag, is to roll back the wide end of the bag before you fill it so you can twist it around the filling – this makes it much easier to keep squeezing the filling towards the nozzle.

Some ideas for savoury choux fillings:

- cooked, finely chopped shallots, mushrooms and roasted walnuts

- diced mushrooms, shallots and tarragon

- goat's cheese combined with ricotta, chopped sun-dried tomatoes and shredded basil

- chicken liver mousse (page 95, 96)

- as above, flavouring the raw paste with very finely chopped garlic and chopped green herbs

- finely diced ham or sautéed chorizo in a thick cheese sauce

- creamed chicken with roasted nibbed almonds

- creamy scrambled eggs with finely diced crisp bacon

Steamed Plaice with Cucumber, Dill and Horseradish

In terms of eating quality, plaice has a near unique slot in the fishy hierarchy. With its mild but sweet flavour, its melting texture that's difficult to overcook, its ready availability and its low price, it's a wonder that it hasn't yet joined the list of fish under threat – cod, haddock, tuna, wild salmon, scallops, lobster. I suppose its association with the fish 'n' chip shop and the other fishy also-rans to be found there – rock salmon, huss – hasn't done its image much good over the years, but perhaps that's something we should be grateful for. Those people who can't cast prejudice aside or look further than turbot or sea bass, at more than twice the price, are missing something special. Try to find large plaice if you can, simply because they make a better mouthful.

Steaming, the most gentle of cooking methods, is ideal for the friable meat of the plaice or lemon sole. Here, the al dente cucumber adds a pleasing textural dimension to a real northern-latitude dish.

1 large cucumber
salt
2 medium to large plaice, filleted to give
    4 fillets, skin removed
3 tbsp chopped dill
25g butter
2 tbsp creamed horseradish
2 tbsp thick yogurt or crème fraiche

Peel the cucumber with a swivel-bladed peeler and remove the core. Cut into long strips, then into 5 mm dice. Place in a sieve or colander and sprinkle liberally with salt. Place a small plate or saucer on top and weight it. Leave for half an hour, then press down to expel a bit more water. Rinse well under running water and pat dry.

Season both sides of the fish lightly with salt and sprinkle fairly liberally with the dill. Fold each fillet into 3 to make a neat parcel. Steam on buttered foil on a trivet over simmering water for about 7 minutes.

Melt the butter in a saucepan and sweat the cucumber for 5 minutes. Add the horseradish and the yogurt or crème fraiche. Spoon the cucumber mixture on to 4 plates and with a spatula or fish slice place the fish on top. Serve with buttered new potatoes.

Cod with Wilted Rocket and Hazelnut Butter

Rocket, unlike that other recent hero the sun-dried tomato, has survived its period on the pedestal of fashion and settled down to become a normal and important member of the family of salad leaves. You can use a lot of it in this dish, as like spinach it rapidly loses bulk when heated. Its mildly nutty flavour chimes well with the hazelnuts.

> 4 fillets of cod, 175g each, skinned
> 25g butter
> a large handful of rocket leaves or more
> beurre blanc (page 26)
> hazelnut butter (below)
> about 20 roasted hazelnuts, chopped

Season the cod fillets and cook in butter over medium heat in a covered pan until just cooked, about 8 minutes. Try to cook them fast enough to keep in the moisture, i.e. so they brown lightly. Remove and keep warm. Throw the rocket leaves into the pan, and stir around in the remaining butter for a minute or so, until the leaves have wilted. Season. Divide the rocket leaves between 4 plates, place the cod on top, and pour the beurre blanc over. Top with a slice of hazelnut butter, and scatter with the hazelnuts. Serve with mashed potato.

Hazelnut Butter

> 15g roasted and ground hazelnuts
> 50g unsalted butter, softened
> salt

Mix the hazelnuts and butter together, season lightly with salt, and roll into a cylindrical shape, about 5 cm in diameter. Chill until hard.

Fish Quenelles, Gratinated

I've never understood the eclipse of the quenelle and the mousseline. Along with bavarian creams, aspics and jellies, they seem to have been consigned to a culinary black hole, unworthy relics of a pre-fusion age, unlike their cousin, the soufflé, which in its unmoulded variations survives untarnished by the tiresome demands of fashion. Were it not for the soufflé, I'd be tempted to ascribe the nation's improved orthodontic health to the passing of the quenelle's denture-friendly textures, but to make it share the same fate as béchamel sauce seems impetuous, to say the least. I suspect that the béchamel's lustre is undimmed at home, even if exiled from restaurants, but I do think the loss of these delectable, airy dumplings which cry out for proper sauces, properly made, is a crying shame. It *is* possible to eat fish in other ways than skin-on, crisply fried, good though that method is. You would think it was the only one, judging by its ubiquity in smart restaurants. In this version, the quenelles are immersed in a béchamel turned into a velouté by using fish stock. The sauce is lightened and refined with an egg yolk liaison, and sprinkled with cheese and browned under the grill.

Although you will need to make choux paste for this recipe (see On Choux Paste and Piping Bags, page 106), the food processor makes the rest straightforward. The results more than repay the time spent.

Fish Mousse

500g boned and skinless, firm-fleshed fish
   (lemon sole, whiting, monkfish, coley,
   turbot or pike), reserving the bones
   for stock
a large pinch of mace
about ½ tsp salt
1 quantity of choux paste (see Fish Pie with
   a Gougère Top, page 104)
4–6 tbsp double cream, chilled

Cut the fish into small pieces and purée in a food processor for 30 seconds. If you want a finer, silkier result, press through a sieve using the back of a ladle (hard work!). Scrape into a large bowl and mix together with the mace, salt, and choux paste. Refrigerate for half an hour and beat in the cream. Test the mix for consistency and seasoning by dropping a blob from a wetted spoon into salted simmering water and poach for 5 minutes. Adjust seasoning and add more cream if necessary. You want lightness but not so much that the mixture disintegrates. Make oval quenelle shapes with 2 wetted dessertspoons and poach in batches in very hot, barely simmering, water. They turn over when cooked through. Remove with a slotted spoon to a large gratin dish, carefully pouring off any water after letting them rest for a few minutes. Keep hot. You should have about 16 large-egg-sized quenelles.

Velouté Sauce

500ml fish stock (page 38)
25g butter
25g flour
1 glass dry white wine
2 egg yolks
200ml double cream
salt

Reduce the fish stock to 300ml. Melt the butter and cook the flour in it, stirring, for 3–4 minutes. Gradually add the stock, stirring at first and then whisking as the liquid thins out the starchy mixture. Pour in the wine and cook gently, whisking until the sauce is perfectly smooth. In a bowl beat together the yolks and cream, and pour in some of the hot sauce, whisking constantly. Return to the saucepan and season. Reduce a little or add a little more cream depending on consistency – better slightly too thick than too thin, as there may be some residual liquid in the gratin dish.

To finish

75g grated Gruyère or Parmesan

Cover the quenelles with the sauce and sprinkle on a good layer of finely grated cheese. Heat through in the oven before serving, then place under a hot grill until the cheese has turned golden brown.

Halibut Fillet with Aromatic Vegetables
and Soft Herbs

This dish makes stars of the usual supporting cast of onion, carrot and celery, using them as the main ingredients of the sauce, which is rich and delicate at the same time. The courgette is there mainly for the colour, and its mild flavour won't interfere with the rest. This is a good sauce for other soft-fleshed fish like sole and plaice, as the vegetables have a pleasing firmness.

25g butter
a 12.5 cm carrot
1 dark green courgette
1 stick of celery, without strings
2 shallots, finely chopped
1 glass dry white wine
150 ml chicken stock
4 tbsp double cream
4 pieces halibut fillet, about 150g each
salt and freshly ground black pepper
1 tbsp chopped dill
2 tbsp chopped chervil

Melt the butter in a large frying pan for which you have a lid (or you can put a big plate on top). Scrub the carrot and cut lengthways into quarters, then across into 2 mm slices. Do the same with the courgette, only make the slices 3 mm. Finally dice the celery very finely. Put the shallots in the butter and cook over moderate heat for 3–4 minutes. Add the carrot, celery and courgette, the wine, stock and cream. Lay the fish, seasoned with salt and pepper, on top of the vegetables, cover and poach/steam for 5 minutes. Remove the fish to warm plates. Now add the herbs to the pan and bubble to reduce to sauce consistency. Check the seasoning and pour over the fish. Serve with another green vegetable if you wish and plain buttered pasta.

Mackerel with Orange Juice and Breadcrumbs

Not a very inspiring name for an excellent recipe for an underrated fish. It's curious that mackerel should still be so cheap, considering how healthy it is (all that oil . . .), how good-looking with its silvery iridescence and sleek hydrodynamic shape, and how distinctive its flavour. It belongs to that small group with a pronounced separateness from most of the fish we are used to – tuna, salmon, the sardine; yet while tuna and salmon are among the great and the good of the fish world, sardines, herrings (though not the smoked version) and mackerel have somehow never become respectable.

Fortunately for us mackerel lovers, we can enjoy this handsome fish knowing stocks are plentiful, it's doing us good and it's remarkably cheap. This recipe is a bit inside-out: it involves a 'stuffing' that is used to cover the fish after cooking, and the fish will be filleted, not left whole with a cavity made by removing the innards. Stuffing the fish in the normal way is convenient to do, but the stuffing tends to get muddled up with the bones which can spoil the fun.

4 mackerel

Marinade
juice of 2 large oranges
juice of ½ a lemon
3 bay leaves, shredded
1 small glass dry white wine

Stuffing
50g pine nuts
8 heaped tbsp coarse, staleish breadcrumbs,
    brown or white
olive oil or melted butter
½ a shallot, very finely chopped

40g sultanas or raisins
4 anchovy fillets, finely chopped
½ tsp grated lemon rind
a large pinch of sugar
25g butter, cold, cut into pieces

With a very sharp knife remove the fillets by cutting them down each side of the dorsal fin, keeping the knife blade against the central bone. Cut each fillet crosswise in half, place them in a roasting tin and cover with the marinade. Leave for an hour or two, turning once.

Preheat the oven to 400°F/205°C/Gas 6.

Toast the pine nuts lightly and carefully (they burn very easily and need to be watched and turned constantly). Brown the breadcrumbs until crisp but not burned over medium heat in 2 tbsp oil or butter, also turning constantly. Remove to a bowl. Add the shallot to the pan, with a little more oil or butter. Soften for 3 minutes, then remove to the bowl. Roughly chop the sultanas or raisins and pine nuts and add to the bowl with the anchovies, lemon rind, and sugar. The mixture should be moist but not clumpy, so add a little more oil or butter if necessary. The anchovies provide enough salt.

Place the marinade tin on top of the stove and turn on the heat. After 1 minute transfer the tin to the oven and bake for about 12 minutes. The fish should be just cooked through. Remove the fillets to a warm gratin dish, keep warm, and pour the cooking liquid through a sieve into a wide pan. Boil to reduce to about 6 tbsp, throw in the butter and boil for a few moments more, until a light emulsion forms. Pour over the fish, scatter over the breadcrumb mix and put under a hot grill for a few seconds.

A warm potato salad would be good with this, dressed with chives, shallots and olive oil.

Home-Salted Salt Cod with Ginger and Tomatoes

Most of the salt cod sold in Britain is well-nigh useless, having been so oversalted that every drop of moisture has been brutally sucked out, rendering the texture of the fish tough, fibrous, and impossible to reconstitute. This may have been fine in centuries past but now we don't need to ensure the fish lasts for many months, nor can we trail it behind our boats as we navigate up the Dordogne from Bordeaux to Capdenac – as the wine barges used to, taking all of seven days. Anyway, salting your own delivers an interesting variation on cod's normal flavour and gives a far better result. It also allows you to vary the salt cure.

You will need one side of a large fish – between 1.5 kg and 2.25 kg is ideal. Sprinkle liberally with sea salt so the fish is covered in an even layer, place in a large roasting tin or on a large tray (you could cut it in two – the fish, that is) and cover with cling-film. Leave in the fridge for 4–7 days. Remove to a bowl and wash the salt off under gently running water for 4 hours, or if you are metered leave in the bowl for 24 hours but change the water a few times.

You can now use the fish without pre-cooking it. Here is a lively recipe that could be just the thing on a wet winter evening.

2 tbsp vegetable oil
1 large Spanish onion, peeled and chopped
1 small carrot, finely chopped
½ a stick of celery, finely chopped
2 cloves of garlic, crushed
1 tin of tomatoes or 225g passata
½ a bay leaf
a 2.5 cm cube of peeled fresh ginger, grated
  or finely chopped
a fresh thyme sprig or ¼ tsp dried thyme
1 glass dry white wine
5 cm piece of orange peel (no pith)
20 fennel seeds
2 hot or mild chillies, finely chopped
½ tsp sugar
4 pieces of salt cod, 175g each, skinned
salt and freshly ground black pepper

In a large frying pan heat the oil and soften the onion, carrot, celery and garlic for 5 minutes. Add all the other ingredients except the fish and the seasoning and cook gently for 20 minutes, stirring occasionally. Season lightly. Place the cod on the top and cover the pan (if you haven't a lid, then use a plate). Cook over a moderate heat for 10 minutes, remove the fish to hot plates, and reduce the sauce if necessary by rapid boiling. Take out the garlic, bay leaf and thyme sprig if using, check the seasoning, and pour the sauce over the fish. Make sure some of the dazzling (we hope) white of the cod is visible against the sauce. Serve with rice or fried potatoes.

Grilled Bream with Parsley and Caper Cream

To avoid the title rhyme, you could replace the bream with bass, snapper or mullet, or even call the cream a sauce, but that doesn't really sound all that appetizing. This is a really fresh-tasting and slightly piquant sauce that is quickly made but tastes very classy. It goes well with the more robustly flavoured fish, as well as those named earlier in this chapter – salmon, tuna, and swordfish would all be suitable. This is a creamy sauce, but we all need fat in our diet.

4 good-sized bream or red mullet, weighing
    about 400g each, cleaned
olive oil
salt and freshly ground black pepper
2 heaped tbsp baby capers
2 shallots, finely chopped
1 small clove of garlic
20g curly parsley, most stalks removed
250ml double cream

Heat the grill to hot. Cut 3 slashes on each side of each fish. Brush some olive oil over a sheet of tinfoil, brush the fish liberally with more olive oil and lay them on the foil. Season with salt and pepper. Place them the furthest distance away from the heat and grill for 6–8 minutes each side, depending on thickness. Remove to hot plates.

Soak the capers in cold water for a few minutes to release some of the salt. Heat 1 tbsp olive oil in a small saucepan and cook the shallots and garlic over moderate heat for 5 minutes. Scrape into the liquidizer jar with the parsley and the cream. Drain the capers and add these to the cream. Blitz together for a few seconds, until the capers have disappeared, and pour back into the saucepan. Heat up again and pour next to the fish, rather than over it, so you can see what you are doing. You probably won't need any more salt. The potato and chorizo gratin would go well with this (page 176).

Smoked Haddock with Curried Lentils

Smoked fish and curry seems an unlikely combination – two very different kinds of cooking treatment from completely different latitudes. On the whole it doesn't seem to work well except in kedgeree, although even there the arguments have come and gone over whether curry spices – particularly turmeric and ginger – should be included. It seems to me that smoked haddock is the exception that proves the rule and takes well to spicing. Here it's applied indirectly, in the lentils, so purists could, I suppose, eat the haddock, pause for a while, and eat the lentils. Or the other way round. But that would look a bit odd, don't you think?

2 undyed smoked haddock fillets, each weighing about 300g, skin and any little bones removed with tweezers or pliers
4 large or 8 small bay leaves
8 thin lemon slices
200g green lentils (they don't need soaking beforehand)
a small bouquet garni of coriander stalks, bay leaf, and parsley stalks, plus 1 lemon grass stem, outer sheath removed, insides bashed with a heavy knife or rolling pin
60g onion, finely chopped
60g carrot, diced
½ a clove of garlic, peeled and finely chopped
1½ tsp salt
250g butter
125 ml double cream
2½ tbsp curry powder
black pepper
a good squeeze of lemon juice
2 tbsp chopped coriander

Cut each fillet in half, folding the tail end underneath the narrow tail fillet. Unroll a sheet of clingfilm and place the fillets on it, and on each fillet place 1 large or 2 small bay leaves and cover these with 2 lemon slices. Wrap tightly with the film and refrigerate for 8 hours or so.

Wash the lentils, and put them in a medium-sized saucepan. Cover with about 500 ml cold water, add the bouquet garni and lemon grass, onion, carrot, garlic and salt and bring to the boil. Skim if necessary, and cook gently, the liquid bubbling occasionally, for about 25 minutes. Taste to see if they are cooked – they should be slightly al dente – and cook a bit longer if necessary. Don't let them get mushy. Drain them in a colander or sieve, remove the bouquet garni and pour back into the saucepan. Keep the liquid as a base for soup, or to cook vegetables in and *then* keep for soup.

Unwrap the fish, discarding the bay and lemon. Heat the butter in a large frying pan and when hot but not foaming put in the fish (which won't need seasoning), unfolded side up. Cook for about 4 minutes, carefully turn over with a fish slice, and cook for 4 minutes more.

While this is going on, heat the lentils with the cream and gently mix in the curry powder, a few turns of the pepper mill and the lemon juice. Check the seasoning. Divide them between 4 hot plates and put a piece of fish on each pile. Sprinkle with the coriander. There's no real need for anything else with this, except maybe a leafy salad.

Tuna Steak with Sweet Peppers, Tomatoes and Lime

This is a dish to exploit the meatiness and sweet flavour of tuna. Best made if you have a ribbed iron grilling pan, but don't *not* do it if you haven't. In this straightforward recipe, all the flavours help each other along, the colours are nice and there are some zingy sweet-sour notes played by the vinegar, lime and sugar.

4 tbsp olive oil
4 shallots, finely chopped
1 red and 1 yellow pepper, stem, ribs and seeds
    removed
1 tbsp red wine vinegar
1 firm dark green lime, grated rind (no pith)
    and 2 tsp juice
2 tsp sugar
4 firm, ripe tomatoes, peeled, seeded and diced
salt and freshly ground black pepper
4 tuna steaks, weighing about 175g each
about 16 basil leaves, torn up

Heat half the oil in a medium saucepan and soften the shallots in it for 5 minutes. Cut the peppers into 1cm dice, add to the pan, and cook gently, covered, for 10 minutes. Add the vinegar, the lime rind, the lime juice and the sugar. Cook a further 5 minutes, uncover and let the liquid evaporate. This should only take 1–2 minutes. Add the tomatoes and cook under the lid for a further 2 minutes. Remove from the heat and season lightly with salt. You can make this ahead up to this point.

Meanwhile, heat the grilling pan to very hot. Brush the steaks with some of the remaining oil, season with salt and pepper, and cook for a couple of minutes each side, depending on how thick they are. This would be sufficient for a thickness of 15mm. Tuna is much better cooked rare like (beef) steak.

Have the sauce very hot and stir in the basil leaves. Place a tuna steak on each of 4 plates and pour the sauce over, finishing off with the remaining olive oil.

Plain pasta tossed in olive oil would be good with this.

Red Mullet with Garlic, Anchovies and Lemon

Although this uses 'French Mediterranean' ingredients, it can go with other kinds of fish, as long as they have a pronounced flavour. Bream or tuna would also be ideal, and stretching a point, cod or haddock would do, but this isn't a treatment for turbot, halibut, sole or plaice. This is more or less a bagna cauda (page 29), but thinner than would be needed as a dipping sauce.

4 cloves of garlic
8 anchovy fillets
salt and freshly ground black pepper
grated rind of 1 lemon and 1 tsp of the juice
8 red mullet or bream fillets
25g butter
1 tbsp olive oil
8 tbsp double cream
4 tbsp olive oil
½ glass dry white wine
1 tbsp chopped parsley

Chop the garlic as finely as you can, and do the same with the anchovies. Mix them together on your chopping board and crush them to a paste with the blade of your largest knife. Season the fish with salt (very little), pepper and a little lemon juice, melt the butter and olive oil, and when the foam has subsided fry the fish for 3 minutes each side. Remove and keep hot.

Heat the garlic and anchovy paste for a couple of minutes in a small pan, add the cream, olive oil and lemon rind, and simmer gently for 5 more minutes. This should provide a loose emulsion. Add the white wine and simmer gently for a further 5 minutes. Dish up the fish, divide the sauce over and sprinkle with the parsley.

A salad of sweet peppers and sliced waxy potatoes would go well, or some green beans finished with finely chopped shallots. You could also serve chickpea pancakes (page 170).

Red Mullet Fillets with Red Lentil Salsa

Does anyone use red lentils any more? I think they make a pleasant change from the earthy little numbers from Le Puy, and not just because of their colour. They have an understated character which carries other flavours well, as in this simple dish. It doesn't need anything else to go with it.

250g red lentils, picked over and washed
½ a red pepper
½ a yellow pepper
2 firm ripe tomatoes
2 shallots, finely chopped
4 tbsp chopped coriander leaves
1 generous tsp curry powder
½ tsp ground cumin
1 generous tbsp sherry vinegar or balsamic vinegar
3 tbsp olive oil
salt and black pepper
4 good-sized red mullet fillets, or 8 small ones

Simmer the unsoaked lentils in unsalted water for about 20 minutes. They must still be al dente so check them during the last few minutes. Drain them and refresh in cold water. Drain again well when they are cold and pour into a bowl. Core and deseed the peppers, cutting out the ribs and removing as much of the skin as you can with a sharp knife or potato peeler, and cut into 1cm dice. Make a cross on the top of each tomato with a very sharp knife and plunge into boiling water for 20 seconds. Remove and put into cold water for a few more seconds. Peel off the skin, cut them into quarters and remove the seeds. Chop into 1cm dice. Add them to the lentils with the peppers, shallots, half the coriander, the spices, vinegar and 2 tbsp of the olive oil. Season as you like and let stand for an hour or so at room temperature.

Season and gently fry the fish fillets in the remaining olive oil for 3–4 minutes, according to thickness. Divide the salsa between 4 heated plates and place 1 or 2 fillets on top. Sprinkle over the rest of the coriander.

Skate Wing with Romesco Stuffing

One of the more interesting fish. *Why? – Ed.* Erm, because it's not a round fish, nor a proper flat fish, because it's really a ray . . . Well, it does have a unique texture, neither chewy nor sludgy, which rather optimistically has been compared to crab. Oh, and it's one of the few fish better eaten after a day or two than straight out of the sea (so that the urea in the fish, which keeps it in osmotic balance in the sea, has broken up and disappeared – an ammoniac smell is a sign that this has happened, and this itself will disappear in cooking). And it has a slightly stronger flavour than most white fish, and doesn't have any annoying little bones. *OK, so it's interesting after all.*

The stuffing was suggested by the excellent Spanish romesco sauce, which could equally well partner this fish, as it does red mullet and hake in Spain. Why are the Spaniards so mad keen on hake? Why the Japanese on tuna? Why the Dutch on herring? Why the British on cod? What interesting questions these are!

Serves 2

2 large firm tomatoes
2 shallots or ½ a small onion, finely chopped
2 tbsp olive oil
1 large clove of garlic, chopped finely and
    then mashed to a paste with a large
    pinch of salt
½ a mild chilli, seeded and finely chopped
50g fresh breadcrumbs, brown or white
40g blanched almonds, lightly toasted
½ tsp salt
a few screws of black pepper
a good pinch of cayenne
2 fairly large pieces of skate wing, each
    weighing about 225g
25g butter
a squeeze of lemon juice

Cut a cross at the top of the tomatoes and plunge into boiling water for 20 seconds, and then into cold water. Remove the skin and seeds and cut into 1cm dice. Soften the shallots or onion in half the olive oil in a small saucepan for 5 minutes, remove to a small bowl and add the tomato, garlic, and chilli. In the food processor whizz the breadcrumbs with the almonds for a few seconds and add to the mixture in the bowl. Season and mix well together.

Preheat the oven to 375°F/190°C/Gas 5.

With a sharp knife remove the fish from its skeleton as neatly as you can. You should have 4 ribbed, roughly triangular pieces. Season each fillet lightly with salt on both sides and place 1 large tbsp of the stuffing in the middle of the underside of each. Fold over the edges to make as neat a parcel as you can and place them smooth-side uppermost in a buttered gratin or baking dish. Cover with a buttered sheet of foil and bake for about 20 minutes, until cooked through.

Heat the remaining olive oil and the butter together in a small pan and pour over the fish. Squeeze a few drops of lemon juice over and serve. Couscous with raisins and maybe some chopped green beans is a good bet to go with this.

Salmon Escalopes with Marinière Sauce

This is an adaptation of a wonderful sauce from Georges Blanc in Vonnas (Burgundy) to embellish any really noble fish – turbot, halibut, Dover sole fillets, bass or wild salmon. I've featured salmon simply because it's easier to buy, but a white fish would make a better colour picture. However, the flavour is the thing, and this goes just as well with salmon.

I say my adaptation, partly because the quantities M. Blanc gives for four would feed eight, and partly because he is at pains to leave the final balance of elements up to the cook, and indeed I have found some juggling to be in order. This is one of those sauces that reflects lustre on to French haute cuisine; not because it involves expensive ingredients or any special knowledge on the part of the cook, but because it relies for its effect on the imagination of its creator (Blanc), the sheer virtue of its ingredients, the interplay of several different processes that culminate in a complex balance that trips off the tongue, and its beguiling appearance.

Rather foolishly, the first time I did this was for a wedding for forty. It took me, alone, four hours, which left me about twenty minutes each for the other four courses. I hadn't been cooking for long then and decided this sort of dish ought really to have a dummy-run beforehand. Although four different stages are involved, the preparation is absolutely not daunting, and the end result is almost bound to be good. The only thing to worry about is making it too runny.

The four components are a concassé of tomatoes; a court bouillon; the olive oil base; and a butter-water emulsion (which is called – but never used these days – drawn butter). Blanc leaves it to the cook to balance the different elements 'until your eye and palate are satisfied'; this is the result I have ended up with.

Serves 6

Marinière Sauce

Concassé of tomatoes

4 large, firm, ripe tomatoes
10g butter
2 tbsp olive oil
15g shallots, very finely chopped
1 peeled clove of garlic, crushed
1 tsp tomato paste
a large pinch of sugar
1 bouquet garni of ½ a bay leaf, 1 sprig
  of thyme, 1 stalk of parsley, ½ a small
  celery stalk cut in half lengthways,
  all tied together (or in a muslin bag)
salt

Cut a cross at the top of the tomatoes and plunge into boiling water for 20 seconds. Take out and put in a bowl of cold water. Peel away the skin, cut into quarters, and remove the seeds. Chop 3 of them roughly, throwing away the stalky bits; cut 1 tomato into 5mm cubes and reserve. Heat the butter and olive oil in a saucepan. Throw in the shallots and cook for a minute over medium heat. Add the garlic, roughly chopped tomatoes, tomato paste, sugar, and bouquet garni. Cook over gentle heat, covered, for 20 minutes. Reduce over medium heat, stirring occasionally, for 15 minutes. Remove the bouquet garni and garlic. Season lightly and set aside.

Court bouillon

¼ bottle dry white wine
125ml water
1 small carrot, thinly sliced
1 medium onion, thinly sliced
2 shallots, finely sliced

½ a bay leaf
1 sprig thyme
1 clove of garlic, crushed
1 small stalk of celery, thinly sliced
thinly pared rind of ½ a lemon
2 parsley stalks
salt

Cook all the ingredients except the salt together for 30 minutes in a medium saucepan. Then season lightly, drain, and reserve the liquid.

Olive oil base

75 ml best olive oil
3 shallots, very finely chopped
the tomato concassé, except the reserved
    tomato dice
the court bouillon
½ a bay leaf
lemon juice
salt
2 tbsp each finely chopped chives and
    basil
1 tbsp finely chopped tarragon

Heat the oil in a saucepan and cook the shallots in it over moderate heat for 5 minutes, without browning. Add the concassé and the court bouillon, stirring well together. Add the bay leaf and cook over moderate heat for 15 minutes. Stir in a good squeeze of lemon juice and a little salt. Remove the bay leaf and stir in the herbs. (Everything can be done ahead to this point.)

Butter-water emulsion

4 tbsp water
juice of ½ a lemon
75g butter, cold, cut into small pieces

Bring the water and lemon juice to the boil in a small saucepan and throw the butter in all at once. Whisk hard until the butter has melted into the water, which should be lightly emulsified.

To finish

Incorporate the butter sauce into the olive oil base, add the reserved tomato dice from the concassé, and check that the seasoning is right. Keep hot while you cook the fish.

Salmon Escalopes

6 salmon escalopes, each weighing about
    150g
salt
1 tbsp olive oil
12g butter

Season the escalopes. In a large frying pan heat together the oil and butter. A few seconds after the foam has died away, put in the fish and cook over moderate heat for 3–4 minutes each side, depending on thickness. They should, I think, still be lightly raw in the middle. Divide the sauce between 6 hot plates and place an escalope on each.

Serve this with well-buttered Jersey Royals or some good buttered pasta – nothing else.

Baked Hake with Cappon Magro Sauce

Hake is a meaty fish which holds its shape when cooked, although that shape, it could be argued, couldn't justify a letter home. More to the point I think is its skin, which like the cod's or haddock's is a rather unappetizing grey. Underneath this though is flesh (I've been trying to avoid that word) of a mild sweet flavour and a firm but yielding consistency that doesn't separate into slippery flakes – good kebab fish, I suppose, if you don't mind throwing some away (and you do – I know you do). The Spanish have the correct view of hake: they value it highly and a great deal of the hake caught by British boats finds its way south, as their appetite for it is insatiable (their own waters, though plentifully supplied, don't meet the demand).

Cappon Magro is (or was – I wonder if it can be found in its traditional form) a Genoese mixture of vegetables, fish, and a green-mayonnaise type sauce, all piled up together in a pyramid shape. I've not tried to reproduce this rather unlikely spectacle but have to admit the sauce is a great one, in the tradition of Continental green sauces, and would be terrific with cold fish or eggs. I've used the cooking juices to dilute some of the sauce, which can be dipped into like aïoli.

To bake the fish

- 2 tbsp olive oil
- 2 large cloves of garlic, finely chopped
- 1 small glass dry white wine
- 4 hake steaks or fillets, each weighing about 175g
- salt

Preheat the oven to 400°F/205°C/Gas 6.

Pour the olive oil into a medium-sized gratin dish and brush it over the base and sides. Sprinkle over the garlic and gently pour in the wine. Place the hake on top, sprinkle lightly with salt, and cover with a buttered/oiled sheet of cooking foil. Bake for 25 minutes in the middle of the oven.

Cappon Magro Sauce

- a bunch of curly parsley, weighing about 10g after the coarse stalks are removed
- 1 large clove of garlic, chopped
- 1 tbsp capers
- 2 anchovy fillets, drained of oil
- yolks of 2 hard-boiled eggs
- 6 large green olives (7, destoned, if using ones with stones in – no seat of the pants here!)
- 3 or 4 slices (1mm thick) of fennel bulb, plus any frondy bits
- 3–4 heaped tbsp breadcrumbs from good bread, brown or white
- grated rind of ½ a lemon
- about 225ml olive oil
- 1 tbsp red wine vinegar

Process the first nine ingredients in the food-processor bowl until the mixture forms a coarse paste – about 20 seconds. Pour the olive oil on, with the motor running, in a thin stream, slowly at first, as if you were making mayonnaise. If it curdles whisk it tablespoon by tablespoon into a fresh egg yolk; however, scraping the mixture out of the processor and into another bowl, and using a spiral whisk to beat the oil into it, is pretty foolproof. The oil can be added faster as the emulsion takes. When the oil is used up beat in the vinegar.

When the fish is cooked and you are ready to serve it, remove to hot plates and in a small bowl mix together the cooking liquid and a few tablespoons of the sauce. Remove the skin from the fish and pour the sauce over. Offer the rest of the sauce separately. All you need with this (and you must have them) is some skinned boiled potatoes, preferably a waxy kind, and a salad of some kind. Well, one other thing that would be quite nice but very incorrect would be some triangles of bread fried in butter as a crunchy counterpart. The sauce is salty enough, but you may want to sprinkle the skinned fish with a little salt and freshly ground black pepper.

Nage of Seafood with Ginger and Saffron

Here different kinds of fish and shellfish are cooked in an aromatic court bouillon made from white wine and fish stock and flavoured with spices and thinly sliced vegetables. This recipe uses ginger, saffron and lemon grass, but other flavourings could easily be used. The point is to have enough of them. The fish is served with some of the broth, with some green herbs – here coriander – scattered over it, and a jug of orange and ginger flavoured beurre blanc offered alongside. This is a good party dish as the court bouillon and beurre blanc base can be made beforehand; the fish takes only 5 minutes or so to cook. It should be a firm-fleshed kind, so it doesn't break up or flake in the liquid.

To make the orange and ginger flavoured beurre blanc follow the instructions on page 26 but add a 2 cm cube of peeled ginger, finely chopped or grated, and 2 pieces of orange peel, 3 cm × 2 cm, to the wine reduction.

> 12g butter
> 4 shallots, finely sliced
> 6 cm piece of white of leek, sliced on the bias into very thin ovals
> middle part (4 cm) of 1 medium carrot, sliced as above
> ½ a stick of celery, finely sliced
> 3 cm cube of fresh ginger root, peeled and thinly sliced
> 2 stems of lemon grass, outer sheath removed, insides bashed with a heavy knife or rolling pin
> 2 bay leaves
> a big pinch of saffron stamens

150 ml fish stock, clear if possible
150 ml good dry white wine (a Semillon-Chardonnay blend would be ideal)
700 ml mussels or clams, cleaned and bearded
500g firm white fish such as haddock, monkfish, sea bass, turbot or brill, free of skin and bone and cut into even-sized chunks, about 4 cm square
8 scallops, cleaned, with coral
salt
coriander leaves

Melt the butter in a large saucepan and cook the shallots, leek, carrot and celery over moderate heat for 15 minutes. Don't let them colour. Add the ginger, lemon grass, bay leaves, saffron, stock and wine. Bring to a very gentle simmer and leave to infuse off the heat for 20 minutes. Bring the nage back up to simmering point and add the mussels or clams, cook for a couple of minutes and add the white fish. The liquid should be just below or at simmering point from here. After about 5 minutes add the scallops and cook for 3 more minutes.

Remove the bay leaves and lemon grass, check the seasoning, and divide the fish between 4 large soup plates, adding a good ladleful of the liquid and vegetables. If you aren't keen on eating pieces of ginger, warn your guests or fish them out. Sprinkle a few chopped coriander leaves over the bowls, and offer the beurre blanc in a hot jug.

All this needs is some boiled waxy potatoes. After all this healthy stuff, especially if you've passed on the beurre blanc (but you shouldn't), you can restore some balance to your diet with a hefty dose of pud.

Omelette Arnold Bennett

This is an all-time favourite. Smoked haddock and Parmesan are excellent companions and combine brilliantly with the eggs and cream. Like all omelettes, this needs to move from pan to table as quickly as possible. If you don't fancy making one after another, increase the ingredients if your pan is large enough. There are more elaborate versions of this omelette, but I think this is the best.

Serves 1

2 eggs
salt and freshly ground black pepper
12g butter
50–75g cooked flaked smoked haddock
3 tbsp double cream in a small jug
1½ tbsp grated Parmesan
chopped parsley

You must preheat the grill to very hot and have your ingredients very handy.

In a bowl beat the eggs together with a pinch of salt and a few grinds of pepper. Melt the butter in a hot, heavy – ideally steel – frying pan. Make sure the butter covers the base and sides of the pan. A few seconds after the foam has died down, pour in the eggs. Immediately, take the pan from the heat and sprinkle the haddock over the eggs. Dribble the cream over, covering about half of the surface, and sprinkle over the cheese. Do all this as fast as possible. Place the pan very close to the hot grill. As soon as the cheese starts to brown, slide the omelette on to a plate. Scatter something green – like chopped parsley – over it and eat.

Fulham Road – a cautionary tale

Naming a restaurant is not an easy thing, unless a) you are French and can add 'chez' to your name (which you have changed to 'Michel' from 'Hyppolite'); b) you are lucky enough to be in an interesting building like an old customs house or c) you are a big brewer and employ an advertising agency to come up with something like 'All Bar One', 'One of Two', 'The Fine Line' or 'Bar 38' that individually have no meaning but when repeated enough start to mean 'a place to drink Australian wine and weak American beer with quasi-Mediterranean food'. Otherwise this is a subject to stretch even the most agile brain and find it wanting, hence the number of restaurants named after their owners (which presupposes there is something 'personal' about them that distinguishes them from their neighbours) or after their addresses. I can't wait for someone to open a restaurant in the street near Waterloo called . . . The Cut.

I admit to having thrown in the towel at an early stage, accepting that I didn't have the chutzpah (or the imagination) to think of names like 'Euphorium' or 'Foxtrot Oscar' or 'Circus' and had to take my place alongside other towel-throwers like the owner of RSJ (Rolled Steel Joist), the Shoreditch Electricity Showroom and the Big Chef. The latter, presumably referring to its owner Marco-Pierre White, didn't last long, as was also the fate of another restaurant which had capitulated altogether and in total if honest desperation came up with No Name Place. It was on a corner site in Battersea, and even *that* would have been a better name than the one it briefly bore.

That most perceptive, kindly and generous spirited of men Jonathan Meades (restaurant critic of *The Times*) understood instantly what I was getting at in putting my name over the door – it was 'a guarantee of gastronomic integrity' – and of course I like to think that it was (and is).

It had, though, never been my intention to do anything as nakedly commercial or as preposterous as to turn myself into a 'brand' and with two restaurants having my name over the door it seemed I was perilously close to being 'rolled out', like Chez Gérard or Café Med – places built around 'a concept' that has more to do with strategic marketing than with offering a product of real individuality. My third London restaurant, in Chelsea, needed therefore to have another name, and although I was going to run it as I ran my two others, I wanted it to develop an identity of its own.

In retrospect, perhaps calling it after an important, well-known and very long road was a bit presumptuous, although I wanted the restaurant to be very good and was confident it would become just as (well, almost as) well known and important. I can't help feeling, though, that if I had more modestly called it 257 (like another restaurant further down, called

755), or if Fulham Road (the road) had somehow been less important, say if I had been in Bow Street – looking at my Monopoly board – then there would have been no hubris and therefore no retribution.

Fulham Road turned out to be a poisoned chalice. Apparently an ordered, elegant and civilized restaurant, it was actually a double-fronted, well-upholstered can of worms. Short of the place burning down (something which I would several times have welcomed, and not for the insurance money) or a customer expiring from anaphylactic shock, I think just about everything that could afflict a restaurant happened there. A number of these things were what are quaintly known as teething troubles and might have seemed less problematic if followed by years of trouble-free operation, but I wasn't at nos 257–9 long enough for the healing balm of time to have any effect, so my memories of the place are largely of one crisis merging into another.

There must have been many days which passed smoothly, but I just can't remember any of them, although I enjoyed the moment the restaurant was laid up properly for the first time – an hour before the first customers arrived. Indeed the place looked so good, so inviting (Michael Winner approvingly wrote that the decor must have cost all of 19/6), that I felt a slight disturbance around my tear ducts, although not enough to be convincing. The run-up to opening hadn't been particularly fraught, as these things go, once I had got rid of the cockroaches and bored out the drains (see the video!), and we managed to open on time.

However, once open and busy, we discovered that trebling the amount of cooking, to match our level of trade, was too much for the ventilation system in the kitchen. Pumping more fresh air in (fresh air? from the Fulham Road?) helped, as did installing the most powerful extractor fan we could find. Unfortunately this resulted in more cooking smells wafting over the rears of the interior design shops and antique dealers around me, so the pipework had to be extended to the roof, and plentiful bunches of flowers and bottles of champagne sent to my fastidious and querulous neighbours. At the same time the fridge motors – for which no one before me had applied for planning permission – had to be given acoustic sheaths and the landscape gardeners called in to disguise them.

In the restaurant things were going well: customers liked the food and the wine, loved my manageress, and were nice about the decor and the furniture. Quite soon though cracks literally started to appear. The chairs, which were a prototype and rather good-looking and comfortable, started to come apart at the seams, occasionally dumping a surprised customer on the floor – once a famed food writer from *Le Figaro*. History doesn't record whether he wrote a review of the place after that. My many attempts to have them strengthened got nowhere until I threatened the makers with a skipful of horse manure on their showroom doorstep. I must have sounded serious because this seemed to work, although the company went bust before they'd all been fixed. Thereafter it was a ritual before lunch or dinner to upend each chair and if it was a dud bang the joints together and hope no one would lean back on it.

In case you're wondering why I didn't replace the chairs, there wasn't the money. Although we were turning over more than £30,000 a week, the profit margins were too low, particularly in the kitchen, where they fluctuated around 53 per cent. The benchmark gross margin in the restaurant trade is about 70 per cent, slightly less in very good restaurants, slightly more in middle-market places. We were so far below these levels that although I wanted to put the chef on a profit-sharing scheme such profligacy scuppered the idea. Staff benefited from the low margins too. I remember being horrified at seeing a tray of a dozen fat pieces of dazzling white turbot being given to the staff one Sunday because 'it wouldn't be good enough by Monday'.

Occasionally the sound of collapsing chairs would be interrupted by that of cold water escaping from the air-conditioning duct above table five – at least table five was under it the first time it happened. True to form, during dinner. Although we moved the table after that, this problem was never properly solved, ice buckets having to be trotted out from time to time to catch the drips. It was mysteriously mirrored by a duct over the pastry section in the kitchen. The efforts of three different specialists couldn't sort this one out: at random intervals about half a gallon of water would gush out on to the marble slab to the consternation and despair of the incumbent. Eventually I had to move the pastry section into a staff changing room, and I dare say that little pipe is still gushing now and again.

Worse, one night the drain on the flat roof above the bar blocked, flooding it, drenching my manageress and, in that mischief-making, unpredictable way water has, knocking out the main switchgear. This of course fused all the lights and cut off the kitchen extraction. It's OK (just) cooking (and eating) by candlelight, as long as you have about five hundred of them, but no extraction means nowhere for the smoke to go, and that means you can't cook. This happened at nine in the evening, so the whole restaurant had to be evacuated. Oddly enough, exactly one week later, there was a power cut at the same time, so the whole pantomime took place again, minus the water.

Unlike my other kitchens, that at Fulham Road seemed to operate like a rather chaotic army run by a volatile general who oversaw a continuous stream of more or less capable soldiers passing through, staying for shorter or longer times depending on their ability to handle the increasing demands of the fighting – sorry, cooking (which earned a star from Michelin in 1995) – and the excitability or passion of the chef (depending on which way you looked at it). Comments (or interference) from the head of state – me – were not welcomed, twice involving threats of resignation, and although we did manage to produce Sunday brunch for all of seven weeks running, the general rebelled. He and his troops just weren't going to do 'that kind of cooking any more'.

Although the Michelin star was an acknowledgement of some sort that the cooking was good, it had not been something I had aimed for when I opened the restaurant, which was intended to be a very good local place offering good value for money but without any great pretensions. The design scheme though had become more luxurious that I had planned, as I realized when I first saw the fabric for the banquette seating. Although it was within budget, it gave out signals of fairly serious opulence which hadn't been my intention when I briefed the designer. However, it would have been impossible to redo the scheme at that stage, and the finished article did look good. So here I was with a restaurant whose design and food were up to Michelin-star level but whose profit margins weren't up to anything, and whose wages bill was nearly 40 per cent of turnover. At least the star was some sort of cover for my having to put the prices up in an attempt to break even, but this was not a long-term strategy as it was bound to alienate some of my less wealthy customers. Not that there were many of them, but you may have noticed that with some people the more they have, the less they spend. I began to get the feeling that things were moving out of my control, or indeed out of anybody's, when I discovered one of the ranks cleaning the kitchen canopy with a clean chef's jacket.

Something had to give; two things, as it happened. My chef left, to apply his Michelin magic to the relaunched Hackney dog stadium. This went belly-up on opening night, so other factors were obviously involved. Anyway, it made a good story and, overall, hasn't done him any harm.

The other thing was that my tireless and charming manager was made an unrefusable (and unconnected) offer and left at the same time to preside over the opening of another, rather larger and more glamorous restaurant.

There was plenty of publicity around these new comings (as opposed to goings) so I was concerned that my turnover would suffer, and indeed it did a bit, although not as much as I'd feared. However, my new head chef, whom I rated highly, didn't find such favour with Fay Maschler, even though her previous review of him had been good. This was not what the restaurant needed at all. Inevitably, turnover fell a bit, but so did losses, and soon we were actually breaking even for the first time, eighteen months after opening. This is a long time in the restaurant business.

But now with my new manager I had a new problem. He turned out to be not only (yes, an awful cliché) drinking the bar dry but putting the cash takings on horses and not, as far as I could see, on clever tricasts. I had noticed profit margins in the bar were sinking rapidly, so put in a lockable shutter and gave the manager the key – after all I had never smelled drink on his breath. *Quis custodiet ipsos custodes?* as Cicero might have said. After this chap had failed to return from a weekend off, and the missing cash had been discovered, I gave him the sack, whereupon instead of slinking off in disgrace – it was quite obvious he had stolen the cash – he took *me* to an industrial tribunal for unfair dismissal. He lost, but I didn't get the money back either, and I can tell you that I'd rather spend a day at the dentist than another one at the Woburn Place tribunal building.

I had hoped life would settle down after that but found my next chef's management style had been learned in the terraces of Stamford Bridge, so after some trouble involving a knife and one of the junior cooks, *he* moved on too.

Quite a bit of the fun had gone out of running Fulham Road by this time – no, *all* the fun – and as the place wasn't really making any money the sudden appearance of a would-be buyer felt like the arrival of the 7th Cavalry and no, it didn't take long to decide to sell. It seemed entirely in keeping with the Fulham Road experience that as I left the place for the last time I saw I had just been given a parking ticket. And I didn't mind at all.

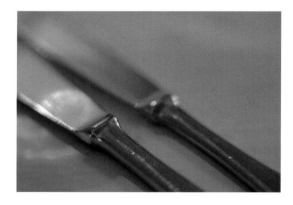

Meat

I'm sure there is nothing I can say about meat cooking that hasn't been better said elsewhere, but I would like to make two observations. The first is that browning meat in hot fat before continuing the cooking elsewhere is not 'sealing' the meat, as if by so doing all the juices would remain inside. It does stiffen the fibres so making it more difficult for the juices to get out, but it certainly doesn't keep them all in. The main purpose of the process ought to be to increase the flavour of the surface of the meat and leave residues of caramelized proteins in the pan to be 'deglazed' with water, stock or wine and then added to the cooking liquid.

The second is that all meat that isn't destined to be cooked until dry will benefit enormously from a resting period, and the bigger the joint or bird, the longer the rest should be – in a warming drawer, a switched-off oven, even near the top of the cooker, but ideally somewhere warm or hot that won't continue the cooking. The ideal place in a restaurant is underneath the grill plate of the salamander, the big wall-mounted overhead grill. It's hot, but away from direct heat. Starting to cook a duck breast, pigeon or a rump of lamb as soon as the order comes in and leaving it just undercooked before it goes to its resting place means it can sit there relaxing for a good ten minutes. During that time the fibres in the meat will have lengthened again and allowed the moisture to spread more evenly through the interior, making the whole thing more succulent.

Smaller cuts of meat will need shorter cooking times, of course, but for any size of meat, cooking for less time at a high temperature is much more likely to keep it juicy all the way through – as long as it can relax. The high heat that gradually penetrates to the inside guarantees that the interior moisture won't escape through the tightened, shortened fibres, and after its removal from pan or oven the residual heat will continue to cook the centre. This applies equally to a breast of chicken, a rib of beef, a leg of lamb or a large turkey. With a naturally dry meat like pigeon, wild duck or pheasant, this technique is not essential but it helps a great deal as what juiciness there is in the meat will stay inside it. If you've ever tried to cook too many pieces of meat at a time in the saucepan you'll know how quickly the meat exudes juice if the pan isn't hot enough.

So high heat and a long period of rest – I suppose we could all do with a bit of that.

Lamb Tagine with Apricots and Almonds and a Raisin Couscous

These Moroccan meat and fruit stews seem to appeal to the British palate, perhaps because we have always liked the idea since it was quite à la mode in Elizabethan times. This style of cooking rather fell out of fashion in Mrs Beeton's day, but was revived somewhat by George Perry-Smith in the 1970s. Claudia Roden, Arto Haroutunian and Paula Wolfert have brought us many different varieties, all worth exploring. Although I've still got quite a few to try, this is my favourite version so far. Quinces are very good instead of the apricots when in season; they need to be peeled, cored and cut into eighths and cooked in the liquid for at least an hour. The unsulphured apricots look a bit murky, but this is another case where taste should triumph over aesthetics.

2 half shoulders of lamb, or one small leg
2 large mild onions, chopped
4 cloves
2 good tsp ground cinnamon
1 tsp cardamom seeds, crushed in a mortar, or ground cardamom
2½ tsp ground coriander
¼ tsp black pepper
4 tbsp vegetable oil
⅔ tsp salt
12 unsulphured dried apricots
4 tbsp crème fraiche
24 blanched whole almonds, lightly toasted
3 tbsp coriander leaves, chopped

Either buy two half shoulders or ask the butcher to cut one in half. Following the muscle separations as closely as you can, remove the meat in as large pieces as possible. (If using a leg, cut it into 4 cm slices first, around the bone, and then follow the muscle separations. The cooking time may need to be extended.) Trim them of membrane and fat and cut into 5 cm chunks. Put the meat into a large saucepan with the next eight ingredients and pour in enough water almost to cover the meat. Bring to a simmer and cook, the liquid bubbling slowly, for about 1½ hours; after an hour put in the apricots. For the last 15 minutes, cook the couscous as below. When the meat is cooked, pour off the liquid and boil hard to reduce to about 250 ml. Return this to the saucepan. All this can be done ahead.

When you are ready to serve it, stir in the crème fraiche roughly and divide between 4 plates. Scatter the almonds and coriander leaves over. Serve this with a raisin couscous.

Raisin Couscous

400g couscous (most of the couscous available is precooked)
350–400 ml water
salt
25g butter
50g raisins, soaked for an hour in a little water

Put the couscous into a bowl and gradually add most of the water, stirring with a fork. Leave to swell for about 15 minutes, stirring occasionally. If you think the grains will take all the water without getting soggy, stir it in. Transfer it to a sieve and place over the top of the tagine, ensuring the bottom of the sieve is clear of the liquid. Leave to heat through in the steam for about 15 minutes, stirring around every 3–4 minutes. Season with salt as you like. Transfer to a hot serving dish and mix in the butter and raisins. Keep hot while the tagine sauce is reducing.

Spiced Lamb Sauté with Tzatziki

Tzatziki is a very, very good salad, but it can't be botched. It must include garlic, the cucumber must be disgorged, and the yogurt should be the best – organic Greek-style. Enjoy it on its own, or pair it with this juicy sauté, the spice striking sparks off the cool astringency of the cucumber.

Tzatziki

a cucumber
salt
1 medium clove of garlic
2 hefty tbsp yogurt or a mixture of crème
    fraiche and yogurt
about 20 leaves mint, chopped

Peel the cucumber (easiest with a swivel-bladed peeler), throw away the watery core and grate coarsely. Place in a colander or sieve and sprinkle with 1 tsp salt, mixing thoroughly. Set over a bowl, place a saucer on top and a weight on top of that and leave for about 30 minutes (if you are short of time, press hard on the weight – after about 30 seconds quite a lot of salted water will come out). Meanwhile, peel and finely chop the garlic and mash to a paste with a large pinch of salt using the flat of a knife. Mix into the yogurt or yogurt and crème fraiche and add the mint. Rinse the salt off the cucumber under the cold tap and use the bowl again to press away the water. Pat dry with a cloth or kitchen paper. Mix into the yogurt and check it's not too salty. If so, add more yogurt.

You could substitute dill or coriander for the mint if eating the tzatziki on its own. This is best made at least an hour before use.

Spiced Lamb

800g lamb leg steaks or leg of lamb
2 heaped tsp ground cumin
2 heaped tsp ground coriander
¼ tsp ground black pepper
4 cloves of garlic, crushed
finely grated rind and juice of 1 lemon
salt
10g butter
1 tbsp sunflower or groundnut oil

Cut the meat into 3cm cubes, getting rid of as much of the sinews and membranes as you can. In a bowl mix the meat well with the spices, garlic and the lemon and cover with clingfilm. Leave to marinate for several hours or overnight in the fridge, turning occasionally. Remove the garlic and sprinkle the meat lightly with salt.

In a large frying pan, heat the butter and oil until the butter foam has all disappeared and throw in the lamb. Over high heat, cook for 5 minutes, tossing (or turning with a spatula) frequently.

Remove from the heat and arrange the meat neatly on a plate, and serve with a dollop of tzatziki. For a fancier presentation use a ring mould for the meat, with the tzatziki spread on top.

Serve with potatoes fried in butter and olive oil with some sliced garlic added for the last 5 minutes' cooking, or red kidney beans heated through with some finely sliced onion and garlic softened in olive oil, or chickpeas dressed with walnut oil and lemon juice.

Chicken with Prunes, Pine Nuts and Sausage

This is my version of a Catalan dish, which I presume came to Spain via the Moors of Africa as it contains so many Moroccan elements. By the time it's finished this dish is quite rich, so you could easily leave out one or two of the dried fruits if you haven't got them, or just disagree with me.

Serves 4–6

a 1.75–2 kg free-range chicken
flour
3 tbsp duck fat or olive oil
1 tsp salt
1 medium onion, finely chopped
1 small carrot, finely chopped
a 10 cm stick of celery, finely chopped
1 kg ripe chopped tomatoes (not necessary
    to peel or deseed them) or 2 tins chopped
    tomatoes
1 glass dry white wine
150 ml chicken stock
½ tsp sugar
2 medium cloves of garlic, peeled and crushed
1 bay leaf
3 parsley sprigs
¼ tsp fresh thyme
¼ tsp fennel seeds
1 tsp ground coriander
a 3 cm piece of orange peel
4 small chorizo or other spicy sausages or
    black pudding
4 tbsp each pine nuts, raisins, diced dried
    apricots, and dried pitted prunes

Remove the breast meat (including the wing bones) from the chicken, and the legs, cut off at the thighs. Make a stock with the carcass as indicated on page 37. Cut each piece of chicken in half to make 8 pieces. Remove the skin if you find it easy (it won't be crisp after cooking). Put some flour in a paper bag and shake the pieces in it one by one.

Get 2 tbsp of the duck fat or oil very hot in a large saucepan. Sprinkle the chicken pieces with some of the salt and brown them quickly on all sides over moderately high heat. Remove to a plate. In the hot fat cook the onion, carrot and celery briskly until they are lightly browned. Add the tomatoes, wine, stock, sugar, garlic, bay leaf, parsley, thyme, fennel seeds, coriander, orange peel, and the rest of the salt, and bring to a simmer. Put in the thighs and drumsticks and cook, covered, for 30 minutes, then add the breast pieces. Cook for a further 5 minutes.

While this is happening, heat the rest of the fat or oil in a frying pan. Prick the sausages here and there and brown them well on all sides and remove to cool a little. Add the pine nuts to the pan and brown them lightly, taking care not to burn them. Add the dried fruit and cook for a couple of minutes, stirring. Cut the sausages into thick slices and add back to the pan. Take the chicken pieces out of the sauce and transfer them to the frying pan. Press the sauce through a sieve on to the chicken and sausage mixture, and heat together for 10 minutes. Check the seasoning (salt and sugar) and boil the sauce down if it needs reducing. Put the chicken pieces in a handsome serving dish and pour everything over them.

As this is a Spanish dish, serve some butter beans, haricot beans or chickpeas, heated in some olive oil and sprinkled with marjoram or oregano leaves.

Chicken Breasts stuffed with Broccoli
and Walnuts

An interesting stuffing for chicken that's half poached, half steamed. This will embellish the bog-standard supermarket 'supreme', or fat fillets taken from two free-range birds. Best use the latter, for flavour for sure, but that way there's a better chance of the little fillet on the inside of the breast remaining intact. It's not difficult removing it yourself. A sharp knife is essential. Cut down along the breastbone and ease the meat away from the ribcage, keeping the knife close to the carcass. Cut down along the wishbone in the same way and remove the breast either with or without the wing bone. If you include the wing bone, chop it off at the first joint and pull off the skin. I would say leave the skin on if you were going to fry the breast, but for this method you should remove it, either before you start cutting or when you've finished. Easy to do if you wrap a cloth around your hand first.

With a small sharp knife make a pocket in the middle of the breast by cutting into the fat end, along the long axis, with the knife nearly horizontal. There must be room for 2 heaped tbsp of the stuffing. Season the apertures lightly with salt and pepper.

Melt the butter in a saucepan and cook the onion or shallots in it over moderate heat for about 8 minutes. Scrape into a bowl. Boil a pan of salted water and plunge in the broccoli. Cook for 3 minutes, drain, and dunk into a bowl of very cold water. Drain well when cold, decant on to kitchen paper, and chop fairly finely.

Add the cream cheese to the onion or shallots, stir in the Parmesan, walnuts, and lemon juice. Season lightly and fold in the broccoli.

Divide the stuffing into 4 and fill the pockets in the chicken breasts. Cover the openings with the flattened fillets, making sure the surfaces are dry, press them on well, and season lightly.

Stuffing the chicken

4 chicken breasts, skinned and boned
salt and freshly ground black pepper
12g butter
½ a small onion or 2 large shallots, finely
 · chopped
250g broccoli florets
80g cream cheese, softened
3 heaped tbsp grated Parmesan
3 tbsp walnut pieces, toasted, rubbed in a
    tea towel and chopped fairly fine
a good squeeze of lemon juice

Place the breasts smooth-side down on a cutting board. Lift off the slender fillets and place them between two sheets of clingfilm. Flatten them with a heavy knife until they are at least twice as wide.

Cooking and saucing the chicken

12g butter
½ a small onion or 2 shallots, finely chopped
½ glass dry white wine
300ml chicken stock
150ml double cream
50g butter, cold, in small pieces
2 tbsp chopped chervil or 1 tbsp chopped
    tarragon or basil
salt

In a large frying pan (or shallow saucepan) with a lid, melt the butter and add the onion or shallots. Raise the heat to moderately high and pour in the wine and half the stock. Add the chicken, fillet sides down, and cook for 8 minutes. The liquid should simmer gently; if it boils the fillets may lift off and the stuffing fall out. Remove the chicken and keep hot. Boil the sauce hard, add the rest of the stock and the cream. When the liquid has reduced by about half, boil in the cold butter. When the butter is incorporated, remove from the heat and add the herbs and a little salt. If the chicken has given off any juice, pour into the sauce. Slice the breasts across at an angle. Divide the chicken between 4 plates and pour the sauce over.

This dish needs something plain like buttered pasta, rice or mashed potato, and maybe some chunky-cut carrots. A bit more broccoli wouldn't be amiss either. Or spinach (just thinking of colours).

Poached Chicken with Walnut Sauce

I love poaching chicken. The meat is always juicy, as it's self-basting by definition, and it makes its own stock at the same time, some or all of which can provide the perfect matching sauce. This dish comes from Turkey (I think), and is simplicity itself to make. It's better with toasted walnuts rather than plain – in fact, I'm not keen at all on the untoasted kind.

Serves 6

a 1.8–2kg chicken
1 medium onion, peeled and quartered
1 medium carrot
1 stalk of celery
1 bay leaf
10 black peppercorns
3 parsley sprigs
salt
75g walnut pieces, lightly toasted, their skins
    rubbed off in a clean tea towel
50g breadcrumbs
150ml single cream
paprika
parsley

Put the chicken in a large saucepan and add water until it's just covered. Add the onion, carrot, celery, bay leaf, peppercorns, parsley, and ½ tsp salt, and bring to simmering point, then turn the heat down, cover, and poach for about 1¼ hours. The liquid should barely bubble. Strain the stock, and measure and pour about 150ml into the liquidizer jar. (Keep the rest of the stock for something else – but add the debris from the jointed chicken and cook again before you do.) Add the walnuts, breadcrumbs, cream and ⅛ tsp salt and blitz to a smooth cream. Joint the chicken, put it in a serving dish and pour the sauce over. Sprinkle with paprika and some very finely chopped parsley.

Try this with sauté potatoes and a green salad.

Poached Chicken with Lemon and Tarragon

It's worth buying the best chicken you can for this, as in poaching the flavour will come through naked and unadorned by the crispy skin that roasting or sautéing provide. We can't go wrong pairing tarragon with chicken, and using the lemon is a safe bet too. This is a fine dish for a family supper. It's also extremely good cold.

1 medium chicken, about 1.2 kg
2 medium leeks, cut into eighths
1 medium onion, quartered
1 medium carrot, sliced lengthways
8 parsley stalks
8 sprigs tarragon plus 1 tbsp chopped
1 bay leaf
1 small clove of garlic, crushed
the grated rind of 1 lemon, plus some of the juice
1 glass dry white wine
½ tsp salt
3 egg yolks
4 tbsp double cream or crème fraiche

Stuff the chicken with some of the leeks and put it in a saucepan just large enough to hold it comfortably and allow a lid to fit. Put in the rest of the leeks, the onion and carrot, parsley stalks, tarragon sprigs, bay leaf, garlic, lemon rind, wine, salt and 1 tbsp of the lemon juice, and pour in enough water almost to cover the bird. Press down on the chicken to expel any air. Bring up to a simmer, and poach gently for 45 minutes, almost covered, the water barely moving. Turn the bird upside down and let everything cool completely. Remove the chicken. Refrigerate the liquid for 30 minutes to solidify the fat, which you can now remove easily. Measure off 1 litre of the liquid and pass through a sieve into a clean, wide pan (keep the rest for something else). Boil it hard to reduce down to about 175 ml.

Remove the leeks from the chicken (these are inside it simply not to crowd the pan). Neatly remove the chicken legs and breasts, cut the legs in half crossways, and do the same with the breasts. If you have a cleaver, chop off the end of the drumstick bones. Keep the carcass and wing bones for stock. All this can be done well in advance.

When you are ready to serve, heat the chicken pieces in the reduced stock in a stainless-steel or enamelled pan and with a slotted spoon place them in a hot serving dish or on hot plates, and keep warm. The liquid should taste quite pungently of lemons. If not, add more juice. The eggs and cream (below) will moderate the flavour considerably.

In a small bowl, whisk together the egg yolks and the cream or crème fraiche. Whisking the while, pour the hot liquid on to this mixture and then return to the saucepan. Place over gentle heat and whisk until the sauce thickens to the consistency of foamy single cream. Make sure the whisk covers all parts of the pan bottom, otherwise the eggs might scramble (you can avoid this by substituting 1 tsp of cornflour for one of the egg yolks, but the flavour will be a bit obscured and it *is* cheating a bit). Add the chopped tarragon, check the seasoning (add a bit more salt or cream if necessary) and pour over the chicken.

Serve this with plain buttered rice and a green vegetable like garlic and lemon flavoured spinach or chard.

Mixed Livers with Lentils and Vinegar

Livers, lentils and vinegar – a fine contrast of textures and savoury flavours. You don't, of course, have to use mixed livers; any of these on their own would be fine, but it's easy to combine different ones in the restaurant and one is really under some obligation to make a restaurant dish interesting. Comparing different livers has, I suppose, an element of that about it. Lamb's liver is, I think, almost as good as calf's liver, and better value for money. The rustic flavour of the humble green lentil is fine for this dish.

400g green lentils, washed and picked over
1 large carrot, finely diced
1 leek, finely diced
1 stick of celery, finely diced
3 bay leaves
about 1.25 litres of chicken stock or water
pancetta trimmings or 3 rashers streaky bacon,
    diced
salt and black pepper
6 duck livers, 6 chicken livers and 6 pieces
    lamb's or calf's liver all cut into pieces
    roughly 4cm square – discard stringy bits
    of veins and nerves
25g butter
3 tbsp balsamic or red wine vinegar
chopped curly parsley (better than flat for this
    dish, I think)

Put the lentils, vegetables, bay leaves, stock or water and pancetta or bacon in a large saucepan, bring to the boil, skim and cook until the lentils are ready – about 25–30 minutes. They must be al dente. Strain, keeping the liquor for another use. Season lightly and keep hot. Remove the bay leaves.

Season the livers, melt the butter in a frying pan, and a few seconds after the foam subsides quickly sauté the livers until they are pink in the centre. Divide the lentil mixture between 4 plates, place the livers on top, and sprinkle over a good-quality vinegar, preferably straight from the bottle (with your thumb over the top, of course). Scatter the parsley over.

Roast Pigeon with Bitter Orange Sauce

Perhaps because they are so common and therefore (relatively) so cheap, the wood pigeon is a grievously underrated bird, with a flavour all its own. More interesting than venison, less extreme than hare, sweeter than much of the wild duck family, for me the pigeon is definitely the poor man's grouse. They do need careful cooking, though, as like all game birds they are lean, muscular and fit – unlike our soft and namby-pamby chickens – so tend to dry out very easily. The trick is (as always with lean meat) to cook at a high temperature for a short time, and then let sit quietly in a warm place for 10–15 minutes – if not longer. The 'warm place' must be hot enough to preserve the bird's temperature, but not so hot that it carries on cooking. In a restaurant the best place is under the cast-iron plate that sits in the centre of the salamander – the overhead grill, where there is plenty of room and, as it's usually sited above the stove, surrounded by indirect heat.

Chefs in restaurants who cook on the meat section – known as the sauce section for some reason – often let their delicate cuts rest at the side of the stove, and then 'flash' them under the salamander before sending them to the restaurant. The trouble with this is that if they have lost heat from the centre, 'flashing' won't bring it back again.

4 fresh pigeons, recently shot, with gizzards, hearts and livers if possible
25g butter
1 medium carrot, onion and stick of celery
1 large clove of garlic
bouquet garni of parsley stalks, thyme sprigs and bay leaf
2 strips of orange peel, 8cm long, no pith
1 glass red wine
200ml stock or water
salt and black pepper

3 tbsp granulated sugar
75ml red wine vinegar
juice of 1 orange, or several Seville oranges if available
1 tbsp lemon juice
1 heaped tsp cornflour
2 tbsp Grand Marnier or orange Curaçao
shredded orange rind, blanched (optional)

Preheat the oven to 450°F/230°C/Gas 8.

With poultry shears or a pair of sharp scissors, cut the backs out of the pigeons, leaving the legs in place, and chop them roughly. Heat the butter in a frying pan and when the foam subsides toss the bones and vegetables (and gizzards, hearts and livers if you have them) until they are lightly browned. Remove to a small saucepan, add the garlic, bouquet garni and orange peel. Pour in the wine and the stock (for preference) or water. Bring to a simmer and cook for about 25 minutes.

Season the pigeon breasts with salt and pepper.

In the same frying pan, adding a little more butter if necessary, cook the pigeons for about 1 minute each side over a high heat, then remove to a roasting dish and put in the oven. Roast for 15 minutes, take out and keep warm. Meanwhile, in a smallish heavy-bottomed saucepan, melt the sugar over a moderate heat, watching it carefully as it gradually forms a pale golden brown, starts to smoke gently, and then, as bubbles form, a darker brown. This will take little more than about 3 minutes. At this stage the brown liquid will start to smoke more heavily. Cover your hand with a cloth, pour in the vinegar, and remove from the heat. When the liquid stops bubbling, strain on the stock (made with the bones, above) and orange and lemon juice, season lightly with salt and reduce to about 125ml. Mix the cornflour with the Grand Marnier or Curaçao and stir in. Cook until the sauce has thickened. Cut each pigeon in half along the breast-bone, lay back to back on 4 hot plates, and pour over the sauce. Garnish with blanched, shredded orange rind if you like.

Serve with potato and spring onion cakes cooked in duck fat and a plain green vegetable.

Potato cakes are mashed potato and finely chopped spring onions, seasoned, formed into cakes, rolled in flour, and fried. They can be made and cooked ahead – warm them up in the same oven.

Sour Cream and Salami Pizzas

I don't think any Italian would recognize this as a pizza, as the dough is, to say the least, rather unorthodox; and the other ingredients, I'm afraid, reek of 'convenience', and lofty spirits might even say it nods in the direction of junk. But it does have Gruyère in it to give it respectability, it doesn't include yeast, and it has a fizzing contrast of savoury (sausage) and sweet (mango chutney). And the pastry is excellent for millefeuilles.

Makes 2 large or 4 small

40g butter, cold
75g plain flour
12g Gruyère, grated
½ tsp salt
3 tbsp sour cream
25g butter for frying
1 medium Spanish onion, fairly finely chopped
small pepperoni or chorizo sausage, sliced into
    circles 3 mm thick
1 tsp tomato purée
50g cooked ham, cut into thin strips
2 heaped tbsp mild mango chutney

Preheat the oven to 375°F/190°C/Gas 5.

Cut the cold butter into small cubes and rub into the flour until it's the texture of oatmeal. Stir in the cheese and salt. Mix in enough sour cream (use both hands for this) to make a smooth, firm dough. Cut the dough into 2 or 4 equal pieces and roll out thinly on a floured surface into discs about 15 cm across for small ones or 20 cm across for large ones. Place on a baking sheet and bake for 15 minutes. They should be lightly browned.

Meanwhile (although they can, of course, be made well in advance, as can the topping), melt the butter and cook the onion over medium heat, stirring often, until brown at the edges. This will take about 10 minutes. Add the sausage and tomato purée and cook for another 10 minutes. Put in the ham and mix in the mango chutney. You won't need to season this mixture. Divide it between the hot pastry discs and serve.

Roast Duck with Limes

Judging from what people have said to me over the years, the domestic duck doesn't have the fans it deserves, largely because of the difficulties of reducing its fattiness. There seem to be three reasons for this: using the wrong sort of duck, not getting rid of the fat properly during the cooking, and then not removing the rest of the fat at the carving stage.

The recipe that follows is guaranteed to make the skin crisp (as the Chinese know, this is the best part) and the meat melting and succulent, and provide you with a supply of delicious duck fat. I served it this way for Elizabeth David once, who sent it back. Dismayed, for she was one of my heroines, I wanted to know why – particularly as, at lunchtimes, I put the duck in the oven at 11.30 a.m. so that it would be perfect by 1.30. It seems the grande dame preferred to have the bird served with a rare breast and a better cooked leg finished under a hot grill, a modish presentation of the time. Well, that way the breast meat is fine but not enough subcutaneous fat runs away, although you can eat the skin; and the leg meat can easily be undercooked, with the skin likely to suffer scorching and blistering without reaching fat-free crispness.

Anyway, both she and her lunchtime companion (who it seemed was meekly following suit) each rejected a perfectly cooked half duck – cooked and carved to order, as it were, with no sign of fat anywhere, the skin crisp, golden brown, without blemish, the meat melting in the mouth. Although taken aback to be exchanging views with the greatest food guru of the time, I stuck to my guns, but I can't deny it was a disappointing experience.

When I say the wrong sort of duck, I mean you must buy a fresh duck that has been dry plucked, not a frozen duck which has almost certainly been wet plucked – that is, plunged into very hot water to open up the pores that hold the feathers. This alters the texture of the skin so it becomes impossible to crisp properly (and the meat is also more likely to dry out). Dry plucking involves coating the bird with hot wax, letting it set, and removing the embedded feathers at one go. The secret of crisp skin involves pricking holes under the skin to allow the fat to run away but not pricking the meat.

This recipe uses limes to go with the duck, but a tart apple sauce with orange rind, or redcurrant jelly melted, acidulated with lemon juice, and jellied again is also very good.

Duck fat is high in polyunsaturates and thus relatively healthy. Keep it for roasting or frying potatoes, sautéing vegetables, and for mixing into a well-dried out swede purée. Three ducks will give you enough fat to make your own duck confit. I'm told goose fat makes good hand cream – I can't say whether duck fat does the same.

1 large, fresh duck, with giblets if possible
1 carrot, chopped
1 onion, chopped
1 stick of celery, chopped
2 tbsp oil or duck fat
600 ml water or light stock
1 clove of garlic, crushed
bouquet garni
salt
3 or 4 limes
50 g sugar
50 ml water
cornflour (optional)
2 tbsp red wine, port or brandy (optional)

Preheat the oven to 450°F / 230°C / Gas 8.

Wipe the duck, and remove any bits of wax, particularly from under the legs. Remove any lumps of fat from inside the cavity and put them in the roasting tin to render down. Remove the feet at the joints and throw them away. Cut off the wing

tips at the second joint in and chop them roughly. Chop the gizzard and heart roughly. Cut off the parson's nose, to allow the duck to fit snugly in a roasting tin, and throw it away. Brown the bits of duck and the vegetables well in the oil or fat, add the water or stock, the garlic and the bouquet garni and cook gently while you are roasting the duck. Let it reduce to about 150 ml.

Prick the duck well along the underside of the breast and where the legs meet the body, taking care not to puncture the meat. Turn the duck over and press down on the middle of the backbone to break it. This allows the duck to sit flat in the tin and to brown evenly, breast side up. Salt the breast lightly and place in the oven for 15–20 minutes to start the fat running.

After this time, pour off the accumulated fat into a tall heatproof jug, turn down the heat to 350°F/180°C/Gas 4 and keep pouring off fat and any brown juices every 20 minutes. The duck should always be sizzling merrily. Cooking time will be about 1 hour 45 minutes, depending on the size and fattiness of the bird, but more cooking to remove more fat will not do any harm. The whole point is to remove all the fat from the breast, and as much from the legs as possible.

Make the lime compote while the duck is cooking. With a very sharp knife remove all the skin and pith from the limes, segment them between the membranes, and chop roughly. Heat the sugar in the water until it is dissolved, stirring, and let the limes steep. You can cut some of the dark green lime skin into fine strips (removing all pith first) if you wish, but blanch them for 30 seconds first and refresh, then add to the compote.

When the duck is cooked, pour off the accumulated fat from the brown residues, strain the stock from the combined giblets and vegetables and reduce it to a gravy, skimming as you go, then add to the residues. Thicken with cornflour if necessary, slaked with red wine, port or brandy. Season. There should be about 4 tbsp of gravy per serving.

Carve the duck into 8 pieces, removing any fat left on the thighs, and arrange on a hot serving dish. Serve the compote and gravy separately.

Duck Stew with Cinnamon, Prunes and Orange

Perhaps 'casserole' would be a more inviting name for this dish, as I've found 'stew' is an apparent turn-off in the restaurants. Can we blame childhood experiences again? Probably. Then again, the notion of stewed prunes is not among most people's treasured memories, so adding a duck is perhaps asking for trouble – or at least neglect. However! Prejudices of this kind must be conquered, children, and eating a dish like this is the way to do it.

This is simply a jointed duck, simmered in wine and stock with aromatic vegetables, orange peel and cinnamon. When the duck is cooked, the skin is very easy to peel off, either before or after serving, so it doesn't in any way make the dish a fatty one. It helps, though, to remove any fat from the sauce. You can always remove the skin first and use it, crisped in the oven, for a salad (page 71).

1 fresh dry-plucked duck, jointed into 8

12 large prunes (those from Agen are the best, sold by some supermarkets and good delis. Buy them without stones if you wish, but they won't look as plump and inviting as those with stones in – but warn your guests)

for the prunes: 1 Earl Grey teabag, a 2 cm strip of orange peel, 1 cinnamon stick

1 large Spanish onion, finely chopped

1 stick of celery, roughly chopped

1 large carrot, roughly chopped

2 bay leaves

4 cinnamon sticks

2 pieces of orange peel, 6 cm long, all pith removed

1 tsp salt

½ bottle of red wine (something from the Rhône Valley or south-west France would be ideal)

575 ml chicken stock or duck stock

1 dsp redcurrant jelly

1 tsp cornflour

1 tbsp brandy

Ask your butcher to joint the duck, which is much the same as jointing a chicken, but ask him to remove the breast meat from the carcass – otherwise it will be difficult to brown, and look unprepossessing. (If you want a perfectly flavoured sauce, keep the carcass, trim it of all fat, chop it up small and brown in a very hot oven for 15 minutes. Add some stock vegetables and herbs and make stock as usual.)

Put the prunes in a bowl with the teabag, orange peel and cinnamon, pour over boiling water and poach gently for 30 minutes.

Brown the pieces of duck, skin-side down first, in a large frying pan (no oil or butter needed – this will release some fat straightaway). Do this for about 5 minutes then turn it over and brown the other side for 3 minutes. Remove the meat and brown the onion, celery and carrot for 10 minutes, stirring a few times.

Put the duck leg pieces and vegetables in a large saucepan or casserole, add the bay leaves, cinnamon, orange peel and salt, and pour over the wine and stock. Add enough water almost to cover (otherwise the sauce will be too strong when reduced – if your stock is weak, of course don't bother with the water). Bring to a simmer and cook part-covered for 45 minutes – the liquid should bubble very gently. After 45 minutes put in the pieces of breast meat. After another 45 minutes remove the pieces of duck with a slotted spoon and keep warm. Pour the cooking liquid through a sieve into another wide pan, pressing hard on the debris in the sieve. Bring back to a boil, skimming off the fat as the bubbles in the liquid push to the fat to the side of the pan. Add the prunes, reduce to about 200 ml and add the redcurrant jelly. In a separate small bowl mix the cornflour with the brandy (using your finger will make sure there are no lumps), whisk into the sauce and cook until it has thickened.

Divide the duck and the prunes between 4 deep plates and pour over the sauce. You don't need much with this – perhaps some carrots cut into thick slices and finished with butter, sugar and lemon juice. A celeriac purée wouldn't go amiss, either.

Paupiettes of Pork with Anchovies and Basil

This is a very savoury and economical dish that enjoys what M&S food selectors call 'good plate occupancy'. I'm sure there are plenty of dishes similar to this in Italian cooking – the saltimboccas, for example – but this is mine. This can also be made with veal from the loin or topside, but will of course be more expensive. You'll need a large frying pan for this.

    1 small pork fillet, about 400g
    1 tin anchovies
    12 basil leaves (optional)
    1 egg
    1 tbsp milk
    25g Parmesan cheese, grated
    50g plain flour
    butter for frying
    salt and pepper

Trim the pork of any fat and membrane, cut it in half crosswise, and then cut each half into 6 slices. Using a heavy knife, a mallet, or even a milk bottle, flatten each slice to a thickness of about 6mm. Cut the anchovies (there will be about 10) to make 12 equal pieces and place them on the pork, followed by the basil (if used – basil increases the flavour of the dish, but it works well without it anyway). Fold each piece of pork over (the end bits might look a bit misshapen but flavour should always win over aesthetics), pressing the edges together tightly. This can be prepared ahead to this point.

In a large bowl or roasting pan mix together thoroughly the egg and milk, and mix the cheese and flour in another bowl. Warm a large serving dish in the oven or under the grill. Dip each piece of pork into the egg wash, then coat well with the flour mixture. Heat some of the butter in a frying pan and fry the pork in batches for about 3 minutes each side. Replenish the butter as needed and keep the cooked pork hot while you make the sauce.

Sauce

    150ml strong chicken stock
    grated rind and juice of 1 lemon (or more)
    25g butter, cold, cut into small pieces
    salt
    sugar
    black and green olives (optional)

Add the stock, lemon rind and half the juice to the frying pan. When it bubbles, add the butter and swirl in. Season lightly with salt, and add more lemon juice and/or sugar according to how tart you like it. Divide the paupiettes and the sauce between 4 plates. Strew with a few slivers of olives if you wish, and serve with pasta and small Brussels sprouts or broccoli.

Braised Pork Rolls

This is my version of a dish I ate at Zafferano in London, where the chef, Giorgio Locatelli, is happy to test his ingenuity on material lesser chefs would disdain. I had an excellent sardine dish there once and some little pork rolls that were very like these. I'm only guessing at the pork belly, but with a little labour these rolls make an extremely tasty, if ungainly, dish for supper. And they are a change from beef olives – if anyone makes those any more.

1 kg pork belly in one piece, without ribs if
    possible, about 15 × 25 cm
25 g salt and 25 g sugar, mixed
40 g soft butter
2 tbsp each parsley and oregano (or marjoram),
    finely chopped
1 tbsp each sage and tarragon, finely chopped
1 tbsp grated lemon rind
3 cloves of garlic
10 anchovy fillets
butter for greasing
1 small carrot, roughly chopped
1 small leek or ½ a Spanish onion, roughly
    chopped
1 stalk of celery, roughly chopped
1 clove of garlic, crushed
1 glass dry white wine
400 ml stock
salt and black pepper
25 g butter, cold, in small pieces

Remove the skin from the pork in one piece using a very sharp knife, slicing it off horizontally, and set aside (see below). Cure the meat overnight in the salt and sugar mixture.

Preheat the oven to 350°F/180°C/Gas 4.

Score the skin crosswise with a very sharp knife, sprinkle with salt, and rub the salt in. Leave for 30 minutes, wash off the salt, and dry with kitchen paper. Roast for 20 minutes or until very crisp, cool and break up to eat at the hour of the aperitif. Lower the oven to 325°F/160°C/Gas 3.

Wash the cure from the pork and dry the meat. Slicing horizontally between the layers of meat and fat, cut as many layers as you can, and as close as possible to the same width and length as the meat. Cut these across to give rectangles of meat/fat about 12 cm × 12 cm. You should be left with 8 thick, flat pieces.

In a bowl mix together the butter with the herbs and lemon rind. You can vary the herbs according to what you have – the exact proportions don't matter very much. Mash the garlic and anchovies to a paste in a mortar or by chopping and then mashing with the blade of a large knife, and mix into the herb butter. Divide into 8 and spread on to each piece of meat. Roll up and tie in two places with kitchen string. Butter a roasting tin and spread the vegetables and garlic out. Season lightly. Place the rolls on top, pour over the wine and stock and sprinkle the meat lightly with salt and pepper. Cover with foil and braise for 2 hours in the oven. Pour the juices through a sieve into a small saucepan, pressing down on the vegetables. Bring to the boil and whisk in the cold butter. Boil until the liquid has thickened a little – there should be about 125 ml. Remove the meat to a serving dish and take off the string. Pour the sauce over the rolls.

A 'risotto' using pearl barley (made the same way) would go well with this dish.

Pork, Chorizo and Chickpea Stew

What Spanish cooking excels at I think is, perhaps surprisingly, winter food. Although the south coast is mild, central and northern Spain can have extremely cold winters. The Spanish have developed thumping great meaty stews – fabulous cocidos – using sausage and ham to line their waist-coats, and rib-sticking soups made from chickpeas or butter beans and black or white pudding. Here is a chickpea stew that uses that most delicious of sausages, chorizo. If you were to add some duck confit you would have something closer to a south-western French cassoulet. This is a dish you must the start the day before you need it.

1 kg boneless, rindless belly pork cured
  overnight in a mixture of 25g salt and
  25g sugar
50g duck or goose fat or lard
50g Bayonne or Serrano ham or bacon, diced
2 cloves of garlic, crushed
1 tbsp herbes de Provence
1 onion, finely chopped
1 carrot, finely chopped
1 stick of celery, finely chopped
1 small turnip, finely chopped
1 leek, finely chopped
2 tbsp tomato paste
250g dried chickpeas, soaked overnight
  and drained
1.2 litres chicken stock
1 small chilli, finely chopped

1 bay leaf
1 sprig of thyme
500g cooking chorizo sausages, sliced 1cm
  thick
1 small spring or Savoy cabbage, shredded
25g parsley, chopped
grated rind and juice of 1 lemon
75g breadcrumbs or brioche crumbs
salt and pepper

Preheat the oven to 350°F/180°C/Gas 4.

Wash the salt and sugar off the pork, and dice it into 1cm cubes. Melt the fat in a large ovenproof casserole dish, and sweat the pork and the ham for 3–4 minutes. Add the garlic, herbes de Provence, onion, carrot, celery, turnip, and leek, and sweat a further 10 minutes. Add the tomato paste, mixing well, then the chickpeas and stock. Bring to the boil, skimming the scum off the top, and simmer for 20 minutes. Now add the chilli, bay leaf, thyme, sausages and cabbage. Bring back to the boil, cover, and put in the oven for 20 minutes.

Meanwhile, mix the parsley, lemon rind and juice, and the breadcrumbs or brioche crumbs, and season. Take the dish out of the oven, sprinkle the breadcrumb mix over the top, put the lid back on and cook until the chickpeas are tender, about 20 minutes. To obtain a light crust on the breadcrumbs, place the dish under a hot grill for a minute or two, but don't burn them.

Serve this in bowls with a leaf salad.

Beef with Stilton and Horseradish Sauce

Stilton isn't one of my favourite cheeses, even the best ones from Colston Bassett or Cropwell Bishop, but it finds a good home here. As the béchamel might indicate, this sauce is an old warhorse of mine. Extremely good with a humble roast, you could make it ahead, and for a quick but distinguished supper use it to deglaze the pan in which you have quickly cooked a couple of slices of fillet or rump steak. Funny that a couple of the emblematic foods of Olde England should marry so well together. Don't use Stilton that's turning yellowy-brown at the edge.

Sauce

12g butter
12g flour
125 ml milk
125 ml meat stock
110g Stilton, crumbled
110g ready-made horseradish sauce (use a
    decent make)
3 tbsp double cream

Melt the butter and stir in the flour. Cook for 2–3 minutes. Add the liquids gradually (in any order), stirring as you go, until the sauce has thickened. Don't do this too quickly or lumps may form, and you'll have to sieve them out. Add the cheese, horseradish sauce and cream, and stir until smooth. You may not need to add any extra seasoning.

Beef

a knob of butter, about 10g
4 slices of fillet or rump steak, 3 cm thick

Melt the butter in a large frying pan. A few seconds after the foam has disappeared, fry the meat over a medium-high heat according to how you like your meat. Not dry, I hope. Remove and keep warm. Pour the sauce into the pan and scrape up any brown residues. Add back any juices that have run from the meat – there won't be any if the meat is rare – and bubble to the thickness of single cream.

Like the other two beef dishes this doesn't need anything elaborate with it, as the flavours are pretty assertive.

Rump Steak Hamburger

In a not completely successful effort at keeping my children away from the burger chains, I have been making these hamburgers for years. Not often with rump steak, I admit, but a pretty good version can be made from minced chuck – better get this from a butcher. Supermarket mince often contains 'mechanically recovered' bits that have an unpleasantly granular texture when cooked, like having a mouthful of small ballbearings. So, use the best mince if not rump, because the dish is worth it. At Blandford Street we used to serve it with foie gras butter (softened butter, mixed half and half with cooked foie gras) and in a brioche bun. A sleek and glistening port sauce would finish it off. A mustard sauce is at least as good.

    750g rump steak, trimmed of all fat and
        connective tissue
    1 medium Spanish onion, finely chopped
    25g butter
    1 tsp fresh thyme or marjoram leaves, chopped
    25g beef marrow, finely chopped (if you can't
        get marrow, use butter)
    1 egg
    1½ tsp salt
    black pepper
    flour
    butter for frying

Chop the meat quite finely with two heavy knives. Cook the onion until soft in the butter, add the herbs, raise the heat, and sauté until the onion starts to brown. With a rubber spatula, mix the onions and herbs into the meat, adding the marrow (or butter) and the egg. Season with the salt and several grinds of pepper, and mix well together well with your hands.

Form into 4 thick hamburgers, roll in flour, and fry or chargrill for 5 minutes each side. Remove and keep hot.

Sauce

    2 shallots, finely chopped
    1 glass red wine
    150ml stock
    6 tbsp double cream
    2 tbsp Dijon or grain mustard
    sugar (optional)

In the same frying pan cook the shallots over medium heat for 3 minutes. Add the wine and boil hard to reduce to about 6 tbsp. Add the stock, reduce again to about 6 tbsp, add the cream and mustard, stirring the sticky pan residues into the sauce. Check the seasoning – a pinch or two of sugar may be needed to balance the wine. Dish up the hamburgers and divide the sauce between them, shallots and all.

What to serve with this? Anything you like, but small new potatoes and a crunchy salad of cos lettuce would be nice.

Persillade of Beef with Anchovy Sauce

This comes into the category of self-indulgence. Although it's good enough for a party, its intense but rustic flavours are probably best enjoyed at home with a bottle of something chunky from the Rhône valley.

The trick with this dish is to have the cooking butter hot enough to cook the meat quickly but not so hot that it burns the persillade. As the meat won't take long to cook, watching the butter and turning down the heat if it starts to brown shouldn't be too taxing.

4 tbsp finely chopped parsley
4 cloves of garlic, finely chopped
grated rind of 1 lemon
4 fillet steaks, each weighing about 150g
    and cut in half horizontally, or 4 pieces
    of rump or rib-eye steak 2 cm thick,
    trimmed of fat and sinew
salt and black pepper
50g butter, cold
1 shallot, finely chopped, or 1 tbsp finely
    chopped onion

150 ml stock
8 anchovy fillets (oil removed with kitchen
    paper), mashed

Mix together the parsley, garlic and lemon rind in a shallow dish and press the pieces of steak into the mixture, covering each side evenly by shaking gently. Season the meat lightly.

Melt about 10g of butter in a large frying pan and, a few seconds after the foam has subsided, cook the meat over medium heat for about 4 minutes each side. To my mind the meat is perfectly done when it feels bouncy if pressed with the thumb. Remove the meat and keep warm.

Add the shallot or onion to the pan and let brown lightly for about 3 minutes. Add the stock and reduce until only about 8 tbsp is left, then the anchovies. Cut the rest of the cold butter into pieces and swirl in until the sauce thickens. Put the meat on plates, adding any juice back to the pan, and pour the sauce over. Serve with spinach and fried potatoes.

On Beef Stews

What? Four recipes for beef stews (not counting the oxtail goulash)? I can't deny it; whatever they're called – daubes, casseroles, sautés – I'm a big fan. I like shoving lots of ingredients into a pot with stock and red wine, letting them cook unmolested for a couple of hours or so and then opening them up to find out what's happened. With a bit of luck there'll be a seriously inviting amalgamation of herbs, garlic, orange peel and wine covering enjoyably chunky and chewable meat. Assuming for a moment that you can buy good stewing meat, chuck, shoulder, topside, even rump (shin if you must), all you have to do is cut the meat into large chunks – small pieces have no chutzpah and imply they have come from a lowly cut that has demanded much interference – brown them quickly and add more or less any ingredients that you think will go well together. Invariably you will need some good stock and a decent fruity unacidic wine – Merlot or Malbec from South America, spicy blends from south-west France or the Rhône valley, robust reds from central Italy would all be fine. Don't be frightened of adding a pinch or two of sugar if you feel your cooking wine hasn't quite enough ripe fruit.

The only problem likely to appear is in the quality of the meat. If you are confident your beef has been hung properly, well and good, but if in doubt, which, of course, means buying meat from a butcher you don't know or in a plastic tub from a supermarket, a marinade will certainly reduce the risk of the end result being old-boots tough, particularly where the only identification on the pack says 'for stewing or braising'. It's more than time these cuts were properly labelled.

A basic marinade should consist of a glass or two or red wine (could be white, depending on the desired outcome, but fatter-bodied whites tend to be expensive – still, a fine cut of veal cooked in good Chardonnay is quite something), some finely sliced onion and carrot, crushed garlic, bruised parsley stalks and finely crumbled bay leaves. Exact quantities aren't that important, but don't overdo the bay. Then you can add orange peel, ginger, crushed juniper or allspice berries, thyme sprigs and so on according to what you have in mind as the finished article. Some olive or vegetable oil can be included as a buffer to the acid and the wine. Turn the meat frequently in the marinade liquid.

Of course you can use a marinade for every stew, but it will shorten the cooking time of good meat. The strained marinade will add considerable flavour to the sauce, but you must be careful not to unbalance the flavours. I usually discard some of the marinade in case the sauce, when reduced, becomes too strong. Obviously, a good recipe will take this into account. For the same reason care must be taken over the quantity of stock used. If too much, there will either be too much sauce or reducing it will concentrate the flavours so much that they cease to taste of anything at all.

So to marinade or not is up to you. What you cannot avoid, though, is trimming the meat extremely thoroughly (unless it's shin) so not a trace of fat or gristle or connective tissue remains.

Finally, thickening the sauce. You can put some flour in a paper bag and shake the meat in this before browning, or thicken later with corn or potato flour or a beurre manié. If you want to emphasize the trouble you have taken, then strain the sauce, discard the vegetables and thicken with cornflour, adding separately cooked vegetables. I think that rather defeats the object. These stews are better a bit rough-hewn.

Beef Stew with Cinnamon and Orange

700g stewing beef
4 tbsp oil
25g butter
1 large Spanish onion
1 large carrot
1 bay leaf
2 strips of orange peel, 3cm × 2cm
1 large clove of garlic, crushed
600ml beef or chicken stock
1 glass robust red wine
1½ tsp sugar
4 tomatoes, skinned, seeded and diced
    (or half a tin of chopped tomatoes)
½ tsp salt
10 turns black pepper

Cut the beef into large pieces, trimming off all fat and gristle, and brown on all sides for 5 minutes in the hot oil and butter. Remove to a large saucepan. Cut the onion into 8 pieces through the root and brown them too but for a bit longer, adding more fat if necessary. Remove and add to the meat. Cut the carrot into 4 crosswise then in half lengthways and brown the pieces in the same way, and add to the pan. Put in the rest of the ingredients, bring to a simmer on top of the stove, and cook for 1½–2 hours. The liquid should only bubble very gently.

When the meat is tender, pour off all the liquid through a sieve and let the meat and vegetables cool a little. Remove the garlic, bay leaf and orange peel. Boil the sauce for a few minutes to concentrate the flavour. By the time it tastes right, it shouldn't really need any extra thickening, but do so with a little cornflour mixed with a little water or red wine if you wish. Add the sauce back to the meat.

Plain buttered rice or noodles would be fine with this.

Beef Stew with Anchovies and Capers

Serves 6

1.5 kg beef rump or topside (it's worth using
    a good cut for this dish)
2 glasses red wine
marinade ingredients listed in On Beef Stews
    (page 155)
500g pancetta or streaky bacon cut into pieces
    2–3 cm square
100g plain flour
25g butter
150g mushrooms, sliced thinly
350g firm, ripe tomatoes, peeled, seeded and
    chopped (or passata)
salt and black pepper
400 ml stock (chicken simmered with the
    browned beef trimmings will do)
10 anchovy fillets
2 tbsp capers
2 cloves of garlic, peeled
2 tbsp chopped parsley
3 tbsp white wine vinegar
3 tbsp olive oil

Cut the beef into large pieces, using the trimmings as in the Beef Stew with Herb Dumplings (page 158). Add the red wine to the other marinade ingredients and marinate for at least 24 hours, turning from time to time.

Preheat the oven to 300°F/150°C/Gas 2.

Blanch the pancetta or bacon for 5 minutes in simmering water. Remove the beef pieces from the marinade and dry on kitchen paper. Put the flour in a paper bag and toss the beef in it.

Heat the butter in a large heavy casserole. A few seconds after the foam disappears, fry the beef and the trimmings, a few pieces at a time, until well browned. Take out the last pieces, discard the trimmings, and put 3 or 4 pieces of pancetta or bacon on the bottom. Cover with some of the marinade vegetables, mushrooms and tomatoes or passata and put in a layer of meat. Season, and repeat until the ingredients are finished, seasoning as you go. Pour in the liquid from the marinade and the stock. Bring to the simmering point on top of the stove, cover and transfer to the oven. The liquid should bubble gently. Chop together very well the anchovies, capers, garlic, and parsley until they almost resemble a paste. Whisk in the vinegar and olive oil. Remove the casserole from the oven after 2½ hours and stir this mixture in. Return to the oven if the meat isn't tender (which it probably won't be, quite) and finish cooking. All together the cooking time, especially for topside, might get up to 3½, even 4, hours. Serve the stew in deep bowls with crusty bread. This is extraordinarily good cold.

Beef Stew with Rum and Olives

50g streaky bacon

1kg chuck steak, cut into 5cm pieces, well
    trimmed

1 Spanish onion, chopped

vegetable oil

1 glass red wine (south-west French would
    be ideal)

½ tsp salt

juice of 1 orange

2 tbsp dark rum

4 tomatoes, skinned, seeded and diced
    (or half a tin of chopped tomatoes)

2 strips of orange peel, 8cm × 3cm, pith
    removed

bouquet garni of 4 parsley stalks, 1 bay leaf,
    3 sprigs of thyme, tied together (or use
    ½ tsp dried thyme and wrap in muslin)

2 cloves of garlic, crushed

1 tsp ground allspice

a good pinch of sugar (optional)

15 black olives

1 tbsp cornflour

Cut the bacon into 2cm pieces and cook over moderate heat in an iron or stainless-steel casserole until the fat has run and the bacon starts to crisp. Remove to a bowl. Raise the heat and brown the meat in batches for several minutes, turning two or three times, until it has coloured well. Don't overcrowd the pan or the heat will drop and the juice start to run, preventing any more browning. Remove to join the bacon, lower the heat a little and add the onion to the pan. Cook until just starting to brown. Add a little vegetable oil if necessary. Pour in the wine and dissolve the brown bits stuck to the pan using a wooden spoon. Return the meat and bacon to the pan with the salt, add the orange juice, rum, and tomatoes, and tuck in the orange peel, bouquet garni and garlic. Add the allspice, and the sugar if the combination of wine, tomatoes and juice seems too tart.

Bring the pan to a simmer on top of the stove and either continue to cook there, covered, for an hour over low heat, or transfer to a low oven (325°F/ 160°C/Gas 3). In any event, the liquid should bubble very slowly. After an hour add the olives and cook for a further 45 minutes. Inferior meat will need considerably longer.

Pour the contents of the pan into a sieve placed over a saucepan and drain. Discard the orange peel, herbs and garlic. Taste the sauce for strength of flavour and seasoning. Boil to reduce a little if required. Mix 1 tbsp of cornflour with 2 tbsp water in a cup (using your finger – you can still do this in the privacy of your own home, but only just) and stir into the sauce. Bring to a simmer for a couple of minutes, replace the meat and the daube is ready. Serve with buttered rice cooked with a good pinch of saffron.

Beef Stew with Herb Dumplings and Damson Cheese

Damsons seem to be one of those quintessential British fruits, like quinces, elderberries and medlars, that come and go all too quickly. Apart, of course, from jams or chutneys, however, they don't feature very much in the cook's repertoire – perhaps because taking out the stones and thus treating them like plums is too labour-intensive. A 'cheese' is nothing but a much-reduced fruit purée made with fruit high in acidity and therefore needing plenty of balancing sugar, and thus achieving that depth of flavour that comes from combining (in the right proportions) opposite characteristics. 1kg of damsons will make more than you need, but damson cheese keeps for ever, and it's difficult handling a smaller quantity.

The sweet-savoury-tart combination of the damsons with the dumplings lifts this straightforward, though good, casserole out of the ordinary into something a bit more special.

Beef

800g stewing beef
12 baby onions
8 small carrots, green tops on
1 tbsp bacon or duck fat
1 fat clove of garlic, crushed
bouquet garni of 4 or 5 parsley stalks,
    1 medium bay leaf, 4 sprigs of fresh thyme
    tied together (or use 1 tsp dried thyme and
    a muslin bag)
1 glass robust red wine
600ml chicken or beef stock
1 tsp salt
2 tsp cornflour

Trim the meat well, reserving the trimmings, and cut into 5cm chunks. Blanch the onions for 30 seconds, place in cold water and slip off the skins. Slice off the little brown root end – only the brown bit or the onions may collapse. Scrub the carrots and leave 3cm of the green tops; or cut one large carrot into three pieces, then quarter each piece lengthways.

Melt the fat and brown the pieces of meat well, including the trimmings. This is simply to obtain maximum 'brown bits' in the pan. Remove the meat, discarding the trimmings, then brown the onions in the same pan, tossing them around frequently. Place the onions and the meat with all the other ingredients in a heavy-bottomed pan. Deglaze the browning pan with some of the stock, scraping the brown bits into the liquid. Decant

back into the casserole. Bring to a simmer and cook gently on top of the stove for about 1¼ hours.

Dumplings

50g self-raising flour
50g breadcrumbs
50g shredded suet
½ tbsp each chopped marjoram and sage,
    mixed
1 small egg
salt and pepper
2 tsp cornflour

Mix together all the ingredients except the cornflour in a bowl, and season well. Divide the mixture into walnut-sized pieces and roll into balls. Add to the stew after the hour and a quarter's cooking, and cook a further 25 minutes. Carefully pour off the liquid and boil down if necessary to strengthen the flavour. Thicken with the cornflour and return to the casserole. Correct the seasoning.

Damson Cheese

1kg damsons, washed, stones left in
sugar

Put the damsons in a heavy-bottomed saucepan, pour in about half their volume of water, simmer for about 20 minutes and rub through a sieve. Weigh, and return to the pan with slightly less than the same weight of sugar. Simmer for about an hour, stirring from time to time. Towards the end of the cooking be careful the purée does not catch and burn on the bottom of the pan. Remove with a flexible spatula to a small dish, cover with clingfilm, and cool. Serve warm or cold with the stew; I prefer warm as it looks a bit tidier on the plate. You can make a good cheese with Bramley apples, but be even more careful not to let them burn.

Nothing else is needed for this.

Rabbit Braised in Red Wine with Orange and Allspice

This is a good way to cook wild rabbit, which has more flavour than the garden bunny but takes more cooking. You'll probably have to buy one from a butcher, so ask him to cut it into six pieces – forelegs, hindlegs, and the saddle into two. I think it's pushing it a bit to get enough for four out of a rabbit, but you could if you served it up with dumplings, say. It pays to marinate the meat, from both the tenderizing and the flavouring points of view. You could also use this recipe for guineafowl, but you would need two birds for four people, and the cooking time would be an hour.

Serves 3

1 × 1.5 kg rabbit, jointed in 6 pieces
1 small carrot, thinly sliced
1 large clove of garlic, thinly sliced
2 bay leaves, crumbled
1 good tsp ground allspice (grind your own
    if possible, or use fresh bought)
½ tsp ground black pepper
1 glass robust dryish red wine – like a good
    fruity Merlot from Chile
grated rind and juice of 1 large orange
3 tbsp dark rum
3 tbsp olive oil
2 tbsp flour
¼ tsp salt
100 ml stock
25g butter, cold, cut into small pieces

Put the rabbit in a large bowl with the next 8 ingredients and 1 tbsp of the olive oil, and mix together well. Leave in the fridge, turning occasionally, for at least 24 hours.

Preheat the oven to 350°F/180°C/Gas 4.

Remove the rabbit pieces and dry them with kitchen paper. Put the flour in another bowl and dip the rabbit in it, covering well. Shake off the excess. Heat the rest of the olive oil in a frying pan and brown the pieces well on each side. Transfer to a casserole dish and season. Pour the marinade into the frying pan and scrape into it any brown bits in the bottom. Pour into the casserole, add the stock, bring to a simmer on top of the stove and then cook, covered, in the oven for 2–3 hours. Keep checking and turn the meat around occasionally. When it's cooked, take the rabbit pieces out and keep hot. Strain the liquid into a clean saucepan, discarding the debris, and over high heat whisk in the butter. Divide the pieces between 3 plates and pour over the sauce, first reducing the sauce by boiling if necessary.

This is good with chunks of carrot and swede sprinkled with a little brown sugar and turned in hot butter.

Saddle of Venison with Juniper and Chocolate

Don't be put off by the sound of this, as the chocolate is merely an embellishment, used to give the sauce a little extra richness and gloss. As the sauce is also based on the red wine used to marinate the venison, there's no danger of it becoming too rich.

The marinade is used to add more flavour to the meat, not to tenderize it.

Venison
about 750g boned and trimmed venison saddle, or the meat from 4 loin chops
300ml stock (chicken, beef or venison)
25g butter, plus 25g refrigerated
12 juniper berries, crushed
1 tbsp cognac
1 dsp redcurrant jelly
20g dark chocolate, grated or chopped coarsely

Marinade
½ bottle medium-bodied red wine
1 small carrot, finely sliced
1 small onion, finely sliced
1 bay leaf, crumbled
3 parsley stalks
10 crushed juniper berries
½ tsp dried thyme

Slice the venison into 8 equal pieces, across the grain, and add to the marinade ingredients in a glass or stainless-steel bowl. Mix well, and leave for 24 hours in the fridge, turning 2 or 3 times.

Remove the meat from the marinade and dry on kitchen paper. Strain the marinade and boil hard to reduce by two-thirds. Do the same with the stock. (If using a cube or paste, be aware that reducing might make it over-salty.)

Season the meat lightly on both sides. Melt the first knob of butter in a frying pan and a few seconds after the foam dies down cook the meat for 3 minutes each side. There should be some bounce in it. Keep warm. Add the reduced marinade and the stock to the pan with the juniper and boil down to about 6 tbsp. Add the cognac, letting it catch fire if you like, and the redcurrant jelly. Cut the cold butter into 2 or 3 pieces and swirl into the sauce, along with the chocolate. If any juice has come out of the meat, pour it into the sauce, which should be lightly syrupy and shiny.

Dish up the meat and pour the sauce over. Serve with fried potatoes and red cabbage (cook small shredded red cabbage slowly for 40 minutes with 1 medium chopped onion, 1 crushed clove of garlic, 3–4 tbsp red wine vinegar, 2–3 tbsp brown sugar, 2 tsp cinnamon, 5 cm strip of orange peel, and salt and ground black pepper).

Venison with Star Anise Sauce and Cornmeal Orange Dumplings

The humbler cuts of venison make good stews and their robust flavour means ingredients with strong personalities can be pressed into service. Star anise commends itself to me because it is more allspicy than aniseedy and its dark woody flavour is a good match for the deep flavour tones of the venison. The dumplings are just a twist on the usual article.

1 tbsp butter
1 tbsp vegetable oil
1 kg venison stewing meat (haunch, shoulder, chine)
1 small carrot, cut into thick slices
⅓ celery stick, cut into 1 cm pieces on the bias
½ a Spanish onion, roughly cut into pieces
350 ml stock
1 glass of red wine
1 bay leaf
1 heaped tbsp orange marmalade
2 tsp cornflour, mixed with 1 tsp brandy

Heat the butter and oil in a frying pan until the butter foam has subsided; a few seconds later brown the meat in 2 or 3 batches for about 5 minutes. Remove to a heavy-bottomed pan or an earthenware casserole and do the same with the vegetables. Remove to join the meat, add the stock, wine, bay leaf and marmalade, bring to a simmer and cook gently, either semi-covered on top of the stove or covered in the oven (350°F / 180°C / Gas 4), for about 1½ hours on top of the stove or a little longer in the oven.

Pour the liquid off through a sieve into a clean pan and whisk in the cornflour and brandy mixture. Cook this for 2–3 minutes and return to the meat, shaking to amalgamate with the juices remaining in the meat pan. Remove the bay leaf.

Cornmeal Dumplings

90 g cornmeal
1 tbsp plain flour
½ tsp baking powder
¼ tsp salt
1 egg
70 ml milk
2 tsp melted butter
grated rind of 1 orange
stock or lightly salted water

Sift together the first four ingredients. Beat the egg with the milk and combine the two mixtures. Add the melted butter and the orange rind. Bring a pan of stock or water to a simmer, turn the heat down a little, and drop blobs of the mixture from a metal teaspoon into the hot liquid. Poach until they rise to the surface and remove with a slotted spoon.

Serve the whole dish with small turnips, quartered and boiled.

Roast Partridge with Black Pudding, Artichokes and Wild Mushrooms

This is a recipe of my Blandford Street chef, Roger Gorman. It may seem rather an exhibitionist dish for cooking at home but is actually straightforward, apart from a bit of labour with the tomatoes and parsnips. On the other hand, the artichokes are out of a jar, the birds are simple to cook and you don't really need anything else except perhaps some potatoes to roast with the birds and maybe some buttered cabbage. The different flavours and textures set each other off very well.

If you can find grey-legged partridges, lucky you, as they have a sweeter, slightly more gamy flavour. Most likely though you'll have to make do with our red-legged variety – although this is no hardship as partridge definitely comes into the treat category. As with all game birds, resting after cooking is essential if the meat is to remain succulent.

You need not truss the birds, but if you don't, cutting them in half with a sharp knife and scissors to serve will make them look neater on the plate.

8 ripe but firm plum tomatoes
2 tsp of oil
75gm cold butter, in small pieces
salt and freshly ground black pepper
4 partridges
1 tbsp shallot or red onion, finely chopped
4 tbsp balsamic or sherry vinegar
200ml reduced meat stock
2 good pinches caster sugar
8 small parsnips, peeled and formed into
    elongated cone shapes
175gm diced black pudding
175gm marinated artichoke hearts, quartered
175gm mixed wild mushrooms
2 tbsp chives, finely chopped

Preheat the oven to 400°F/200°C/Gas 6.

Cut a slit at the top of the tomatoes, plunge them into just-boiled water for 20 seconds and remove the skin. Quarter them and remove the seeds.

Heat the oil with a small lump of the butter in a heavy pan (preferably an ovenproof one), season the birds inside and out and brown the breasts and legs well for about 8 minutes. Roast in the oven, if possible in the same pan, for 15 minutes, remove and keep hot.

Add the shallots or onion to the pan and cook fairly briskly for 3 minutes. Add the vinegar and boil away almost completely, then add the stock and 1 pinch of sugar. Reduce to about 8 tbsp and set aside.

Meanwhile, heat a little more of the butter in another pan and gently roll the parsnips in it until they are golden brown. Season, sprinkle with the other pinch of sugar and roast in the oven for about 10 minutes, until crisp and tender. Remove and keep warm.

In a frying pan heat a little more of the butter and fry the black pudding until it becomes crisp – 3 minutes – add the artichokes and mushrooms, fry for 2 minutes then add the tomato pieces and chives. Season.

Heat up the pan containing the sauce until it bubbles and swirl in the remaining butter.

Divide the black pudding mixture between 4 hot plates, put a partridge on each and arrange 2 parsnips alongside. Pour over the sauce (through a sieve if you like) and serve.

Oxtail Goulash with Caraway Noodles

Goulash is one of those dishes that deserve to represent a nation's cooking. And paprika and sour cream are one of those combinations where you couldn't find better partners for either, and the addition of caraway, another of Hungary's favourite flavours, in the pasta along with a few poppy seeds argues a vigorous case for goulash to be included in the list of the world's great dishes. Here I am using oxtail to celebrate the virtue of the beef bone – you can, of course, use stewing beef or veal, but the sauce won't be quite as rich. It's important to use really fresh paprika.

2 kg oxtail, washed, dried, and cut into 5 cm pieces (ask your butcher to do this: if you have a cleaver you could cut up the oxtails yourself as they do have joints; it does, however, take an expert to spot them)
2 tbsp duck fat or butter
2 Spanish onions, finely chopped
2 cloves of garlic, finely chopped
2 tbsp paprika
1 tsp caraway seeds
1 tsp each dried marjoram and thyme, or 2 tsp each of fresh
400 g chopped tomatoes (tinned are fine)
150 ml beef or chicken stock
110 g mushrooms, sliced
2 red peppers, thinly sliced
1 tsp salt
cornflour (optional)
150 ml sour cream

In a large stainless-steel or enamel pan, brown the meat on all sides in the fat for about 10 minutes. Remove to a bowl, add the onion and garlic to the pan and cook for about 5 minutes. Replace the meat and add all the other ingredients except the sour cream. Cover, bring to a simmer and cook over very low heat, or in a low oven, for about 2½ hours. Pour the cooking liquid though a sieve into another pan and skim off the fat as you bring it back to the boil. Reduce to sauce consistency (thicken with a little cornflour if you wish, but the gelatine from the tail should give the sauce enough body). Check the seasoning and tip the meat into a warm serving dish. Cover with the sauce and just stir in the sour cream, to contrast it with the warm red of the paprika. Serve with the caraway noodles.

Caraway noodles

300 g ribbon pasta
25 g butter
1 tsp ground caraway seeds
½ tsp poppy seeds

Cook the pasta in salted water until al dente. Melt the butter in the hot pan and add the caraway seeds and the poppy seeds. Toss the pasta well in these.

No-Shows

A fascinating subject? No, but one capable of arousing strong emotion, particularly in smaller restaurants where no-shows can make the difference between profit and loss. Some while ago, there was a story in the trade that a restaurateur rang at 3 a.m. the number of a booking which had failed to arrive and asked if they minded if he let his staff go home now. Sometimes I feel so exercised by this question that I'm almost ready to stay up till 3 a.m. Certainly if he had managed to speak to somebody at the end of the line that would have been an achievement in itself. More often than not, the contact number we all take with bookings is, for no shows, a dud, especially if the name attached to it is, for example, Roland Butter, C. Lion, or Michael Hunt (it's time he changed his pseudonym), and believe it or not bookings under these names do get taken (OK, maybe we deserve it if we fall for those tricks). However, my apologies to S. Tinker who turned out not to be one after all.

Alternatively, the perpetrators may have booked at several different restaurants, a) to make sure of eating somewhere, b) to offer, so considerate of them, their guests a choice. You know this because of the odd occasion when someone does reply (the au pair/nanny/housekeeper/ secretary) and says, 'They've gone out to a restaurant.' 'Yes, but they should have been at *this* restaurant an hour ago.' 'I'm sorry, but they didn't say where they were going.' 'Well,' a bit crossly but you can't browbeat the innocent parties too much, unfortunately for your anger management programme, 'please tell them we are still waiting when they return, and that we will have to send them a bill.' 'I'm sorry, but I'm not allowed to give out the address.'

Otherwise, the answering voice will most likely say, 'There's no one of that name here.' Sometimes it will say, 'Oh dear – didn't my secretary cancel it?' Sometimes it will say, 'But I cancelled it this morning' (actually this is a bit of a fib). Sometimes it will say, at least half an hour after arrival time, 'Oh dear, can I cancel it now?' We answer, 'Well, it's a bit late now. You confirmed your table over the phone this morning and we held it for you, turning away somebody else who wanted it. We weren't able to offer it to anyone else. I'm afraid in these circumstances we'll have to send you a bill – not a very large one – to cover our loss of revenue as the law entitles us to do. May we therefore have the name and address of your company?'

Pause. In tones of mild but increasing outrage: 'No, you may not. It was never made clear to me when I booked that a cancellation charge would be made, and the law does not allow you to make one anyway.' 'But it is the case, when you make a restaurant booking, even over the phone, that you are entering into a contract. Failure to honour the booking or to cancel within a reasonable time puts you in breach of that contract, so we are therefore entitled to recover damages. So please, may we have your address?' 'No.' And down goes the phone.

I don't know whether you've ever rung up the number of a company whose name you weren't sure of, to find the answering voice completely unintelligible. Easy if you know it, of course. In the case of the foregoing, after several different staff members tried, we gave up. Dogged persistence might have paid off, but there are after all other miscreants to chase. I must say, though, that I've never managed to take anyone to the small claims court or otherwise recover any money, even though I've tried hard. I suppose it doesn't help if, when the no-show's secretary throws herself at your mercy, tearfully stuttering 'He'll absolutely kill me if he finds out,' your natural chivalry never allows your dogged persistence to get going.

I'll do it one day, though.

Vegetables

Haricot Bean Purée

This is a dish which can be used as a dip with cauliflower and broccoli florets, as a purée to go with lamb, pheasant, guineafowl or even tuna, as a sauce likewise, or as a soup. And as Tommy Cooper said about rice pudding, it's so good you could even do your bathroom out with it.

500g dried haricot beans
bouquet garni: bay leaf, 6 parsley stalks,
    8 peppercorns, 4 sprigs of fresh thyme
    (or ½ tsp dried), 2 crushed cloves of
    garlic and a 5 cm piece of lemon peel,
    all wrapped in muslin; if you haven't
    any muslin, it simply makes removing
    the bits later a little messy
½ a Spanish onion, peeled and quartered
    through the root
1 medium carrot
2 large cloves of garlic, peeled and finely
    chopped
⅓ tsp ground mace
1 good tsp paprika
½ tbsp lemon juice
125–175 ml olive oil
salt and black pepper

Soak the beans overnight. Pour off the water and put the beans into a large saucepan. Add enough cold water to cover by about 3 cm and put in the bouquet garni, onion and carrot. Bring to the boil and simmer gently for 1½ hours (if the beans are old you'll probably need longer). Remove the bouquet garni and the vegetables. Pour off and reserve the liquid. Ideally, there should be about 150 ml; boil to reduce if necessary.

Pour the beans into the bowl of a food processor, purée with the garlic, spices and lemon juice and add back the cooking liquid. Add olive oil in a thin stream with the motor running until you have the consistency you want. Season well with salt and pepper.

To bring this purée to dip or sauce consistency, simply add enough light chicken stock.

Chickpea and Walnut Purée

This is good as a substitute for mashed potato or polenta, to go with garlicky roast lamb, a tagine, or red mullet, say, cooked with lemon and capers.

250g chickpeas, soaked overnight and drained
1 litre water
1 small carrot, quartered
½ a Spanish onion, quartered
2 cloves of garlic, crushed
1 sprig of thyme
1 bay leaf
4 parsley stalks
6 pieces of lemon peel, 1cm × 3cm
25g walnuts
25g butter

Cover the chickpeas with the water in a saucepan. Add all the other ingredients except the walnuts and butter. Bring to a simmer and cook gently for about 45 minutes, skimming two or three times early on. Pour off the liquid through a sieve (reserve for soup) and cool the chickpeas for 5 minutes. Remove the vegetables, herbs and lemon peel. Toast the walnuts lightly under the grill and chop them. Rub in a tea towel if you want to remove some of the (slightly) bitter skins. Pour the peas and nuts into a food-processor bowl and run until smooth, adding some of the reserved liquid and the butter, until you have a consistency just stiff enough to allow you to form quenelle shapes with two dessertspoons. Alternatively, if you want it more like a creamy mash, let it down with a little more liquid to the consistency of soft polenta.

Chickpea Pancakes

An interesting way to serve chickpeas. Good with any strong-flavoured dish with Mediterranean overtones.

Makes about 12

350g (cooked weight) chickpeas, tinned or
    dried (you'll need about 200g if dried)
1 egg plus 1 egg white
2 tbsp double cream or crème fraiche
1 tbsp chickpea flour or plain flour
½ tsp baking powder
½ tsp ground cumin
1 large clove of garlic, very finely chopped
1 tsp lemon juice
2 tbsp coriander leaves, finely chopped
⅓ tsp salt
black pepper
50ml milk, scalded and cooled
olive oil

Combine all the ingredients except the milk and oil in the bowl of a food processor and run the motor for 15 seconds, pouring the milk in steadily. Heat the olive oil in a frying pan and when very hot but not smoking drop in the mixture 2 tbsp at a time. Cook each side about 3 minutes, in batches of two or three.

White Cabbage cooked with Sweet Peppers and Onions

This is an example of how my feelings about mixing the latitudes can't be cast in stone. I was a bit stumped one day for an interesting vegetable to go with some fish and didn't have much to play around with, so I thought I would try cooking together sliced onion, sweet pepper and shredded cabbage, with some chopped garlic to start them off. I think it worked really well, and my wife says it's her favourite way of eating cabbage (I have to admit the choice offered to her hasn't been extensive, but it is a good dish).

2 tbsp olive oil
25g butter
2 cloves of garlic, finely chopped
1 Spanish onion, finely sliced
2 red or yellow peppers, cored, seeded and finely sliced
1 small, heavy white cabbage, weighing about 600g
salt

Heat the olive oil and butter together in a large saucepan and throw in the garlic. Let this cook gently for 3–4 minutes. Add the onions (finely sliced means finely sliced) and cook over moderate heat for 10 minutes, covered. Don't let them brown. Uncover, add the peppers and the cabbage, season lightly and put the lid back on. Carry on cooking over moderate heat for about 15 minutes and give everything a good stir. Cover again, raise the heat a little and cook for a further 15 minutes. By this time the onions should be melting and the cabbage al dente, or ideally a bit less firm. Check for saltiness and add a bit more salt if you need to, and serve.

This goes well with most white fish cooked fairly plainly. It's also very nice if you add some sliced pepperoni halfway through the cooking and eat it on its own. The addition of herbs doesn't really improve this, oddly enough.

Fennel with Saffron and Orange

This is good as a vegetable with grilled or fresh fish like red mullet or sea bream, or with roast lamb, but, as with most things that taste good, could have a life of its own, cold, and as a salad. It has a lovely colour which could be dramatized by adding some black olives. The addition of some quartered hard-boiled eggs would give it substance.

Serves 6

2 large, fresh fennel bulbs, preferably with the feathery fronds attached
1 glass good dry white wine (Chardonnay works well with this)
grated rind and juice of 1 large orange
a large pinch of saffron
2 big pinches of salt
a pinch of sugar
black pepper

Cut off the fennel fronds and reserve. Remove any coarse and/or discoloured outside leaves, cutting off the green shots at the top and removing the protruding base, but don't cut off so much that good leaves go with it. Cut each bulb in half across the short axis then in half again, at right angles, then cut each quarter into four neat wedges. Place in a gratin dish or smallish roasting tin.

Heat the wine and orange juice and rind gently with the saffron and let them infuse for 10 minutes. Pour over the fennel, turning so all is covered. Leave to marinate for an hour or so.

Take a large saucepan or frying pan and transfer the fennel and liquid into it, add the salt and sugar, and cook, covered, at a gentle simmer for 12–15 minutes. Transfer to a warm serving dish and give it a few turns of the pepper mill. Chop the fronds and sprinkle over the dish.

Beetroot, Celeriac and Orange Ragout

Another excellent beetroot dish (see Beetroot Bavarois, page 44). Beetroot and orange make good companions, and the addition of celeriac gives this dish an extra dimension. The really important thing, though, is the marmalade, which must be good quality and bitter – home-made? This goes brilliantly with venison, wild boar or hare, but is very good on its own.

Serves 6–8

225g Spanish onion, finely chopped
50g butter
grated rind of 2 large oranges
4cm cube of fresh ginger, peeled and finely chopped
2 tbsp plain flour
200ml stock
1 tbsp red wine vinegar
2 tbsp creamed horseradish
2 tbsp orange marmalade (chop any large pieces of peel)
juice of 1 orange
1 orange, peeled of all skin and pith
450g raw beetroot, peeled and thinly sliced
900g celeriac, peeled and thinly sliced
salt and pepper

Preheat the oven to 350°F/180°C/Gas 4. Butter a gratin or casserole dish.

Cook the onion in the butter with the orange rind and ginger until lightly browned, about 15 minutes. Stir in the flour, cook a further 2 minutes, then add the stock, vinegar, horseradish, marmalade and orange juice. Simmer until the marmalade melts. Season lightly. Cut the peeled orange cross-wise into very thin slices. Put alternate layers of beetroot and celeriac into the buttered dish, seasoning as you go. Pour over the sauce and finish with the slices of orange. Cover with buttered foil and bake for 2 hours.

Grated Courgettes with Cream and Basil

This is so good you could almost eat it on its own. Use it with fish or chicken, cooked without any really strong flavours. Squeeze those courgettes really hard!

4–6 courgettes (about 450g), preferably with dark green skins
25g butter
4 tbsp double cream
2 tbsp torn basil leaves
salt

Wash, dry, top and tail the courgettes and grate coarsely into a bowl. Take up handfuls and squeeze hard over the sink to expel as much moisture as possible. Repeat until you have dealt with them all.

In a large saucepan melt the butter with the cream and over moderate heat reduce by half. Stir in the courgettes and the basil and cook, stirring two or three times, for 2 minutes. Season lightly and serve straight away.

Corn and Courgette Fry-up

Hardly a dish for a restaurant, but surprisingly good given the humdrum-looking ingredients, and without the chillis finds favour with children (ours, anyway). It wouldn't upset me too much if I never ate another standalone chilli (i.e. unless in something like chilli con carne or chorizo) but the little kick of mild chilli gives a useful edge to this dish.

4 mild green European chillis
4 cobs of corn
4tsp light vegetable oil
1 medium onion, finely chopped
3 courgettes or different squash, diced
salt
1 tbsp fresh oregano, finely chopped
black pepper

Deseed the chillis and chop finely. Remove the corn from the kernels by slicing down with a sharp knife. Heat the oil in a large frying pan, add the onion and sweat for a few minutes until the onion is golden and starting to brown at the edges. Add the courgettes or squash, salt and oregano, cover, and cook over moderate heat until the courgettes are slightly softened. Add the chillis, corn and a few twists of black pepper, and cook another 3–4 minutes. Divide between 4 plates.

To make this a more substantial dish you could add a poached egg to each plate, or include some chorizo or cotechino-type sausage. You would need about 200g, diced, and you should add it along with the onion. It will leak out some delicious fat, so cut down on the vegetable oil.

Garlic Custards

A very light custard, this is for those who like the sweet, muted but compelling flavour of cooked garlic floating on a background of herbs. I make this as a 'vegetable' to go with roast lamb.

300ml creamy milk
20 cloves of garlic, peeled and crushed
2 shallots or ½ a medium onion, thinly sliced
1 bay leaf
16 peppercorns
parsley stalks
2–3 sprigs of thyme or marjoram, or ½ tsp
    dried
4 egg whites or 2 whole eggs (according to
    what colour you want), beaten and strained
    (use the same strainer – see below)

Preheat the oven to 350°F/180°C/Gas 4. Butter well 4 ramekins about 9cm diameter, and place a circle of buttered paper, butter side up, in the bottom of each.

Infuse the milk with all the ingredients except the eggs or egg whites, over low heat, for 45 minutes. Don't let it boil. Strain the milk into a bowl, and retrieve the garlic from the debris. Discard the debris and push the garlic through the sieve into the milk. Let this cool slightly, beat in the whole eggs or egg whites, divide between the 4 buttered ramekins, and bake in a bain-marie for 40 minutes. Cool slightly before turning out.

Apple and Onion Gratin

This is very good with roast pork, duck and venison, the Bramleys as usual providing the basis for that satisfying tension between sweet and tart, with the onions offering a savoury counterpoint. You could add a herb like marjoram or sage if you like, but I prefer the simplicity of this dish, the crunchy crumb topping reacting well with the soft mixture underneath.

500g Bramleys, peeled, cored, and finely sliced
1 dsp lemon juice
50g butter, and more for greasing
salt
55g soft brown sugar
500g large onions, finely chopped
40g coarse breadcrumbs, brown or white,
    from good bread

Preheat the oven to 350°F/180°C/Gas 4.

In a bowl toss the apple slices in the lemon juice as you cut them. Butter a large gratin dish and strew the apple evenly over the bottom. Sprinkle lightly with salt and half the sugar. Cover evenly with the onions, salt lightly, and cover with the remaining sugar. In turn cover this with the breadcrumbs. Melt the butter in a small pan and drizzle over the crumbs, covering as much of the surface as you can. Bake for 1¼ hours, until the breadcrumbs have crisped and browned.

Potato and Chorizo Gratin

It's taken a long time for chorizo to become available over here, more's the pity. Spain hasn't quite the variety of sausages of Italy or Germany but the quality is in no way inferior, and in chorizo Spain has a world-beater anyway. It's less fatty than salami and more highly spiced, especially with pimentón (sweet paprika) and chilli in the picante versions. As such, a little goes a fairly long way.

This gratin is a highly savoury mix of potato, chorizo and garlic, with a little finely diced porcini to round it off. This would be good with a plain piece of beef or venison but it's better I think on its own as a main course, with a plain salad or green vegetable. You can, of course, vary the amount of meat in the gratin.

If you can find it, use the hard Spanish ewe's milk cheese Manchego. Otherwise use Gruyère or a medium Cheddar.

1 large clove of garlic, peeled and finely
    chopped
750g firm-bodied potatoes like Reds or King
    Edwards, peeled and cut into slices 3mm
    thick
salt and pepper
6–8 pieces dried porcini mushrooms, very
    finely chopped (no soaking required)
about 100g thick chorizo, cut into about 30
    slices 0.5mm thick (ask at the meat counter
    to have it sliced; if you have to use thinner
    chorizo, make the slices a bit thicker – and,
    of course, use more of them)

250 ml double cream
110g hard cheese (see above)
butter for greasing

Preheat the oven to 325°F/160°C/Gas 3. Butter a gratin dish of about 30 cm × 23 cm.

Sprinkle half the garlic into the gratin dish. Place a slightly overlapping layer of potatoes in the dish and season lightly with salt and black pepper. Sprinkle over one third of the porcini. Cover with an overlapping layer of chorizo. Add another layer of potatoes, sprinkle on the rest of the garlic, more porcini, season, cover with chorizo. Add another layer of potatoes and porcini, season, cover with the rest of the chorizo and finish off with more potato. Season again. Pour on the cream around the edges of the dish and cover the top with the cheese. Bake for 1½ a hours or until the potatoes are soft.

Variation: omit the porcini and replace with 2 tsp very finely chopped rosemary, thyme or marjoram leaves.

Potato Latkes

Gratinated with garlic, mountain cheese and cream; sautéed in duck fat with rosemary; grated into rösti; and latkes – these are the potatoes for me. With latkes, it's a question of what to serve alongside, not the other way round. They are, basically, shallow-fried grated potato pancakes, but given a notch more gravitas by the garlic and bicarbonate. They are possibly at their best with something like sour cream, perhaps smoked eel or mackerel, as an excellent substitute for blinis. A plain steak with a dollop of sour cream has considerable charm, too, as does a slightly tart apple sauce.

Makes about 8–10

350g potatoes, peeled and grated (almost any variety will do for this – except new or salad spuds, of course)
½ tsp bicarbonate of soda
1 small onion, grated
37g plain flour
1 small clove of garlic, finely chopped
1 egg, beaten
75 ml single cream
½ tsp salt and 10 turns of the pepper mill
oil for frying

Soak the potato with the bicarbonate in water just to cover for an hour. Drain well and pat dry with a cloth or kitchen paper. Mix well with the other ingredients (except the oil), and season. Drop about 1 good tbsp of the mixture into 1–2 cm of very hot vegetable oil, spreading and flattening a little with the back of the spoon. Fry in batches until well browned and drain on kitchen paper.

Kitchen Porters

There's a riveting account in George Orwell's *Down and Out in Paris and London* of pre-war life in the service areas of the Hôtel Crillon, particularly of the *plongeurs* who led a troglodytic life of unremitting toil in the hotel's hot and fetid bowels. The lowest in the highly structured pecking order of the staff, the *plongeurs* were the most despised and exploited, with no one beneath them to assuage their feelings of insignificance. Their mechanism to combat this and generate some self-respect was to convince themselves they were the only ones who could endure their horrendous workload and inhuman conditions, and thus protect themselves from the knowledge that they weren't at the toe of the world's boot. They could then even look down on the lowest cooks and waiters as namby-pambies who would faint at the sight of an encrusted, burnt-on, fifty-kilo copper stockpot. '*Je suis dur. Je suis dur,*' was their incantation. If you repeat it for long enough, does it work? I've tried doing it but I haven't the stamina.

Although they are rather better treated now, the modern version of *plongeur*, feeble in its euphemism 'kitchen porter', can sometimes be more an unsung hero than a downtrodden victim. His old skills of cleaning tinned copper with salt and lemon juice have been replaced by the simple elbow grease needed for stainless steel; the pre-wash spray, the pass-through dishwasher and detergents in pumps have reduced even this physical labour. Quite right, too, because in theory it has freed the KP to do other things. A good one will not only keep the kitchen clean, but will prepare vegetables, wash and pick salads and herbs, descale fish, and generally improve the lives of the cooks. In short, to quote an Australian chef of mine, a good one's worth his weight in wallaby droppings.

Unfortunately, there aren't that many good ones and I've seen a fair few KPs. In spite of the improvements in conditions, the change in the demands it makes, it's still not a job which seems to offer much of the dignity of labour, although I'm old-fashioned enough to think there ought to be some satisfaction to be gained from doing any job well, particularly if the results are quickly evident. At the moment this isn't an idea received with much enthusiasm by most of the KP population, and, if forced, I suppose I can understand that.

The best I had was my first, Betty Williams, who did the necessary for me in North Wales. Betty, who had had nine children, which I suppose was good training for the job, was short and twinkly and over the years had developed a barrel-like shape, exaggerated by her small stature. How she had done this was a mystery because in the three years she worked for me I never saw her eat anything at all, or even drink a cup of tea. Unlike other KPs, she was never drunk, never turned up late, never misunderstood or refused a request, had a tantrum, or otherwise introduced an extra unwanted dynamic into the sometimes brittle atmosphere of the average kitchen. Betty was a true treasure, but then, she was Welsh.

In London, home to so many immigrants, there is always a reservoir of KPs to draw from – or I should say different reservoirs – and restaurants tend to be fed a continual supply through the separate extended networks of Irish, Poles, Spaniards, Moroccans, Venezuelans, Algerians, and this year Ivoiriens. Where are all the French, Dutch, Belgian, and German KPs – they can't all be middle class and driving BMWs, can they? The Italians I imagine all go to Italian restaurants. There is even a dedicated job centre for them, in Denmark Street. Years ago, it was the norm to employ these people in the black economy, an endless stream of desperate, nomadic and sometimes rootless people who would come and go at the whim of head chef, proprietor or probation officer. In our paradoxical age of expanding civil liberty and suffocating bureaucracy, KPs are now visible and respectable with NI numbers, bank accounts and holiday entitlements. No one would wish otherwise, but the constant ebb and flow of people with unpronounceable names and ephemeral addresses, besides adding to the paperwork, frequently leads to farce when the Inland Revenue, which *always* loses its bit of the P45 sent when an employee leaves, is trying to track down someone who worked for you for ten days two years ago, and whose name, try as you might, you don't recognize at all.

When I worked in Richmond there were fewer to choose from and one had to take one's chances. They were, on the whole, less efficient than foreign workers grateful to be here and in work, but, as long as you knew you couldn't rely on them for long, more entertaining. There was Ron, about forty-five, ex-RAF ('I used to be a supervisor'), in and out of rehab. You could tell his bad days because he would carefully comb his greasy hair over and over again, between washing the odd cup, as he slowly sank closer and closer to the floor. For years after he moved on, he would suddenly appear, unavoidable in the kitchen, and touch me for a fiver. Luckily he was tall so he was easy to spot and dodge in the street, where he eventually spent a good deal of his time. There was elderly John, who had trouble with both his back and his live-in partner, who kicked him out one day so he had to sleep on East Sheen station, where he fell down a manhole and disappeared for two days. There was Seamus, who was in constant and intimate conference with his hip flask and one evening, assailed by demons, had an altercation with himself, decided to leave without telling anyone, and halfway through changing his clothes rushed off leaving his shoes behind.

There was Serge, who upset a box of live eels into the potwash sink, which was full of dirty water. He lost his presence of mind and instead of taking the plug out tried to catch them in his hands (you try it). There was Abdel, who was pretty good until Ramadan came round and his consequent low blood sugar meant frequent periods of repose interspersed with bouts of ferociously bad temper, although to give him credit he was tolerant of people tripping over his prayer mat; and there was Pepe, who was fifty, five foot tall and twelve stone, who had two jobs. He had a family in Portugal for whom he toiled seven days a week. When this burden wasn't shortening his temper (he once threw my largest frying pan the length of the kitchen, by some miracle missing everybody), he was serenading in Portuguese one of my cooks, a pretty girl of about twenty, with a smile of foolish rapture on his round face. Eventually, it all became too much for poor Pepe, who felt ill one day and had to lie down on the foam mattress we kept for my then manager, who also had a bad back (yes, what a pantomime). I drove him home. Next day he didn't show up so I went to find him. He had had a heart attack and died; at least he was in hospital, with someone to look after him and, I hope, wearing his foolish smile.

Puddings, ice creams and cakes

Apple and Almond Pudding with Calvados Cream

This is a simple nursery sort of pud but, Harry Potter-like, it can be eaten very happily by grown-ups, especially with the Calvados cream. You can alter the proportions of sponge to apple if you like: here the top is about twice the thickness of the apple base. Just add more apples if you wish. The sponge is also good on its own, flavoured with vanilla or orange rind.

Gluten-free

500g Bramley apples, peeled, cored and
    roughly chopped
50g soft brown sugar
100g soft butter
100g caster sugar
2 eggs, beaten
100g ground almonds
double or whipping cream
Calvados
caster sugar

Preheat the oven to 350°F/180°C/Gas 4.

Stew the apples with the brown sugar, covered, until they make a soft purée. Uncover, and boil off some of the moisture, stirring from time to time, for 5 minutes. Remove to a baking or gratin dish. In a bowl cream together the butter and caster sugar until pale, light and fluffy. Beat in the eggs little by little. Fold in the almonds. Spread the mixture over the apples and bake for about an hour.

Whip some cream until semi-stiff. Stir in some Calvados then enough caster sugar to balance the rough edge of the Calvados. Serve the pudding warm.

Seville Orange Pudding

It is a shame that the Seville orange (which these days seems to come mainly from Cyprus and Sicily) has such a short season, as its tangential relationship to the sweet orange (like the lime to the lemon) can offer interesting variations on familiar themes. It can be used successfully in Sussex Pond Pudding, in marinades for hare, wild duck, and venison, in ceviches and indeed as a substitute for limes in salsas and syrups.

This is one of those sponge puddings that forms its own sauce at the bottom of the dish. Very easy to make.

Serves 4–6

85g soft butter
225g caster sugar
grated rind and juice of 3 Seville oranges
5 large eggs, separated
50g plain flour, sifted
280ml milk

Preheat the oven to 350°F/180°C/Gas 4. Butter a 20cm soufflé dish.

Cream the butter in a bowl with an electric beater (or in the food processor), gradually adding the sugar. When the mixture is very pale, add the orange rind (if the oranges are difficult to grate, remove the peel thinly with a potato peeler or very sharp knife and chop finely), the juice, then the egg yolks one by one. Don't worry if the mixture curdles. Beat in the flour alternating with tablespoons of the milk. Beat the egg whites until stiff and fold into the orange mixture. Decant into the dish and place the dish in a roasting tin. Pour boiling water to come halfway up the side of the dish and bake for about 50 minutes. Serve hot or warm.

Steamed Maple Pecan Pudding

Steamed puds have enjoyed a revival over the last three or four years, some of them a world away from the syrup puds of childhood, but all showing the inevitable contrast of airy sponge with sticky sauce. This is a very good one from across the pond.

Serves 6–8

150g unsalted butter
150g soft dark brown sugar
3 eggs
a large pinch of salt
1 tsp vanilla extract
225g self-raising flour
50ml milk
110g pecan nuts, roasted and roughly
    chopped
70ml maple syrup, and more for serving

Butter and sugar a 1kg basin.

Cream together the butter and sugar until light and fluffy, then mix in the eggs; add the salt and vanilla extract. Sift the flour and beat in, followed by the milk and half the nuts. Cover the bottom of the basin with the maple syrup and the remaining nuts. Pour the mixture on top, cover with a greaseproof lid, place inside a large saucepan containing 2cm simmering water, and steam for about 1¾ hours. Keep an eye on the water level. Serve with more maple syrup (both butterscotch or chocolate sauce would also go well). Cream too if you like.

Pithiviers

There are probably thousands of delicious, eponymously named cakes, sweet tarts and biscuits to be found throughout the small towns of France, but very few of them seem to have crossed the Channel. Perhaps pithiviers owes its presence here to the proselytizing of Jane Grigson, who wrote about it in her excellent book *Good Things*. She mentions a variant of the filling – frangipani – which includes a pig's kidney, added to give an interesting granular texture to the almond cream. Not an idea I've tried myself, but this straightforward, if slightly finicky, pud needs the embellishment of only brandy, rum, Kirsch and the like to justify its unparochial status. It's just puff pastry enveloping a frangipani filling, which can be used so successfully in open fruit tarts.

Serves 6–8

50g soft butter
65g caster sugar
1 large egg, beaten
½ tsp vanilla extract
1 tbsp brandy, dark rum, Grand Marnier
  (reduce the sugar a little if using),
  or Kirsch
50g ground almonds
50g plain flour, sifted
340g puff pastry
1 egg for glazing, beaten with a little water
  or milk

To serve
double or whipping cream

Cream together the butter and sugar, add the egg, vanilla extract and liqueur, then fold in the almonds and the flour. Form into a thick disc about 9cm × 4cm and refrigerate for 1 hour.

Cut the pastry crosswise into halves. On a floured board roll out into 2 squares, one about 23cm wide, the other about 24cm. Using saucepan lids or cake tins or springform tin bottoms, cut or mark out and then cut the largest possible circle from each square (a pizza wheel does this easily; a knife a bit more slowly but well enough). Put them in the fridge for 30 minutes.

Preheat the oven to 400°F/205°C/Gas 6.

Place the smaller pastry disc on baking parchment on a baking sheet. In the centre put the frangipani cake. Brush the entire exposed surface of the disc, not occupied by the cake, with water, and carefully place the larger disc of pastry on top, pressing gently from the centre outwards to avoid any air pockets forming, and then firmly press the pastry rims together. As wrinkles form in the top disc cut out narrow wedges with scissors. Above all, make sure that there is a good seal to prevent the filling from escaping.

If you wish, you can scallop the edges by placing a deep cake tin upside down over the whole thing to leave a rim of about 1cm. At 4cm intervals, press the pastry against the tin with the flat of a knife.

Brush the egg wash well all over the pastry, trying not to get any on to the parchment. With the point of a small knife, describe lines in a spiral from the centre to the edge, hitting the edge at 4cm intervals. Cut a small cross in the very centre to let any steam escape. Bake for about 50 minutes. Serve this warm (it reheats well) with whipped, sweetened cream flavoured with whatever alcohol you used in the filling.

Chocolate Praline Ice Cream

This is really a frozen mousse, but it matters not. I think this is the world's greatest ice cream, although that obsessive chap in the high Andes with his twenty-eight varieties (including chilli) might not agree. Nor have I tasted the Fisherman's Friend ice cream at El Bulli near Barcelona. My senior pastry chef, George Harvey, who has nearly earned himself a mantelpiece clock for his long service, always blanches his own almonds. You really must do the same.

Serves 6–8

Praline

100g almonds in their skins
100g sugar
3 tbsp water

Preheat the oven to 350°F/180°C/Gas 4.

Pour boiling water over the almonds and leave for 5 minutes. Remove in batches with a slotted spoon, push them out of their skins (do this in front of a wall as they tend to pop out and irritatingly skitter about the floor) and roast to golden brown. While this is going on melt the sugar in a smallish pan over heat with the water, swirling until the sugar dissolves. Boil the syrup until it just starts to smoke and turns a mid-brown colour. Add the nuts and turn the lot out on to a flat, oiled surface – preferably not the kitchen table (the back of a roasting in or a tin tray will do). Let cool for half an hour, break into bits, and pulverize in a food processor.

Ice Cream

100g sugar
4 tbsp water
2 tbsp instant coffee granules
225g bitter chocolate, broken into pieces
425ml whipping cream

To serve
double cream

Melt the sugar with the water over heat, add the coffee granules and then the chocolate. Turn the heat right down, and when the chocolate has melted remove from heat and cool.

Whip the cream until semi-stiff. Fold the cooled chocolate mixture into the cream along with all but 1 tbsp of the praline, amalgamating well. Pour into dariole moulds or ramekins and freeze. To serve, turn out, dribble some double cream over, and sprinkle with the reserved praline.

Brown Bread Ice Cream

This has always been one of my favourite ice creams, with its interesting granular texture and nutty flavours. It's essential, I think, to caramelize the breadcrumbs. It may sound unduly pernickety, but the better the bread the better the bread-crumbs. You could serve a strawberry, raspberry or chocolate sauce, white or dark, with this, but it doesn't really need it.

6 egg yolks
125g caster sugar
425ml single cream, or single cream and milk
1 vanilla pod
75g brown breadcrumbs
10g butter
1 tbsp sweet sherry or Madeira

In a bowl whisk the egg yolks and 50g of the sugar until pale and mousse-like. Meanwhile, bring the cream or cream and milk to the boil with the vanilla pod. Remove the pod and pour the cream on to the egg mixture, whisking hard. Pour back into the saucepan and heat again, whisking hard, until it thickens. Don't overheat – stop as soon as you see the mixture starting to bubble. Pour into a freezer container.

Fry the breadcrumbs in the butter until crisp, sprinkle the rest of the sugar over them evenly and heat until the sugar starts to caramelize. Remove from the pan and let cool completely. If you've made the breadcrumbs in the processor, return them and run the motor for a few seconds. Otherwise crush with a rolling pin. Mix into the cream mixture, add the sherry or Madeira, and freeze. The air trapped in the mixture will prevent the ice cream from becoming rock-like and an enemy to spoons. Still, it's not a bad idea to let it soften in the fridge for 20 minutes before serving.

Never-a-Failure Cake

An unorthodox recipe which is guaranteed to work – its name an implicit rebuke to those recipes that look good on paper, but *don't* work. The origin of this one is lost in the mists of time, or at least in my mother-in-law's memory, but the important thing is that it's very good, easy and quick, and will work equally well warm as a pudding with cream or custard or as a cake that keeps well.

450g mixed fruit, including a decent amount of cut mixed peel and diced unsulphured apricots; if you like glacé ginger put some of that in too
200 ml water
225g caster sugar
110g butter

2 eggs, beaten
1 tsp ground mixed spice
½ tsp bicarbonate of soda
275g self-raising flour

Preheat the oven to 325°F/160°C/Gas 3. Grease a 20cm cake tin and put a buttered disc of greaseproof paper in the bottom.

Put the first 4 ingredients in a saucepan and boil gently, stirring, for 4 minutes. Remove from the heat, pour into a large bowl and cool for 10 minutes. Stir in the eggs. Sift together on to the mixture the spice, bicarbonate, and flour, and mix in thoroughly. Spoon into the cake tin and bake for 1½ hours. Turn off the oven, open the door and leave for 10 more minutes, then allow to cool before turning out.

Semolina and Almond Cake

This is a moist cake with a fine flavour of almonds and lemon. Sandwich it with whipped cream folded into home-made lemon curd, or crème pâtissière with more chopped toasted almonds or almond praline (see chocolate praline ice cream, page 185) folded into it. Alternatively, drizzle over it a chocolate glaze.

3 large eggs, separated
125g caster sugar
125g blanched almonds, lightly toasted and finely ground (see below)
100g semolina flour
1 heaped tsp grated lemon rind
1 tbsp lemon juice
a pinch of salt
orange juice (if necessary)
50g bitter chocolate, chopped
12g butter

Preheat the oven to 375°F/190°C/Gas 5; butter 2 20cm cake tins and put a circle of buttered baking parchment or tinfoil at the bottom of each.

In a bowl beat the egg yolks and sugar until thick and pale, about 3 minutes. Stir in the almonds, semolina flour, lemon rind and lemon juice. In another bowl beat the egg whites and the salt to stiff peaks and carefully fold into the batter. Add orange juice to loosen the batter if necessary – if it's too thick it will be difficult to fold in the egg whites without knocking the air out of them.

Divide the batter between the tins and bake for about 40 minutes. Test with a skewer, which should come out clean. To bake a whole cake, use a 23cm springform tin, buttered and lined, and cook for 10 minutes longer.

For the glaze melt the chocolate and butter together in a small pan, and pour over the cake.

Omelette Soufflée

Paperback cookery books aren't really designed to last twenty years or more if they have any sort of usage, but my copy of Elizabeth David's *French Provincial Cooking* is now brown, wrinkled and infirm, the pages held together by a corset of elastic bands, and threatening to collapse altogether when its stays are removed. Plenty has been written over the years about its influence on the eating habits and attitudes of the nation, and it certainly had an effect on me – someone with the zeal of the recent convert – in its pictures of a country where the pleasures of the table rose above all others.

Oddly enough I didn't cook much from it, but refer to it still for its picture of a vanished world, emphasized by ED's own inclusion of cameos from what was to her the fairly distant, but not remote, past – Escoffier on a shooting weekend in Haute Savoie, a glimpse into a bourgeois household of the 1870s, cooking the same things that ED was herself encountering on her travels around France – but I can remember now how impressed I was at her recipe for potage bonne femme. This couldn't be any more straightforward: potatoes, carrots, leeks, water, and some butter. Furthermore, the carrots aren't even essential. I was deeply impressed that something so apparently banal could have so much flavour. This woman really knows her stuff, I thought, and still do, in spite of our problem with the duck (page 144).

This dish is also simple but you have to pay attention in the cooking or you will end up with a delicious but shapeless mess. It is something that has to be done just before it is eaten, so it will take you away from the table for five minutes, but the result is spectacular. You can use different alcohols to flavour it, but I think Grand Marnier is best.

You will need a large frying pan you can put in the oven, preferably a 25cm or 30cm heavy steel pan, but a non-stick one will do.

Serves 2 or 3

3 large eggs, separated
3 tbsp caster sugar
grated rind of 1 orange
2 tbsp Grand Marnier
15g butter

Preheat the oven to 450°F/230°C/Gas 8.

Put the egg yolks in a bowl about 20cm in diameter and the whites in a large bowl – copper if you have it, otherwise steel or glass. Using a whisk or an electric beater, beat the yolks very well with the sugar, orange rind and Grand Marnier, until the mixture has thickened and become pale, and the sugar has dissolved. Quickly wash the beaters, dry them thoroughly, and whip the egg whites until they stand in stiffish peaks. With a rubber spatula scrape the egg yolk mixture on to the egg whites and fold them together, cutting down through the middle, and up the sides and over, turning the bowl slightly with each stroke.

While you are doing this, heat an ovenproof frying pan, a large flat dish and 2 or 3 plates. The pan must be pretty hot but not so hot that the butter burns. In other words, put in the butter, which should foam and splutter straightaway. It's essential that the butter covers every inch of the pan rim to facilitate turning the thing out. Do this by tipping the pan, or better by using a pastry brush. This should ensure the omelette doesn't stick. A few seconds after the foam has died down, pour in all the mixture, shake the pan, and leave it over the heat for about 30 seconds. Remove from the heat and put in the hot oven for 1 minute to heat and set the upper part of the omelette. Remove from the oven and slide half the omelette out of the pan on to the large, flat dish, folding the rest over the top. Divide between the plates using a fish slice or something similar. Wow!

Peanut Butter Cheesecake

Quick, easy, and irresistible to children (mine, anyway).

Serves 8–10

50g butter
10 digestive biscuits (bought or home-made, see page 217)
150ml whipping cream
225g cream cheese
110g icing sugar
150g smooth peanut butter
½ tsp vanilla extract

Melt the butter, crush the biscuits and mix together. Press them evenly into a 22cm springform or loose-bottomed cake tin. Half whip the cream – until soft peaks but not stiff – and set aside. Using a food processor or a wooden spoon beat the cream cheese and sugar well until light. In a separate bowl cream the peanut butter until very light, then fold the two mixtures together. Add the vanilla extract and fold in the half-whipped cream.

Transfer to the cake tin and smooth the top. Refrigerate for several hours, run a knife blade between the cheesecake and the tin, and remove to a large plate.

Light Lemon Cheesecake

I first served this at Blandford Street. When George arrived in the pastry kitchen there he thought we would be different – not better, mind you, but different – which is why we do things like the peanut butter one now . . . This is a kind of spiritually pure cheesecake, as it hasn't any gelatine, and could be the better for it.

Serves 10

175g unsalted butter
10 digestive biscuits, bought or home-made (page 217)
150g caster sugar
3 large eggs, separated
finely grated rind and strained juice of 2 lemons
200g light cream cheese, softened
300ml whipping cream
icing sugar

To serve
orange segments macerated in caramel sauce

Preheat the oven to 350°F/180°C/Gas 4. Cover the bottom of a 22cm springform tin with greaseproof paper.

Melt 50g of the butter, crush the biscuits and mix together. Press them evenly into the tin. Cream the remaining butter and the sugar together until light and fluffy. Beat in the egg yolks, lemon rind and juice and cream cheese. Whip the cream until it just holds its shape; whisk the egg whites until stiff and fold both into the cheese mixture. Pour into the tin, and chill for at least 2 hours.

Unmould the cheesecake from the tin. Dust with icing sugar and cut into serving size sections. Serve with the orange segments.

Butternut Squash and Cornmeal Cake

This is a recipe I've borrowed from our friend Vicky Jones, who wrote an excellent book called *Dordogne Gastronomique* and is the guiding spirit behind (of all things) the Abergavenny Food Festival. Always on the lookout for good gluten-free recipes, I jumped on this one because it's such a good vehicle for butternut squash, and mercifully a fair distance away from pumpkin pie. My small daughter loves this in her school lunchbox. It's very easy and the rum-soaked raisins give it a grown-up appeal. Its Périgourdine name is milassou, and prunes are sometimes used instead of raisins. Soaking them in some Armagnac sounds a nice idea, too. The alcohol, by the way, can be dissipated by heating it with the fruit, leaving the flavour behind. You probably knew that.

If you want to use this as a pud, serve warm with orange custard or non-flavoured sweetened cream.

Serves 6

2 tbsp rum
50g raisins
280g butternut squash, peeled, seeded, and cut
    into pieces
150ml milk
40g butter
100g polenta flour or fine polenta
75g caster sugar
1 tsp vanilla extract
2 large eggs, separated

Warm the rum and soak the raisins in it for 1 hour.

Preheat the oven to 400°F/205°C/Gas 6. Butter a 22cm cake tin and to be on the safe side put a buttered disc of greaseproof paper in the bottom.

Cook the squash in the milk until it's soft and purée them together. Transfer to a bowl and stir in the butter, polenta flour or polenta, sugar, and vanilla extract and mix well. Beat in the egg yolks with the raisins and rum.

In a separate bowl whisk the egg whites until stiff and, using a rotary motion, starting in the centre and turning the bowl a little each time, fold them in. Pour the mixture into the tin and bake in the middle of the oven until lightly browned – about 25 minutes. Cool in the tin a little before turning out. Serve it whichever way up you prefer. It's better eaten warm, I think.

Nasty Moments: 3

I was giving a speech one afternoon to a conference of chefs (yes, chefs do have them too), as it happened on the process of opening a restaurant. This was not long after I started in Marylebone. I thought I would find out how lunch service had gone so I rang at 2.30 p.m. Everything had been fine, apart from a couple of things. Apparently no fish had been delivered, as the delivery van had broken down in Lewisham. Fish dishes were therefore reduced to one, which ran out at 1.15. The kitchen ventilator fan had come loose from its mounting and had vibrated so hard that the screw-in bulbs lighting the customers' loos had all fallen out, plunging the basement into darkness. A customer on table twenty, who had perhaps been marooned in the gents, or was simply horrified by his lunch, had some kind of seizure and collapsed on the floor. As if that wasn't enough, two of my hand-picked female staff had had a falling out and had started hitting each other as the first customers arrived.

Suddenly it seemed rather frivolous to be making a speech at a conference – I should have been back at the restaurant, taking charge. Then nothing like that would have happened, would it?

Chocolate, tarts and fruit

Chocolate Cake

How many chocolate cakes are there? Do we need another? Maybe not, but this is worth a try, as it's another straightforward recipe that tastes very good, keeps well and strikes that happy note between being moreish and cloying. Furthermore my young daughter can eat it; she calls it 'black cake'. It's fine on its own, too.

Gluten-free

100g butter
150g good dark chocolate
100g caster sugar
4 eggs, separated
1 tsp vanilla extract
50g potato flour or cornflour
1 tsp baking powder
a pinch of salt
filling: raspberry jam and stiffly whipped
    cream, or chocolate buttercream (below)

Preheat the oven to 350°F/180°C/Gas 4; butter a deep 20cm or 23cm cake tin, and line it with buttered greaseproof paper.

Melt the butter and chocolate over hot water in a large bowl. Add the sugar, egg yolks and vanilla extract, and remove from the heat. Sift and fold in the potato flour or cornflour and baking powder.

Beat the egg whites with the salt until stiff and fold into the batter, cutting down from the centre to the edges in a circular motion, turning the bowl a little with each fold. Keep folding until there are no flecks of white left. Pour into the tin and bake until it has risen well and a skewer comes out clean, about 40 minutes.

Let cool and turn out upside down. This cake makes a regular shape, but the top may need a slight levelling (with a sharp knife) before turning it over to become a neat cylinder. Slice in half and fill with the jam and cream, or this simple buttercream.

Buttercream

50g plain chocolate
2 egg yolks
50g icing sugar, sifted
170g butter, softened

Melt the chocolate in a large mixing bowl over hot water, and add all the other ingredients. Beat with an electric whisk for about 4 minutes, until smooth and creamy.

Alternatively, simply melt together 100g chocolate, 50g butter and 1 tbsp rum, brandy or Grand Marnier, and pour over the cake.

Chocolate and Hazelnut Tart

This is a recipe developed over the years by my long-suffering and peerless pastry chef, George Harvey, who is the most reliable person I know – in all the ten years he has worked at my Blandford Street restaurant, I've never known him serve anything that wasn't as good as it should have been. In a lesser person this would look like perfectionism bordering on the obsessional, but with George it is as normal as getting from Land's End to John O'Groats (he cycles for charity). Too good to be true, really.

This is a more elaborate variant of the Chocolate Mousse Tart in Orange Hazelnut Pastry (page 195) and is worth the little extra effort. The pastry is very buttery, and needs to be worked quickly, but is very good-tempered, too; patching together if it breaks up won't hurt, and it doesn't shrink. Use plenty of flour on your rolling-out surface and keep turning the pastry. If it breaks up, put it in the freezer on a flat surface for a few minutes, and try again. This quantity of pastry makes two shells; if you halve the quantities you'd do better to make the pastry by hand.

Pastry

85g butter, cold, cut into small pieces
45g sugar
40g ground almonds
110g plain flour
a pinch of salt (if using unsalted butter)
1 egg yolk
1 tbsp cold water

Preheat the oven to 350°F/180°C/Gas 4.

Place the first five ingredients in the bowl of a food processor and run the motor until the mixture resembles breadcrumbs. Add the egg yolk and water and run again until the dough adheres in a lump.

Refrigerate for a few minutes. Roll out quickly on a well-floured board and line a 2cm high 20cm flan ring, or a 23cm shallower ring. Bake the pastry case blind as in the courgette tart recipe (page 87), but take it out when just beginning to brown. Remove from the oven and cool a little.

Filling

110g hazelnuts
110g light brown muscovado sugar
2 tsp vanilla extract
2 eggs and 1 egg yolk
50g butter
110g good dark chocolate
1 tbsp brandy or rum (optional)

To serve
raspberries or cream (see below)

Roast the hazelnuts until the skins start to flake and the nuts are a light golden brown. Rub off the skins in a tea towel. Put them in a food-processor bowl with the sugar, 1 tsp of the vanilla and 1 whole egg. Run the motor for 1 minute. Scrape out the mixture into the pastry shell, level it, and bake again (at the same temperature) for about 12 minutes, until the mixture is firmish.

Meanwhile, melt together the butter and chocolate in a bowl over hot water. When amalgamated add the second egg and the yolk with the remaining vanilla extract (with the alcohol if you want it – the tart is pretty rich and good without) and whisk with electric beaters or a spiral whisk until pale and thick – about 3 minutes using the former. Spread this on top of the hazelnut layer and return to the oven for about 15 minutes. It will puff up slightly and sink as it cools. This is really good with raspberries in one guise or another, but cream alone would do fine.

Chocolate Mousse Tart in Hazelnut Orange Pastry

I make no apology for including two chocolate tarts, as they are different enough from each other to justify an appearance. This one is more straightforward, and contains for me the best chocolate mousse mixture of all the variants, made with butter, eggs and cream – as it should be. This mixture is stiff enough to slice if poured into a loaf tin – double or treble the quantities accordingly, and serve with a proper custard flavoured with an orange liqueur or brandy. Remember to slice with a hot knife if using it this way.

Serves 6

Pastry

65g ground hazelnuts (to grind your own, toast under the grill or roast in the oven until a light golden brown and the skins start to flake off, rub together in a tea towel and grind in a food processor or coffee mill)
110g plain flour
50g butter, cold, cut into small pieces
1 tbsp caster sugar
grated rind and juice of 1 orange
a large pinch of salt

Preheat the oven to 375°F/190°C/Gas 5.

Put all the ingredients except the orange juice into the food-processor bowl and run the motor for about 7 seconds. Remove to a large bowl and, using a wooden spoon, mix in enough of the orange juice to make a firm dough. Be careful not to make it too wet. It is helpful to use your hands to amalgamate all the loose bits into the main mass, rather than adding more moisture and beating with the spoon; better the dough is too dry than too wet though if it is too dry it will be difficult to roll and if too wet it will become leathery.

Flatten the dough into a thick disc about 12cm across and refrigerate for 20 minutes. This should make it easier to roll into a circle. Now roll it out to fit a 20 or 23cm flan ring. Bake blind as in the courgette tart recipe (page 87). Set aside to cool completely.

Filling

150g dark chocolate
50g butter
1 tsp instant coffee granules, dissolved in 1 tsp water
2 large eggs, separated
a pinch of cream of tartar
a pinch of salt
1 tbsp caster sugar
1 tbsp orange liqueur
120ml double or whipping cream
12 skinned hazelnuts

Melt the chocolate and butter together in a medium bowl set over hot water. Stir occasionally and when melted stir in the coffee and egg yolks. In a clean, dry medium mixing bowl, whizz the egg whites with the cream of tartar and salt until soft peaks form. Sprinkle in the sugar and beat until stiff – a minute or two. Scrape the chocolate mixture on to the whites and fold together carefully, adding the liqueur, until all traces of white disappear. Scrape the whole thing into the cold tart case and smooth over the top. Refrigerate at least 2 hours before serving.

To garnish, whip the cream until semi-stiff and with a star nozzle pipe 12 small rosettes of cream around the rim of the tart, and place a hazelnut on each. Serve the rest of the cream separately.

Pleyels – Little Chocolate Cakes

This is an excellent recipe I have adapted slightly from the Maison du Chocolat in Paris. These little cakes are rich (of course) but light. You can fill the muffin holes to the brim – the mixture will spread a bit as it cooks, but is light enough to hold together nicely as it rises. The tops ought to be dome-shaped, and fissured with deepish cracks.

Gluten-free
Makes 12 little cakes

170g good dark chocolate
150g butter
4 eggs, size 3, separated
180g icing sugar
65g ground almonds
80g cornflour
1 tsp vanilla extract

Preheat the oven to 400°F/205°C/Gas 6. Butter and flour well a 12-hole muffin tin. This mixture will fill a muffin tin generously.

Melt the chocolate and the butter together in a bowl over hot water, gently stirring with a wooden spoon. Remove from the heat. Stir in the egg yolks. In a separate bowl, sift together the icing sugar and the almonds, stir into the chocolate mixture and amalgamate thoroughly. Sift the cornflour into the mixture and stir in with the vanilla extract. Beat the egg whites until stiff-peaked and fold into the mixture carefully, leaving no bits of white. Fill the muffin tin and bake for 10 minutes, then lower the heat to 350°F/180°C/Gas 4 and cook for a further 15–20 minutes. Let cool a few minutes. Run a knife around the holes and turn out.

They are really good on their own or served with cream and a simple sauce of chocolate melted in a little water.

Just about the quickest possible chocolate pud

If you happen to have a fair bit of chocolate in the cupboard and some cream in the fridge – double or whipping – and have a sudden craving, this will deal with it as well as any, and quicker than most. Not sophisticated, but very good and extremely quick. The better the chocolate, the better the result.

200g good, dark chocolate
1 tbsp instant coffee granules
50ml water
250ml whipping cream

Melt together in a saucepan, over very low heat, the chocolate, instant coffee granules and water. Pour into a bowl and cool in the freezer for 20 minutes, taking out after 10 minutes and stirring well. In another bowl, whip the cream until semi-stiff and fold into the chocolate. Don't do this thoroughly – do it halfway, leaving a pronounced ripple effect. The contrast of the chocolate with the cream is very moreish. Turn into a decent serving dish and leave to set in the fridge for half an hour. If you like, sprinkle with chopped, toasted almonds. You could substitute brandy or an orange liqueur for some of the water.

Chocolate and Dried Fruit Brownies

I know there are plenty of brownie recipes around, because in the search for the perfect example I think I've tried most of them. These meet the chewy criterion head on, and are dense with chocolate flavour, but the addition of the raisins, sultanas and candied peel makes these, for me, transcend the best. I'm not too keen on nuts in brownies, unless they are roasted, as in the next recipe. They would be OTT here. Another good thing about this recipe is the way the mix can go straight on to the foil – no buttering and flouring to bother with.

Gluten-free
Makes 12–15

75g butter
225g caster sugar
3 heaped tbsp cocoa – the best you can find
50g rice flour
1 tsp baking powder
100g mixed fruit, with a good proportion of peel
2 eggs, beaten
½ tsp vanilla extract

Preheat the oven to 350°F/180°C/Gas 4.

Melt the butter. In a large bowl mix together the sugar, cocoa, flour, baking powder, and fruit. Mix in the eggs, vanilla extract and melted butter. Line a 20 cm × 23 cm tin with foil (no need to butter it) and scrape in the mixture. Bake for 30 minutes. Cool in the tin, remove, and cut into squares.

Chocolate Brownie Thins

In a way these aren't true brownies, as they are too thin to have a chewy middle and crisp outside – they're more like an American cookie in texture. We developed these to go on a plate of mixed chocolate puds and they are better than you might think – given the chocolate element is provided by cocoa.

Makes 16–20

115g hazelnuts
250g butter
85g cocoa powder
4 eggs
425g sugar
85g plain flour
¼ tbsp vanilla extract
icing sugar

Preheat the oven to 350°F/180°C/Gas 4; line two Swiss roll tins (or a flat-bottomed roasting tin would do) with buttered baking parchment.

Roast the hazelnuts until the skins start to flake and the nuts are a light golden brown. Rub off the skins in a tea towel and process for a few seconds with the metal blade of your food processor. Melt the butter with the cocoa, then beat the eggs and sugar together, and amalgamate the two mixtures. Add the flour, vanilla extract, and nuts, pour into the tins, and bake for between 15 and 20 minutes. When cool, cut into squares and dust a diagonal half of each square with icing sugar. Serve with the chocolate praline ice cream on page 185.

Chocolate Chip Macaroons

These are halfway between macaroons and meringues, and can be turned into a pretty rich and luxurious pudding quite easily by sandwiching around hazelnut, praline or coffee buttercream.

Gluten-free
Makes about 12

100g blanched almonds
5 tbsp caster sugar
37g dark chocolate, grated
3 egg whites at room temperature
¼ tsp vanilla extract

Preheat the oven to 350°F/180°C/Gas 4; line a baking sheet with buttered foil or baking parchment.

Grind the almonds in batches with the sugar in a spice grinder (for preference) or a food processor, and mix with the chocolate in a large bowl. Whisk the egg whites until they hold soft peaks, and fold into the mixture along with the vanilla.

Using a piping bag, pipe out circles about 5 cm across and 2 cm apart (you can, of course, use a spoon but the shapes won't be so regular). Bake for 25 minutes. Slide the foil on to a rack and let them cool.

Chocolate Soufflés

A recipe to win over anyone intimidated by the mystique of the soufflé myth. These are useful for a supper party as they are very easy to make, requiring about 10 minutes' absence from the table and a further 10 minutes' cooking. They have the authentic smack of chocolate truth, underlined by the sympathetic resonance of Grand Marnier. These are made in individual ramekins (200 ml). Use a bigger dish (1.2 litre) if you want, but cook for 20 minutes longer.

Serves 6

butter for greasing
50g caster sugar
110g good dark chocolate, chopped
4 eggs, separated, and 3 egg whites
2 tbsp Grand Marnier
juice of ½ a lemon

To serve
double cream

Butter well 6 ramekins and dust with about half the sugar. Do this in advance and place in the fridge. Preheat the oven to 400°F/205°C/Gas 6.

Melt the chocolate in a metal bowl over just simmering water. Remove from the heat and stir in the egg yolks and Grand Marnier. In a large bowl whisk all 7 egg whites to hold soft peaks. Whisk in the lemon juice and the rest of the sugar, and continue whisking until they are stiff and still very shiny. Scrape the chocolate mixture on to the whites and fold together well until all white flecks have gone. Fill the ramekins with the mixture, place on a hot baking sheet, and bake for 10 minutes. Serve with double cream separately to pour into the middles.

Pecan Butter Tart

Of all the pecan tart recipes I have tried and tasted, this is the best. Jon Bentham, a very talented chef who has worked with me on and off over the years, gave me the recipe. I don't know where he acquired it, but it must have been a distant ancestor who settled in the Carolinas, as this tart is much admired by Americans, and has been published in *Bon Appetit*.

When we serve it we cut a thinnish wedge, as it is so rich, and accompany it with a ball of Bourbon or coffee ice cream. Plain cream is fine too.

Serves 10

Pastry

230g plain flour
a pinch of salt
30g caster sugar
155g unsalted butter, chilled and diced
1 egg yolk, size 2, mixed with 1 tbsp icy water

Preheat the oven to 400°F/205°C/Gas 6; you will need a 25.5cm loose-based deep flan tin or spring-form tin.

Sift the flour, salt and sugar into the food-processor bowl, add the butter and process until the mixture resembles fine crumbs. With the machine running add the egg and water mixture through the feed tube. Run the machine until the dough comes together in a ball. It should be soft but not sticky. If this hasn't happened after a minute and there are dry crumbs, add more water, 1 tsp at a time. Wrap and chill for 15 minutes.

On a floured work surface, roll out the dough to a circle about 33cm in diameter, and line the tin. Prick the bottom of the pastry case all over with a fork, then chill for 10 minutes. Bake the pastry case blind as in the recipe for Courgette Tart (page 87), then leave to cool while making the filling. Reduce the oven temperature to 300°F/150°C/Gas 2.

Filling

280g dark muscovado sugar
230g unsalted butter
170g maple syrup
170g Golden Syrup
5 eggs, size 2
1 tsp vanilla extract
170g raisins
500g pecan nuts, roughly chopped

Put the sugar, butter and syrups into a large saucepan and bring to the boil. Cook over moderate heat for 5 minutes, stirring frequently to prevent sticking, then remove from the heat and set aside. Put the eggs into a large bowl and beat well, then stir in the vanilla extract, the raisins and the nuts. When thoroughly blended, add the syrup mixture and mix well.

Pour the filling into the baked pastry case and bake for 1 hour or until the filling is fairly firm to the touch. Serve either warm or cold.

Lime Parfait

If the thought of doing complicated things with sugar makes you want to move on hastily – don't. It's not at all difficult to make this kind of meringue (Italian, as opposed to the more common Swiss) and apart from that this recipe is a breeze. Not only that, but you can make it with any really tart fruit – blackcurrants, damsons and passion fruit are particularly delicious and good to look at.

> 6 limes – juicy ones (you may need one or two
>   more if not very juicy)
> 200g caster sugar
> 6 tbsp water
> a pinch of salt
> ⅛ tsp cream of tartar
> 6 egg whites
> green colouring (optional)

Line a 1kg loaf tin with clingfilm. Have a bowl of iced water ready.

Wash and dry the limes and grate as much of the zest as you can, concentrating on the dark green areas (and don't grate the bitter pith). Squeeze out the juice into a small bowl. Put the sugar and water into a saucepan and bring slowly to a boil, swirling the pan occasionally. When the sugar has melted and the water is clear, reduce to a simmer. Add salt and the cream of tartar to the egg whites and beat until they stand in stiff peaks. By this time the sugar should be at the soft ball stage (238°F on a sugar thermometer if you have one); boil the sugar rapidly and as the bubbles thicken use a teaspoon to drop the syrup into the bowl of iced water: at the right temperature the sugar will form into malleable droplets in the water.

Slowly pour the hot syrup on to the egg whites, beating constantly, until all the syrup is used up. Continue beating until the mixture is cold (this is easier with a stand mixer); but you could carry out the lime squeezing now, alternating with beating the egg whites. If you stand the egg white bowl in a larger bowl of iced water, you'll save about 5 minutes. Once cool, fold in the lime juice and zest. Add more lime juice (or lemon, if you've run out of limes), as this parfait stands or falls by its sweet–tart balance. Gently fold in a few drops of green colouring – you don't have to but these will make the finished article a delectable, translucent green.

Pour the mixture into the tin, tapping it a couple of times to settle it, and freeze. Stir 2 or 3 times while it is freezing. Unmould, remove the clingfilm, and slice. Crumbly biscuits or shortbread would finish it off beautifully.

Orange and Caramel Trifle

The trouble with a good trifle is that one helping just isn't enough, and as it is one of the most filling dishes known to man, this can lead to a condition of extreme seam-stretching. Nor, in its magnificence, is it something to eat all the time. Perhaps one day a month should be set aside as Trifle Day, when it becomes the entire contents of supper . . . with perhaps a salad of spinach sprinkled with Brewers' Yeast as a sop to one's conscience.

No doubt everyone has a favourite kind: orange and caramel is mine. Any trifle, of course, will benefit from being made with the best ingredients. This one can be made with ordinary wheatflour, but the rice flour improves the sponge (which is a classic génoise).

Gluten-free
Serves 6

For the sponge cake

3 eggs
80g caster sugar
½ tsp vanilla extract
75g rice flour, sifted

Preheat the oven to 350°F/180°C/Gas 4; line 2 20cm shallow cake tins with buttered and floured foil or non-stick baking paper.

In a bowl over hot water beat the eggs with the sugar and vanilla extract for 3–4 minutes until the mixture is pale and has at least trebled in volume. Fold the flour, half at a time, into the mixture gently but thoroughly. Divide between the tins and bake for about 25 minutes. Cool and remove.

Pastry cream

40g caster sugar
3 egg yolks
50g rice flour, sifted
300ml milk, heated to boiling
½ tsp vanilla extract
1½ tbsp orange liqueur
150ml whipping or double cream

In a mixing bowl gradually beat the sugar with the egg yolks and continue beating until the mixture is pale and forms an unbroken stream when the beaters are lifted a few centimetres above it. Beat in the flour and gradually beat in the milk. Pour the mixture back into the hot pan and place over a medium to high heat. Now beat with a wire whisk,

covering all the bottom of the pan, until the mixture boils. Whisk for a couple more minutes (rice flour loses its rawness quicker than wheatflour), add the vanilla extract and liqueur and let cool, covered.

Whip the cream until semi-stiff and fold in to the cold custard.

Caramel

150g sugar
2 tbsp cold water
50ml warm water

Melt together the sugar and cold water, swirling the pan, and cook over moderate heat until the syrup turns a darkish brown. As soon as you see the liquid starting to smoke, pour in the warm water. Do this at arm's length, with your hand covered by a cloth, because the liquid will splutter and spit for a moment or two. Remove from the heat and let cool.

Assembling the trifle

3 large oranges
2 tbsp orange liqueur, preferably Cointreau

Squeeze the juice from 1 orange and mix with the alcohol. Remove the skin and all the pith from the others with a sharp knife and slice across very thinly. Put one of the sponge cakes, cut to fit, into the bottom of a 20cm soufflé dish or break up into a glass bowl, and sprinkle over half the juice/liqueur. Cover with half the slices of orange, drizzle with half the caramel, and cover them with half the pastry cream. The other cake goes in next, followed by the juice/liqueur, the pastry cream, the remaining oranges, and finally the rest of the caramel. Refrigerate for a few hours but serve at room temperature.

If you think a trifle isn't a trifle without toasted almonds, you can pipe some rosettes of whipped cream on top and scatter a few almonds on each.

Peaches stuffed with Macaroons

Not an ultra-sophisticated pud but extremely good. Sprinkle with more crumbled amaretti or toasted flaked almonds. Nectarines are just as good, but not so large.

Serves 6

6 large ripe peaches
1 egg yolk
50g caster sugar
100g stale macaroons or amaretti biscuits, crushed to powder
¼ tsp vanilla essence
2 pinches grated nutmeg
25g unsalted butter at room temperature

Preheat the oven to 325°F/160°C/Gas 3; butter a gratin dish.

Place the peaches in a bowl and cover with boiling water. Leave for 15 seconds then refresh in a bowl of cold water and take off the skins. Halve them and remove the stones.

Beat the egg yolk well in a small bowl and gradually add the sugar, beating until the mixture is light and fluffy. Add the macaroons or amaretti biscuits, vanilla and nutmeg, mix well, then work in the butter. Fill the cavities of half the peaches with this and cover with the rest of the peach halves, and bake for 20 minutes.

Serve hot or warm with double cream, slightly sweetened, and flavoured with vanilla essence or vanilla sugar, and the amaretti or almonds.

Peaches with Strawberry Cream

6 large, fragrant peaches
juice of ½ a lemon
110g brown sugar
1 tbsp water
110g ripe strawberries
25g or more caster sugar
1 tbsp Kirsch or orange liqueur
150ml double cream, whipped

Place the peaches in a bowl and cover with boiling water. Leave for 15 seconds, then remove to a bowl of cold water. Peel off the skins, halve and cut into thickish slices. Toss gently with the lemon juice.

In a small saucepan combine the sugar and water. Bring gently to the boil, swirling the pan to dissolve the sugar. As soon as it boils pour it over the peaches, scraping the pan with a rubber spatula. Cover and chill.

Purée the strawberries with the caster sugar and alcohol. Fold into the cream and chill 1–2 hours. Spoon over the peaches just before serving. Serve with shortbread too if you like.

Strawberries with Cointreau Cream

Peter Langan used to serve these at Odins in the summer as part of his rather perfunctory pudding menu – the serious business of eating having been completed by then; any puds were there, I felt, as rather a sop to the namby-pamby. Even the (at the time) rather admired 'Mrs Langan's chocolate pudding' was a bit of a cop-out, consisting simply of beaten egg white folded into creamed egg yolks, sugar and cocoa, baked, and sandwiched with whipped cream. Chocolate sauce was then applied. On the other hand, you could say it was a neat and economical answer to the 'What kind of chocolate pud?' question.

This is another simple recipe that works well and shows the affinity strawberries have with orange.

Take any number of ripe strawberries, washed, patted dry and hulled, place them in one layer on a roasting tray and sprinkle fairly generously with caster sugar. Chill for a few hours. Whip some double or whipping cream until semi-stiff and fold in the pink strawberry juice that will have appeared. Add some Cointreau (Grand Marnier is OK but sweeter) to taste – 1 tbsp to 150 ml cream is about right, and sweeten further if you like. Serve the strawberries in bowls with the cream on top.

Marinated Figs

We can't all be lucky enough to eat figs straight from the tree, as I could in my south London garden. This rather pleasant experience was mitigated by the small production, which in a good year would supply about enough for this pudding. Look for figs which are purple-black in colour. They have a long season in southern Europe so should be easily available throughout the summer.

12 ripe fresh figs, quartered then halved
½ tsp ground cinnamon
1 tbsp grated orange rind
4 tbsp brandy
4 tbsp medium or sweet sherry
2 tsp (or less) caster sugar
300 ml double or whipping cream
2 tbsp toasted almonds

Place the figs in a large bowl. Mix together the next five ingredients, easing up on the sugar if using sweet sherry, and fold the figs in the mixture carefully but thoroughly. Cover with clingfilm and refrigerate for a couple of hours or more. Whip the cream to soft peak stage and fold in the marinade juices. Divide the figs between 4 bowls, pour over the cream and sprinkle with toasted almonds.

Unmoulded Mango Soufflé, Brunoise of Fruit

This is rather a tricky dish, but if you have the bottle for it, it's worth a try. The tricky part is the unmoulding: you need to make sure that the soufflé mixture has cooked through otherwise the top half might fall off when you turn it out.

Serves 6

1 large ripe mango
2 tsp lime juice
2 tsp caster sugar and more for dusting the
    moulds
2 egg whites
a pinch of salt

Preheat the oven to 400°F/205°C/Gas 6. Butter and sugar very well 6 dariole moulds or large ramekins, rims included, and refrigerate.

Peel the mango (easiest with a swivel-bladed peeler) and remove the flesh from around the stone, avoiding the fibrous centre as much as possible. Purée in the bowl of a food processor. Remove to a medium-sized bowl, mix in well the lime juice and 2 tsp of the sugar. Whisk the egg whites in a large bowl with the salt until they make stiff peaks. With a rubber spatula scrape the mango purée on to the whites and fold together using a rotary motion, cutting down from the centre, turning the bowl a little with each fold. Divide the mixture between the moulds, place on a baking sheet and bake for about 15 minutes until well risen.

Sauce

75g caster sugar
75 ml water
8 ripe strawberries
1 ripe papaya
1 tbsp Kirsch, brandy or orange liqueur
3 wrinkled passion fruit
lemon juice

Boil together the sugar and water for 5 minutes and let it cool a little. While the soufflés are cooking (you can make the sauce beforehand of course, but heat it up to serve) hull the strawberries and peel and deseed the papaya. Chop both into very small dice. Add the diced fruit to the syrup with the alcohol. Cut the passion fruit in half and scrape the contents into the saucepan. Add a good squeeze of lemon juice.

Unmould the soufflés as best you can by up-ending the contents of the moulds on to warmed plates. This isn't an exact science, but should be easy enough to do as long as the soufflés are cooked through. Pour the warm sauce over and serve.

Cold Lemon Soufflé

This is a pretty retro dish but doesn't deserve to be forgotten as, along with lemon curd, I think it takes its place at the top of the lemon pudding list. Making this is also a good way to hone your skills at folding in beaten egg whites. The lemons must have firm, slightly rough skins; if firm but smooth you won't be able to grate the zest so easily.

Serves 6–8

3 large eggs, separated
500g caster sugar
grated rind and strained juice of 2½ lemons
12g gelatine
275 ml double cream

Place the egg yolks, sugar, and lemon rind and juice in a medium saucepan and whisk over low heat until thick. Remove from the heat into a large bowl and whisk until cold. Put the gelatine to dissolve in 70 ml water, over very low heat, and stir in. Half whip the cream and fold in. Chill the mixture, checking that it doesn't set too firmly to accept the egg whites; it should be on the point of setting. Stiffly beat the egg whites. With a large metal spoon place a good spoonful on the centre of the mixture, and, with a rotary motion, cut down through the whites to the bottom of the dish, bringing some of the mixture up and over them. Turn the bowl about 5 cm, and repeat the motion. Carry on until the white flecks have all disappeared. If you do this with a firm but light touch your finished soufflé will be – well, a gossamer cloud springs to mind. Lemon-flavoured, of course. Refrigerate for at least 2 hours. For an old-fashioned look, tie a strip of foil or greaseproof around the top of a soufflé dish to project upwards by 2–3 cm. When set peel off. Either way, serve with buttery shortbreads.

Snares and Pitfalls of Menu Writing

In the dim, dark days of long ago when windows meant glazed openings you looked out of, I used to hand write my menus. Interrupted at the wrong moment I wrote, I found out later, 'crab salad with marinated customers' instead of 'cucumbers', something which I would like to have done to a few, then spitted them and roast over a slow flame. But more of that later.

This sort of picturesque boob is less likely to happen in updating a file in a PC, but the increasingly polyglot character of cooking in Britain, even when its horizons are only European, can flummox those toiling over the keyboard even if they are literate enough otherwise. I must be one of the few people who regret the arrival of the spellchecker, not because it's helpful with menu-speak, but because it steals my thunder: the one area of human endeavour in which I really shine, and can thus generate awe and respect from my staff (perhaps we'd better forget the awe bit), is menu spelling, and not just in English, but French and Italian too. There's no point in being falsely modest about this because it's not much of a claim, coming into the category of knack, about on a par with being able to ride a penny-farthing (what dat?). And it has absolutely no market value at all. However, it does mean that I'm better at it than anyone else around me, which occasionally (about twice a day) can be useful.

There are quite a lot of sneaky words lurking in the modern vocabulary of the menu and I'm surprised there isn't a dedicated menu-writing spellchecker. (Hey – that may be my big chance after all. Must speak with my agent. Must find an agent.) The biggest danger seems to be the doubling of consonants – Moroccan, piccalilli, radicchio, focaccia, carpaccio, cinnamon, Taleggio, Mediterranean, Caribbean, even broccoli have a perverse tendency to appear with the wrong one doubled, and sometimes an extra one thrown in just in case. Accents are annoying too. If you haven't learned at school, or aren't actually French, what on earth is the difference between the grave and acute, where does the circumflex go? (And don't even talk to me about a cedilla or a diaeresis.) It may seem pedantic to fuss about these things, but really it's no more so than being pedantic about wanting the cooking to be done properly – and that's a different thing from being anal about measuring quantities to the last gram.

Anyway, it can certainly pay to avoid solecisms of this kind. London's most feared restaurant critic is quick to point them out, and a rap on the knuckles will also swiftly follow errors of grammar, particularly tautologies. Happy the reviewee who escapes without a 'sic' or an 'otiose', although the latter can equally describe what's on the plate as descriptions on the menu. Thank goodness for us non-Arabs there are some friendly names to give us a breathing space – words like hummus, tabbouleh, b'stilla, caldareida, skordalia seem to have no definitive form, which is probably just as well, although there are a few stinkers around like esquixadas (Portuguese salt cod salad) and salchichón (Spanish sausage) to trip you up. Still, who's to know?

The alert restaurateur or manager also has to have an eye open for the infiltration of kitchen expressions. We restaurateurs know what an 'anglaise' is, but it's a bit presumptuous to assume you do, as in 'steamed marmalade pudding with orange anglaise'; who or what is celeriac Anna, dauphinoise rosemary, vegetable boulangère, or a balantine – is it a ballottine, a galantine, or trying to be both at the same time? Chefs can't be blamed for this, any more than bricklayers can for not being architects.

I don't expect my chefs to get their tongues around shoritho or morthilla but my waiting staff must, just as my wine servers and managers must know how to pronounce Pago de Carraovejas or Rais Baixas, Roero Arneis or Pacherenc du Vic-bilh. Wine lists now are a million miles away from the days when the burning issue was how to pronounce 'Bollinger'. Not only are wines characterized by style and variety; wine lists have to give the country, area, domaine, vineyard, alcoholic strength, time in oak or stainless steel, type of oak, phase of the moon, when the malolactic finished, name of grower/winemaker, how many croissants he had for breakfast. I exaggerate only slightly. In fact, wine lists, like everything else in modern life, are becoming more and more complicated, but wine is becoming better and better – except perhaps in Bordeaux, where there is very little value for money. There's no excuse now for not having a decent list, although it would be nice if you, the public, would be a bit more experimental and put your trust in conscientious restaurateurs. We've been exploring those areas in south-west France, with obscure names like Marcillac, Pécharmant and Montravel, producing wonderful wines at affordable prices. You should too. Isn't it nice to know how much work we're doing on your behalf?

Restaurant Rage

Talking of marinated customers (see previous page) there have been quite a few whom I would have liked to pickle in vinegar, impale on skewers or give a thorough gratinating, for although most restaurant-goers are out for a good time there are quite a lot who wish they were somewhere else and make it plain from the start that nothing is going to make them happy. Tyrannizing the waiters because you want to impress a client or a girlfriend or because you are ill at ease in an unfamiliar environment and are busy overcompensating are the kinds of behaviour we amateur psychologists encounter all the time, but that doesn't make it any less tiresome. Rejecting a perfectly good bottle of wine or sending food back unnecessarily may be signs of a childhood deprived of security and approval but costs money and can lead to scenes of bloody attrition if a Stand Must Be Made. I very nearly became involved in litigation with a customer who insisted his rib-eye steak was no such thing, and had to be shown the meat in the kitchen before he would agree. Unfortunately, it turned out to be first cut from the only tough rib-eye I had ever received, so it had been sent back. One thing led to another and eventually the police turned up. This piece of nonsense fizzled out after a few lawyers' letters but created a lot of stress for nothing. The worst thing possible had happened, of course: the customer had been proved wrong. Things were bound to go downhill after that.

The evolution of restaurant culture has distorted what once was properly a restorative process into one where more demanding norms apply which provide new kinds of social pressure. Good food and wine are only part of the mix these days: sharing the same space as 'celebrities' (and I don't mean the chefs), trying to reinforce one's self-worth by going to the 'right' places, engaging in mental combat with arrogant maîtres d' (and loath as I am to admit it, they do exist), fretting over the right outfit to wear or over whether the service might be too slow – eating out will soon be up there on the 'life's most stressful' list. It's not really any wonder that customers can be fraught. I've seen a minor opera critic literally stamp his foot in rage because he thought he wasn't being given a good enough table. I've seen customers lose their temper because their wine wasn't being poured for them (in one of my places) and do the same because it was (somewhere else). In one of mine two adjacent sets of customers complained because the air conditioning was too cold for one lot, and when turned off it became too hot for the others. After some interesting exchanges of views, *both* tables made an early departure. One man's charming and attentive waiter is another's intensive, over-familiar nuisance. One man's rapacious, hustling and condescending sommelier is another's helpful, polite and thoughtful adviser.

In restaurants, as in life at large, you can't please everybody, but it's a pity the British don't have a more straightforward and enlightened attitude to eating instead of being bothered by their position in the pecking order and becoming ever more demanding and difficult. Having said that, most customers are very civilized – it's just that the unpleasant ones are becoming more unpleasant. There's a restaurant run by a Brit in London where you can have a massage after your sushi; perhaps we'll all have this 'dedicated facility' soon – but will it be enough?

Nasty Moments: 4

When I bought it, my Marylebone restaurant was one of the only two Kosher Chinese restaurants in London (which possibly was why it was for sale). The first time my little band of shareholders convened for me to show them our exciting new premises, we found the locks changed and a sign on the front door announcing that the lease had been forfeit. As we had just paid £160,000 for it we were rather alarmed; although we weren't quite sure what forfeit meant we knew it sounded sinister. We were aware the restaurant business was risky, but we thought this was taking risky a bit far. Panic meetings with our solicitors ending with our taking the landlord to the High Court to obtain an injunction to allow us to resume possession; this, it turned out later, had been his subtle way of bringing us to the table to negotiate a new lease at a higher rent. An unsuccessful tactic, as it happened, but one which brought to light the shortcomings of our solicitors and wasted lots of time and money in deciding whether to sue them or not. We didn't, taking silk's advice that our chances were 50:50. Nerves were pretty well racked, though.

Anyway, I rolled up to the injunction hearing at the law courts at eleven in the morning. That day there was a good eighteen-runner handicap at Newmarket, where the ground was soft, which would suit three horses I fancied strongly. Their odds would be good because of the number of runners. I had six new fivers in my pocket which I wanted to put on them to finish first, second and third – a bet called a tricast, £5 on each of six permutations. Hardly a heavy bet, but enough to make the outcome interesting. I didn't have a credit account, so couldn't place the bet by phone, but although I didn't know where the nearest betting shop was, there was plenty of time to find one as the race was the three forty-five. I thought we'd be in at eleven, and out again, win or lose, pretty soon after. In fact, there was no time set for our hearing. By one o'clock we were still waiting, by two, by three we still hadn't been called, by which time I was cursing myself for not having done a recce beforehand so I could have least have sprinted out, laid the bet, and sprinted back before the beak muttering some excuse about nerves detaining me in the men's room.

In the event three forty-five came and went, and as these things do in such circumstances (people who place bets even in a small way will know this), conviction grew that the horses – Pinctada, Burkaan and Sutosky – were bound to have come in, simply because I didn't have the money on, not because of my skill in picking the right horses. Finally at four o'clock we went before the judge, whose name, I remember thinking at the time, was completely absurd: he was Judge Judge, or given that we were in England and not Chicago, Mr Justice Judge. Mr Justice Judge found for us against the landlord, who had to pay the costs. I should have been delighted, but all I could think of were the names of those three horses up on the results screen. When I finally found a Ladbroke's near the LSE, there they were, at odds of 16–1, 14–1 and 11–1. The tricast paid £1,860 to £1, so I would have won £9,300 for the modest outlay of £30. The knowledge that our £160,000 was not now lost was far outweighed by the bitter gall of knowing my skilful exercise of knowledge, judgement and boldness had been cruelly thwarted, and that this opportunity was unlikely ever to come again. And, of course, it hasn't.

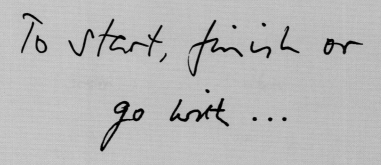

Cheese Sablés

The high fat content of these little biscuits gives them their sandy (sablé) texture. I've been serving these with drinks at Blandford Street for years. They need to be highly seasoned. It's worth making a big batch as they disappear quickly. They also freeze well.

Makes 50–60

200g plain flour
1 tsp salt
¼ tsp cayenne pepper
200g grated strong Cheddar or blue cheese
200g cold diced butter
1 egg, beaten

Put the flour, salt and cayenne pepper in the food-processor bowl, mix quickly, and add the cheese and butter. Run the motor until the mixture forms a smooth ball, taking care not to overwork the mixture (it would get too soft). Wrap in clingfilm and keep in the freezer until needed.

Preheat the oven to 375°F/190°C/Gas 5.

Use the pastry cold, a quarter at a time. Beat with a rolling pin a few times. Roll on a lightly floured board to a thickness of 2 mm. Cut into circles with a 5 cm or 6 cm cutter, or into squares. Form the trimmings into another ball, and roll out as before.

Put on a baking tray (no greasing necessary). Chill for 5 minutes and then eggwash the sablés, which helps to hold them together. Try to avoid the eggwash dripping on to the tray. Bake for about 12 minutes, until golden brown.

Pear Chutney

Excellent with hard cheeses, cold lamb or pork, and chicken liver parfait (page 98).

125g onions, finely chopped
125g sultanas
1 tbsp grated orange rind
juice of 2 oranges
300g sugar
½ tsp cinnamon
1 tsp nutmeg
1 tsp cayenne pepper
50g ginger, finely chopped
300ml white wine vinegar
1.2 tbsp salt

2 pinches of saffron
750g pears, peeled, quartered, cored and coarsely chopped
125g cooking apples, peeled, cored, and roughly chopped
250g tomatoes, peeled, seeded and diced

In a saucepan combine everything except the last three ingredients and cook gently for 30 minutes, stirring now and then. Add the fruit and tomatoes and cook for 20 minutes more, uncovered. Pour off any juice, boil down to a syrup and return to the pan. Cook and pour into clean jam jars. It's worth making quite a lot as it keeps well in the fridge.

Parmesan, Garlic and Parsley Sticks

Crunchy savoury breadsticks to go with that seven o'clock gin (or whatever you drink at seven – I hope you drink something).

6 slices of good, slightly stale, white or granary bread, 2cm thick
2 large cloves of garlic, peeled and finely chopped
40g Parmesan, finely grated
2 tbsp parsley, finely chopped
25g butter
2 tbsp olive oil
salt (if using unsalted butter)
black pepper

Preheat the oven to 375°F/190°C/Gas 5.

Cut the crusts off the bread and cut each into 5 or 6 sticks lengthways – about 2cm wide.

Combine together in a bowl the garlic, Parmesan and parsley. Melt the butter and add to the olive oil in another bowl. Using a pastry brush, coat liberally each side of the breadsticks with this mixture, and roll them individually in the parsley mix. Place on a baking sheet, season lightly, and cook for 10 minutes. Turn them over with a spatula or fish slice, season again and cook for a further 5–10 minutes, until golden brown and crisp.

These are good cold, but can be reheated if you prefer.

Manchego and Serrano Puffballs

This is another version of cheese profiteroles. I like the idea of all-Spanish or all-Italian, and I especially like the taste of sheep's milk cheese.

25g butter
4 tbsp water
50g plain flour
2 eggs
25g finely chopped ham, Serrano or Parma
25g finely grated Manchego or Pecorino
1 level tsp finely chopped shallots
salt and cayenne pepper
oil for deep frying

Bring the butter and water to the boil, remove from the heat and shove in the flour all at once, stirring hard with a wooden spoon until the mixture thickens and starts to leave the sides of the pan cleanly. Cool slightly and beat the eggs in one at a time until completely absorbed and the mixture takes on a dull shine. Add the other ingredients, allowing the salt to dissolve and checking the seasoning. A good pinch of cayenne should be enough.

Heat the oil in a saucepan until a 2cm cube of white bread turns golden brown in 60 seconds. Drop teaspoonfuls of the mixture in and cook for 4–5 minutes, removing with a slotted spoon on to kitchen paper.

These can be reheated but aren't quite as good, like most deep-fried things. Best kept hot and consumed on the spot.

Sarah Fairbairn's Bloody Mary Mix

I'd always thought Bloody Mary rather an indifferent drink (not in the same league as a Manhattan or even a Negroni), even using the best tomato juice, until Sarah brought this recipe to Blandford Street. The (small) problem is that celery seeds are quite hard to find, but you can substitute a pinch of celery salt without doing too much damage. A few drops of this mix turns Bloody Mary into a proper drink.

550ml dry sherry
3 cloves of garlic, peeled and bashed slightly
3 green chillis
1 tsp ground black pepper
1 tsp grated horseradish
a generous pinch of celery seeds (or salt)
tomato juice
vodka

Leave all the ingredients except the tomato juice and vodka in a bottle for at least 24 hours.

Put ice cubes in a tall glass, shake in a few drops of the mixture and add whatever amount of vodka and tomato juice you like, and maybe a lemon slice. I can do without. Although I hesitate to name a brand, Libby's is the one.

Parmesan Rosemary Wafers

More biscuits for drinks.

> 50g unsalted butter
> 2 scant level tsp caster sugar
> white of 1 egg
> ½ tsp salt
> 6 tbsp plain flour
> 3 tbsp grated Parmesan
> 3 tbsp rosemary, very finely chopped

Cream the butter and sugar until fluffy, add the egg white and salt, and beat at low speed for 15 seconds. Lightly fold the flour and 2 tbsp of the cheese into the mixture. Cover and chill for 30 minutes.

Preheat the oven to 400°F/205°C/Gas 6.

Roll into a cylinder about 4 cm in diameter and cut into rounds about 4 mm thick. Roll out on a floured board to a thickness of about a 10p piece. Place on a greased baking sheet, spread liberally with the rosemary and remaining Parmesan, and bake for about 10 minutes until golden brown.

Garlic Croutes

Garlic toasts, really, which in the Bull household seem to appear at weekends around 7 p.m. I think these arrived – evolved is hardly the word – when there was nothing else in the fridge one day and something had to be eaten right now. You need granary baguettes if you can find them, but any good granary or white bread will do, as long as it's not sliced. It should be a bit stale. If using a baguette, cut slices on the bias about 5 mm thick; if an ordinary loaf, cut slices of the same thickness, and stamp out rounds or just cut across diagonally in half. Remove the crusts if using an ordinary loaf. Use good olive oil and firm (i.e. juicy) garlic cloves.

Put the bread slices under the grill, but on the lowest level. Put the grill on at about half strength and dry the bread out until it starts to get crisp. Turn over to crisp the other side. Don't let it toast. Take the slices out and brush or sprinkle generously with olive oil. Peel and chop very finely several fat cloves of garlic and spread over the bread. I find each clove is good for 3–4 baguette slices. Season with salt and ground black pepper. Return them to the grill, turn the heat up, and toast them until the garlic turns a pale brown. A delicious smell will tell you when the garlic has started to feel the heat. Better watch them at this stage, as the garlic will brown quite quickly. Take them out again, sprinkle over some more olive oil, and there they are.

A slightly more sophisticated version is to mash the garlic with finely chopped green herbs – thyme, parsley, marjoram or oregano. I suppose it depends how impatient you are.

Digestive Biscuits

Blue cheese (preferably Harborne Blue or Roquefort), a good apple and a couple of digestives present an ideal combination of taste and textures which I could happily eat at any time of day. The digestives, salty and sweet at the same time, crispish but melting in the mouth, seem the perfect bridge between the salty crumbliness of the cheese and the crisp sweetness of the apple. This cosy arrangement was one of life's small pleasures until I found out, during the BSE neurosis, that 'my favourite brand' contained beef marrow. I had nothing against that, but looking at the ingredients list there, prominently, was the dreaded hydrogenated vegetable oil (page 36). As I had from time to time wondered what a home-made version might be like (surely it had to be better, even if the favourite brand was pretty good), this seemed like the moment to try.

George Harvey and I had several goes at it and ended up with this recipe, which I felt I could serve in the restaurants. Some snobbery in me prevented offering the 'f.b.' with the cheeses – I've never sold anything in my restaurants which hasn't been made on the premises (except for a really good granary bread I used to buy for one of them, which we couldn't then better).

Makes about 16 biscuits

100g oatmeal
100g wholemeal flour
45g soft light brown sugar
75g butter
½ tsp bicarbonate of soda
¾ tsp salt
3–4 tbsp milk
a good squeeze of lemon juice

Preheat the oven to 400°F/205°C/Gas 6.

Put all the dry ingredients in the food-processor bowl and run the motor for a few seconds. Add the milk and lemon juice and process for a few more seconds to make a dryish paste. Scrape out on to a floured surface (same flour) and roll out to a thickness of slightly less than the f.b. Cut out circles with an 8cm cutter, place on a sheet of buttered baking parchment or tinfoil and prick 3 or 4 times in a regular pattern with a fork. Bake for 10–12 minutes, until starting to brown at the edges. They need to be crisp.

This will make about 16 biscuits; once you have found the right balance for you between sweet and salt it's obviously worth making a double quantity. These have never lasted long enough for me to find out if they keep well or not. Sorry.

Scones

If I were to be for ever denied, as retribution for some imaginary transgression, my single favourite thing to eat, it would be the scone. Never mind chocolate cake, crème pâtissière, a cream cheese Danish (I'm giving myself away here), let alone a grey-legged partridge or a caramelized scallop, the removal of the humble scone from my diet would be a dreadful punishment. I'm not sure why this should be; the scone is, in baking terms, one of the lower invertebrates – hardly a sophisticated confection (think of gâteau opéra) – but this may be the key to its appeal. Good bread has the same sort of admirable simplicity, which can take only very limited embellishment.

I like the scone's straightforwardness, its lack of pretension (unlike this paragraph – Ed.): here I am, it seems to say, I offer nothing more than a simple pleasure, the chance to assuage a small hunger with the minimum of fuss. On these terms a good scone is a brilliant success. The addition of clotted cream and good jam has some justification but I prefer the unadorned article – and without the cream a second one isn't at all unreasonable, and a third might even come into consideration were it not for iron self-discipline. That's the real key: a scone is for ever because one can never have a surfeit of reticence . . .

Cheese and Air-Dried Tomato Scones

After my rhapsodizing over the sweet scone's simplicity, it may seem odd to include a couple of savoury recipes. But these are different articles, designed to hold another place in the scheme of things, to play a supporting role. The cheese scone can be eaten on its own, but reaches maturity as the topping for a stew or as part of a breakfast or supper dish with scrambled eggs and good bacon.

Makes 10 using a cutter

225g plain flour
2½ tsp baking powder
2 tsp salt
a large pinch of cayenne pepper
25g butter, cold, in pieces
75g grated Cheddar
3 tbsp air-dried tomatoes, soaked in water,
    covered, for 8 hours, drained (reserve
    3 tbsp of the water), and finely chopped
1 large egg
100ml milk, or slightly more
4 tbsp finely grated Parmesan, Gruyère or
    Cheddar

Preheat the oven to 425°F/220°C/Gas7.

Put the flour, baking powder, salt, cayenne pepper and butter in the bowl of a food processor, and run for 5 seconds. Remove to a large bowl and mix in the Cheddar and the tomatoes. In a small bowl, beat together with a fork the egg, reserved tomato soaking water and milk, and transfer this mixture to the larger bowl. Use the fork to make a sticky but firmish dough. Add more milk sparingly if it's too dry. Knead for 30 seconds on a floured surface and pat into a circular shape 2–3cm thick. Cut out rounds of whatever size you like, using the leftovers kneaded together quickly and patted out in the same way. Place on a lightly oiled baking sheet and sprinkle with the finely grated Parmesan, Gruyère or Cheddar. Bake for 12–15 minutes.

Onion Scones with Poached Eggs and Sweet Onion Purée

Not a dish that photographs well, but it has a rewardingly homely quality. The scones can stand on their own or be turned into sandwiches, but make an excellent supper with the addition of the light, foamy onion purée and the poached eggs.

2 tbsp duck or bacon fat, or butter
½ a large Spanish onion, finely chopped
2 tbsp leek, white and pale green part, finely sliced
225g plain flour
2 tsp baking powder
½ tsp bicarbonate of soda
½ tsp salt
50g butter, cold, cut into bits
40g grated Parmesan
200g yogurt
4 eggs

Preheat the oven to 400°F/205°C/Gas 6.

Heat the fat in a frying pan and cook the onion over medium heat, stirring often, until lightly browned. Remove the onion to a small bowl and cook the leek for 5 minutes without browning. Add to the onion.

Sift together into a large bowl the flour, baking powder, bicarbonate and salt. Transfer to a food processor and add the butter. Run the motor for 3–4 seconds (or blend the butter by hand until the mixture resembles oatmeal). Transfer back to the bowl and stir in the onion and leek mixture together with half the cheese. Mix in the yogurt but keep a little back and only add it if the mixture is very dry; the dough should be a bit sticky but not wet. Transfer to a floured surface and knead for a few seconds. Pat it out until it's about 2cm thick. Using a pastry cutter, cut out 5cm rounds and place in the oven. Bake for about 15 minutes.

To poach the eggs, pour about 10cm of water into a small saucepan and heat to simmering point. Turn the heat down a little to banish the bubbles. Crack an egg into a saucer. With a fork, make a vortex in the hot water, and slide the egg into the centre. The circular motion should wrap the white around the yolk. Poach the egg for about 4 minutes for a still-runny yolk, and remove with a slotted spoon to a hot plate. Repeat with the other eggs.

To serve, cut each scone in half horizontally. Place an egg on each base, and arrange the top to lean against the base.

Sweet Onion Purée

25g butter
150g onions, thinly sliced
a large pinch of salt
130ml hot milk

Melt the butter in a medium saucepan and cook the onions gently with the salt under a lid for 30 minutes. Tip into a liquidizer jar, pour on the milk and liquidize. Pour over the poached eggs. You could replace some of the milk with double cream if you're reckless.

Spiced Oranges

This is a simple but very good counterpoint to the chicken liver parfait (page 98) but would be very at home on a plate of sheep's cheese and/or country ham and salami. Hot black pudding, wild duck or even cold leftover lamb would go well, too, but this is one of those things that seems awfully good late at night with Cheddar cheese and several (home-made) digestive biscuits (page 217).

Enough to keep you going for a bit

6 oranges of a good size, but not huge and
   pithy
550g granulated sugar
300ml cider vinegar
½ a cinnamon stick
⅓ tsp ground cloves
6 whole cloves
2 blades mace

Wash the oranges and cut into slices about 1cm thick, discarding the end bits. Place in a large stainless-steel or enamel pan and just cover with water. Bring to the boil and simmer gently for 40 minutes.

Preheat the oven to 275°F/130°C/Gas 1.

Drain off the water. In a separate, oven-going pan boil together the sugar, vinegar and spices for 10 minutes. Add the oranges, cover with greaseproof paper, and cook in the oven for around 4 hours. The oranges should become very soft and translucent.

Meanwhile prepare 3 clean jam jars or a litre Kilner jar and their lids. Sterilize them by placing in a wide pan or on a rack of some kind, covering with cold water and bringing this to the boil. Continue boiling for 5 minutes, then drain, but do not dry them. Invert them on to the rack to drain. Do this fairly soon before use. Thirty minutes before filling, place the jars and lids in the oven. This will sterilize them and prevent them cracking as they are filled.

Pack the oranges into the jars, filling them to the tops, and seal. Store for 2–3 weeks before using; this and similar pickles are best used within a month after opening. Keep in the fridge unless you use Kilner jars or self-sealing lids.

Serve them as they are or drain them, chop roughly, and mix with some of the syrup, as a sort of runny marmalade.

Never a Dull Moment

One thing about opening and running restaurants is that you never fall into a comfortable or boring routine (depending on how you look at it). Opening them is always exciting because you are sustained by a vision of restaurant perfection, all the obstacles en route merely the steps necessary to the realization of this vision: an efficient machine for turning base metals into gold, for generating delight and well-being in the customer, for pleasurably oiling the wheels of commerce, and for lining the pockets of the owner (hang on – how did that get in?).

Running them is exciting because a) no day is ever like another and b) every day brings new hope that *this* will be the day when everything does work perfectly and customers can walk out saying, 'Well, that was great.' Of course, one doesn't want this degree of achievement to happen every day, because life would soon become too predictable: perfection does need the occasional blemish just to underline its perfectness, if nothing else. I think this is why I never got much of a thrill from eating in three-star restaurants, where the performance is so practised, back and front of house, that the only real excitement comes from wondering how big the bill's going to be. Perhaps it's just that at this level, because all the systems are so seamless, a bit of electricity and tension has gone out of the air.

There's never been much danger of that happening in my own places, especially when the menu changes twice a day, and you're never *quite* sure that a) all the cooks will turn up and b) the mise en place will all be ready on time. In fact, they nearly always do, and it always is (now that I'm no longer head chef, anyway), and I've found that the stimulus of dealing with what the 'market' throws up (if you'll excuse the phrase) produces cooking with more zest than sticking to the same things for weeks at a time. This in turn involves front-of-house staff in daily briefings to mobilize their faculties and bring that gleam of purpose and concentration to their eye. It's certainly true that far more mistakes happen when pressure on staff is low, presumably because the mild stresses of the kitchen wondering if everyone is going to arrive at once, and out front the waiters trying to remember dish descriptions and which ice creams and cheeses are on today, have the effect of getting the adrenalin going and generally sharpening up the faculties.

This daily changing tableau is enough to keep the proprietor interested, too, but other things come along to provide diversion – apart from all the machines that are just waiting to blow a fuse, pop a bearing, expire in a cloud of ozone or spring a leak, and the customers, mercifully few, who have hidden allergies, low alcohol tolerance or the odd seizure.

Mice, for example. Twice these ingenious creatures have tried to commit suicide by jumping off the mezzanine floor at Smithfield, each time (of course) during lunch. (Neither was successful – they just staggered around until rescued by a caring waiter. And not a single customer jumped up on the table, to their credit.) I hasten to say I don't have a mouse problem, and these incidents happened years apart, but there are so many old buildings in London constantly being rebuilt that the mouse population must be constantly on the move. I caught a rat once, with kitchen tongs, when his home next door was being excavated to make my new bar. This excavation, in an old sausage-making factory (we are in Smithfield, after all) exposed a three-foot high heap of putrefied pigs' intestines which produced a stink that can have been only a bit less toxic than mustard gas.

Talking of stinks, for a year or two an unidentifiable but seriously bad one reeking of the sewer would appear and disappear for short spells, always in a different place. This peculiar phenomenon was the closest I have come to a poltergeist as there seemed be no rational explanation for it or its arrival or its ultimate disappearance.

Now that I am running a pub in Herefordshire, I hope life will be a bit more predictable: my staff don't have to use public transport, no-shows are mercifully few, neighbours are less likely to be difficult, madmen or dodgy characters with bulging suitcases are less likely to stray in off the street – but I do have a septic tank with a complicated pumping system, and the River Wye is only a small sandbag's throw away . . .

Recipe Index

all-purpose dressing 33
allspice and orange, in braised rabbit in red wine
    160
almond
    and apple pudding with Calvados cream 181
    and apricots with lamb tagine and a raisin
        couscous 134
    feta and fennel soup 64
    pastry 94
    and semolina cake 187
    and watercress soup 57
anchoïade 34
anchovies
    with aubergines and garlic 41
    and basil, with paupiettes of pork 148
    and capers, in beef stew 157
    cream, with haricot bean and sweet pepper
        salad 75
    garlic and lemon, with red mullet 118
    sauce, with persillade of beef 154
apple
    and almond pudding with Calvados cream 181
    and onion gratin 176
apricots and almonds with lamb tagine and a raisin
    couscous 134
artichokes
    globe
        asparagus and broad bean salad 69
        black pudding and wild mushrooms, with
            roast partridge 164
    Jerusalem
        soup 59
        terrine of 52
asparagus, artichoke and broad bean salad 69
aubergine with garlic and anchovies 41
avgolemono, jellied, with dill 60
avocado, cucumber and tomato salad with mustard
    and chervil 72

bagna cauda 29, 118
baked hake with cappon magro sauce 124
basil mayonnaise, with cold tomato soup 58
bavarois
    beetroot 44
    sweet pepper 46

beans
    broad
        asparagus and artichoke salad 69
        mousse 48
    cannellini, soup 60
    haricot
        purée 169
        and sweet pepper salad with anchovy
            cream 75
Béarnaise sauce 23
beef
    persillade of, with anchovy sauce 154
    rump steak hamburger 153
    stew 155–6
        with anchovies and capers 157
        with cinnamon and ginger 156
        with herb dumplings and damson cheese
            158–9
        with rum and olives 158
    with Stilton and horseradish sauce 152
beetroot
    bavarois 44
    celeriac and orange ragout 174
beurre
    blanc 26–7
    rouge 27
biscuits
    caraway 43
    cheese sablés 213
    chocolate brownie thins 198
    digestive 217
    Parmesan and rosemary wafers 216
bitter orange sauce, with roast pigeon 142–3
black pudding, artichokes and wild mushrooms,
    with roast partridge 164
Bloody Mary, Sarah Fairbairn's mix 215
bouillon, court 122–3
braised pork rolls 150
bread soldiers 41
breadsticks, Parmesan, garlic and parsley 214
bream, grilled with parsley and caper cream
    114
broad beans
    asparagus and artichoke salad 69
    mousse 48
broccoli and walnut stuffing for chicken 138–9

brown bread
 ice cream 186
 and turnip soup 63
brownies 198
browning meat 133
brunoise of fruit, with unmoulded mango soufflé
 206
bulgur salad 73
buttercream, chocolate 193
butternut squash and cornmeal cake 191

cabbage
 red, salad 74
 white, cooked with sweet peppers and onions 171
cakes
 butternut squash and cornmeal 191
 chocolate 193
 chocolate and dried fruit brownies 198
 never-a-failure 187
 pleyels 196
 semolina and almond 187
Calvados cream 181
cannellini bean soup 62
capers
 and anchovies, in beef stew 157
 and parsley cream, with grilled bream 114
 vinaigrette 35
cappon magro sauce, with baked hake 124
caramel and orange trifle 202–3
caraway
 biscuits 43
 noodles, with oxtail goulash 166
 and orange vinaigrette 35
cardamom and crab salad 70
cauliflower and Gorgonzola soup 64
celeriac, beetroot and orange ragout 174
celery à la grècque, with monkfish 103
ceviche 50
 of salmon or sea trout with passion fruit 51
chard, feta and pine nut tortilla 47
chargrilled salmon cured with orange and juniper 104
cheese
 and air-dried tomato scones 219
 cream, and black olive pâté 42
 damson 158–9
 feta
  almond and fennel soup 64
  chard and pine nut tortilla 47
  and courgette tart 87
 goat's, soufflé, twice-cooked 84

Gorgonzola and cauliflower soup 64
Manchego and Serrano puffballs 215
millefeuille of three cheeses 89
Parmesan pastry, vegetables in 80
sablés 213
cheesecake
 light lemon 190
 peanut butter 190
chervil
 and mustard, with avocado, cucumber and
  tomato salad 72
 sauce, with porcini custards 78
chestnut soup 61
chicken
 breasts stuffed with broccoli and walnuts
  138–9
 livers 93
  marjolaine of 94–5
  mousse, cold 96
  mousse, hot 95
  parfait 98
 poached
  with lemon and tarragon 140
  with walnut sauce 139
 with prunes, pine nuts and sausage 136
 stock 37
chickpea
 pancakes 170
 pork and chorizo stew 151
 walnut and cumin salad 72
 and walnut purée 170
chocolate
 brownie thins 198
 cake 193
 chip macaroons 199
 and dried fruit brownies 198
 and hazelnut tart 194
 and juniper, with saddle of venison 162
 mousse tart in hazelnut orange pastry 195
 pleyels 196
 praline ice cream 185
 pud, just about the quickest possible 196
 soufflés 199
chorizo
 pork and chickpea stew 151
 and potato gratin 176–7
choux paste 106
chutney, pear 214
cinnamon
 and orange, in beef stew 156
 prunes and orange, in duck stew 146–7

cod
>   home-salted salt, with ginger and tomatoes
>   112
>   with wilted rocket and hazelnut butter 108
Cointreau cream, with strawberries 205
cold chicken liver mousse 96
cold lemon soufflé 207
cold tomato soup with basil mayonnaise 58
concassé of tomatoes 122–3
coriander and sesame seed dressing 33
corn and courgette fry-up 175
cornmeal
>   and butternut squash cake 191
>   orange dumplings, with venison and star anise
>   sauce 163
courgettes
>   and corn fry-up 175
>   and feta tart with nut topping 87
>   grated with cream and basil 174
court bouillon 122–3
couscous, raisin, with lamb tagine 134
crab and cardamom salad 70
cream cheese and black olive pâté 42
creamy mustard dressing 34
croutes, garlic 216
cucumber
>   avocado and tomato salad with mustard and
>   chervil 72
>   dill and horseradish, with steamed plaice 107
>   tzatziki 135
cumin, chickpea and walnut salad 72
curried lentils with smoked haddock 115
custards
>   garlic 175
>   leek and mushroom 77
>   porcini, with chervil sauce 78

damson cheese and herb dumplings, with beef stew
>   158–9
digestive biscuits 217
dill
>   cucumber and horseradish, with steamed plaice
>   107
>   with jellied avgolemono 60
dressings
>   all-purpose 33
>   anchoïade 34
>   caper vinaigrette 35
>   creamy mustard 34

general 22, 32
ginger vinaigrette 35
green herb 33
green peppercorn vinaigrette 34
mustard and chervil 72
orange caraway vinaigrette 35
sesame seed and coriander 33
dried fruit and chocolate brownies 198
duck
>   roast, with limes 144–6
>   skin, walnut and orange salad 71
>   stew with cinnamon, prunes and orange 146–7
dumplings
>   cornmeal orange 163
>   herb 158–9
>   porcini 79

eggs
>   feta, chard and pine nut tortilla 47
>   omelette Arnold Bennett 127
>   poached, with sweet onion purée and onion
>   scones 220

fennel
>   feta and almond soup 64
>   with saffron and orange 172
feta
>   almond and fennel soup 64
>   chard and pine nut tortilla 47
>   and courgette tart with nut topping 87
figs, marinated 205
fish 101–2
>   bream, grilled with parsley and caper cream
>   114
>   ceviche 50
>   cod
>   home-salted salt, with ginger and tomatoes
>   112
>   with wilted rocket and hazelnut butter 108
>   haddock, smoked
>   with curried lentils 115
>   in omelette Arnold Bennett 127
>   hake, baked with cappon magro sauce 124
>   halibut fillet with aromatic vegetables and soft
>   herbs 110
>   mackerel, with orange juice and breadcrumbs
>   111
>   monkfish with celery à la grècque 103

nage of seafood with ginger and saffron 126
pie with a gougère top 104–5
plaice, steamed, with cucumber, dill and
horseradish 107
quenelles, gratinated 108–9
red mullet
fillets with red lentil salsa 119
with garlic, anchovies and lemon 118
salmon
in ceviche, with passion fruit 51
cured with orange and juniper, chargrilled
104
escalopes with marinière sauce 122–3
sea trout, in ceviche, with passion fruit 51
skate wing with romesco stuffing 120
stock 38
tuna
steak with sweet peppers, tomatoes and lime
116
tartare of 51
frangipani, in pithiviers 184
fritters, split pea 86

gammon 54
garlic
anchovies and lemon, with red mullet 118
croutes 216
custards 175
Parmesan and parsley sticks 214
ginger
and saffron, with nage of seafood 126
and sweet pepper soup 58
and tomatoes, with home-salted salt cod 112
vinaigrette 35
gluten-free recipes 181, 191, 193, 196, 198, 199,
202–3
gnocchi
pumpkin 83
semolina, with porcini cream 82
goat's cheese soufflé, twice-cooked 84
Gorgonzola and cauliflower soup 64
gougère topping, fish pie with 104–5
goulash, oxtail, with caraway noodles 166
grated courgettes with cream and basil 174
gratin
of apple and onion 176
of fish quenelles 108–9
of potato and chorizo 176–7
green herb dressing 33

green peppercorn vinaigrette 34
grilled bream with parsley and caper cream 114

haddock, smoked
with curried lentils 115
in omelette Arnold Bennett 127
hake, baked with cappon magro sauce 124
halibut fillet with aromatic vegetables and soft herbs
110
ham, jellied 54
hamburger, rump steak 153
haricot beans
purée 169
and sweet pepper salad with anchovy cream 75
hazelnut
butter, with cod and wilted rocket 108
and chocolate tart 194
and orange pastry, chocolate mousse tart in 195
herb dumplings and damson cheese, with beef stew
158–9
hollandaise sauce 23–4
home-salted salt cod with ginger and tomatoes 112
horseradish
cucumber and dill, with steamed plaice 107
and Stilton sauce, with beef 152
hot chicken liver mousse 95
hummus 43

ice cream
brown bread 186
chocolate praline 185

jellied avgolemono with dill 60
jellied ham 54
Jerusalem artichokes
soup 59
terrine of 52
juniper
chargrilled salmon cured with orange and 104
and chocolate, with saddle of venison 162
just about the quickest possible chocolate pud 196

lamb
spiced sauté with tzatziki 135
tagine with apricots and almonds and a raisin
couscous 134

latkes, potato 177
leek and mushroom custards 77
lemon
    cheesecake, light 190
    garlic and anchovies, with red mullet 118
    soufflé, cold 207
    and tarragon, with poached chicken 140
lentils
    curried, with smoked haddock 115
    red, salsa of, with red mullet fillets 119
    and vinegar, with mixed livers 141
light lemon cheesecake 190
limes
    in ceviche 50
    parfait 202
    with roast duck 144–6
    sweet peppers and tomatoes, with tuna steak
        116
livers
    chicken 93–8
    mixed, with lentils and vinegar 141

macaroons
    chocolate chip 199
    peaches stuffed with 204
mackerel with orange juice and breadcrumbs 111
Manchego and Serrano puffballs 215
mango
    salsa 30
    soufflé, unmoulded, with brunoise of fruit 206
maple pecan pudding, steamed 183
marinades for beef 155–6
marinated figs 205
marinière sauce, with salmon escalopes 122–3
marjolaine of chicken livers 94–5
mayonnaise, basil, with cold tomato soup 58
meat 133–66
milassou 191
millefeuille of three cheeses 88
mixed livers with lentils and vinegar 141
monkfish with celery à la grècque 103
mousse
    broad bean 48
    chocolate, in tart 195
    cold chicken liver 96
    hot chicken liver 95
mushrooms
    and leek custards 77
    porcini

cream, with semolina gnocchi 82
custards with chervil sauce 78
dumplings 79
wild, artichokes and black pudding, with roast
        partridge 164
mustard
    and chervil, with avocado, cucumber and tomato
        salad 72
    dressing, creamy 34

nage of seafood with ginger and saffron 126
never-a-failure cake 187
nivernaise sauce 25
noodles, caraway 166
nut topping for courgette and feta tart 87

oils 22, 32
olives
    black, and cream cheese pâté 42
    and rum, in beef stew 158
omelette
    Arnold Bennett 127
    soufflée 188
onion
    and apple gratin 176
    scones with poached eggs and sweet onion purée
        220
orange
    and allspice, in braised rabbit in red wine 160
    and caramel trifle 202–3
    caraway vinaigrette 35
    celeriac and beetroot ragout 174
    chargrilled salmon cured with juniper and 104
    and cinnamon, in beef stew 156
    duck skin and walnut salad 71
    and hazelnut pastry 195
    juice, and breadcrumbs, with mackerel 111
    prunes and cinnamon, in duck stew 146–7
    pudding, Seville 182
    and saffron, with fennel 172
    sauce, bitter, with roast pigeon 142–3
    spiced 221
oxtail goulash with caraway noodles 166

pancakes
    chickpea 170
    latkes 177

papaya salsa 30
parfait
    chicken liver 98
    lime 202
Parmesan
    garlic and parsley sticks 214
    pastry, vegetables in 80
    and rosemary wafers 216
parsley
    and caper cream, with grilled bream 114
    Parmesan and garlic sticks 214
partridge, roast, with black pudding, artichokes and
        wild mushrooms 164
passion fruit, in ceviche of salmon or sea trout 51
pastry
    almond 94, 194
    choux 106
    cream 203
    hazelnut orange 195
    Parmesan 80
pâté, cream cheese and black olive 42
paupiettes of pork with anchovies and basil 148
peaches
    with strawberry cream 204
    stuffed with macaroons 204
peanut butter cheesecake 190
pear chutney 214
peas, split, fritters 86
pecan
    butter tart 200
    and maple pudding, steamed 183
peppercorns, green, vinaigrette 34
peppers, sweet
    cooked with white cabbage and onions 171
    bavarois 46
    and ginger soup 58
    and haricot bean salad with anchovy cream
        75
    tomatoes and lime, with tuna steak 116
persillade of beef with anchovy sauce 154
pigeon, roast, with bitter orange sauce 142–3
pine nuts
    feta and chard tortilla 47
    prunes and sausage with chicken 136
pineapple salsa 30
piping bags 106
pithiviers 184
pizzas, salami and sour cream 143
plaice, steamed, with cucumber, dill and horseradish
    107

pleyels – little chocolate cakes 196
poached chicken
    with lemon and tarragon 140
    with walnut sauce 139
porcini
    cream, with semolina gnocchi 82
    custards with chervil sauce 78
    dumplings 79
pork
    chorizo and chickpea stew 151
    jellied ham 54
    paupiettes, with anchovies and basil 148
    rolls, braised 150
potato
    and chorizo gratin 176–7
    latkes 177
praline ice cream, chocolate 185
prunes
    orange and cinnamon, in duck stew 146–7
    pine nuts and sausage with chicken 136
puddings 181–4
pumpkin gnocchi 83
purées
    chickpea and walnut 170
    haricot bean 169
    sweet onion 220

quenelles, fish, gratinated 108–9

rabbit braised in red wine with orange and allspice
    160
raisin couscous, with lamb tagine 134
red cabbage salad 74
red lentil salsa, with red mullet fillets 119
red mullet
    fillets with red lentil salsa 119
    with garlic, anchovies and lemon 118
resting meat 133
roast duck with limes 144–6
roast partridge with black pudding, artichokes and
        wild mushrooms 164
roast pigeon with bitter orange sauce 142–3
rocket, wilted, with cod and hazelnut butter 108
romesco sauce 28
romesco stuffing, with skate wing 120
rosemary and Parmesan wafers 216
rum and olives, in beef stew 158
rump steak hamburger 153

sablés, cheese 213
saddle of venison with juniper and chocolate 162
saffron
    and ginger, with nage of seafood 126
    and orange, with fennel 172
salad dressings *see* dressings
salads
    asparagus, artichoke and broad bean 69
    avocado, cucumber and tomato, with mustard
        and chervil 72
    bulgur 73
    chickpea, walnut and cumin 72
    crab and cardamom 70
    duck skin, walnut and orange 71
    haricot bean and sweet pepper with anchovy
        cream 75
    red cabbage 74
salami and sour cream pizzas 143
salmon
    in ceviche, with passion fruit 51
    cured with orange and juniper, chargrilled 104
    escalopes with marinière sauce 122–3
salsas 21–2
    mango 30
    papaya 30
    pineapple 30
    red lentil, with red mullet fillets 119
    tomato 31
salt cod, home-salted, with ginger and tomatoes 112
Sarah Fairbairn's Bloody Mary mix 215
sauces 21
    anchovy 154
    bagna cauda 29
    Béarnaise 23
    beurre blanc 26–7
    beurre rouge 27
    brunoise of fruit 206
    cappon magro 124
    chervil 78
    hollandaise 23–4
    marinière 122–3
    nivernaise 25
    orange 142–3
    romesco 28
    star anise 163
    Stilton and horseradish 152
    tomato 27
    turnip cream 29
    velouté 109
    walnut 139

sausage, pine nuts and prunes with chicken 136
scones
    cheese and air-dried tomato 219
    general 218
    onion, with poached eggs and sweet onion
        purée 220
sea trout, in ceviche, with passion fruit 51
semolina
    and almond cake 187
    gnocchi with porcini cream 82
Serrano and Manchego puffballs 215
sesame seed and coriander dressing 33
Seville orange pudding 182
shellfish
    crab and cardamom salad 70
    nage of seafood with ginger and saffron
        126
skate wing with romesco stuffing 120
smoked haddock
    with curried lentils 115
    in omelette Arnold Bennett 127
soufflés
    chocolate 199
    cold lemon 207
    mango, unmoulded 206
    omelette 188
    twice-cooked goat's cheese 84
soup
    cannellini bean 62
    cauliflower and Gorgonzola 64
    chestnut 60
    cold tomato, with basil mayonnaise 58
    feta, almond and fennel 64
    jellied avgolemono with dill 60
    Jerusalem artichoke 59
    sweet pepper and ginger 58
    turnip and brown bread 63
    watercress and almond 57
sour cream and salami pizzas 143
spiced lamb sauté with tzatziki 135
spiced oranges 221
split pea fritters 86
squash, butternut, and cornmeal cake 191
star anise sauce, with venison and cornmeal orange
    dumplings 163
starters
    cold 41–54
    hot 77–89
steak, rump, in hamburgers 153
steamed maple pecan pudding 183

steamed plaice with cucumber, dill and horseradish
107
Stilton and horseradish sauce, with beef 152
stock
    chicken 37
    fish 38
    general 36–7
    meat 38
strawberries with Cointreau cream 205
strawberry cream, with peaches 204
stuffing
    broccoli and walnut 138–9
    romesco, with skate wing 120
sweet peppers
    bavarois 46
    and ginger soup 58
    and haricot bean salad with anchovy cream 75
    and onions, cooked with white cabbage 171
    tomatoes and lime, with tuna steak 116

tabbouleh 73
tagine, lamb, with apricots and almonds and a raisin
    couscous 134
tarragon and lemon, with poached chicken 140
tartare of tuna 51
tarts
    chocolate and hazelnut 194
    chocolate mousse in hazelnut orange pastry 195
    courgette and feta, with nut topping 87
    pecan butter 200
terrine, Jerusalem artichokes 52
tomatoes
    air-dried, and cheese scones 219
    avocado and cucumber salad with mustard and
        chervil 72
    concassé of 122–3
    and ginger, with home-salted salt cod 112
    salsa 31
    sauce 27
    soup, cold, with basil mayonnaise 58
    sweet peppers and lime, with tuna steak 116

tortilla, feta, chard and pine nut 47
trifle, orange and caramel 202–3
tuna
    steak with sweet peppers, tomatoes and lime 116
    tartare of 51
turnip
    and brown bread soup 63
    cream sauce 29
twice-cooked goat's cheese soufflé 84
tzatziki, with spiced lamb sauté 135

unmoulded mango soufflé with brunoise of fruit
206

vegetables 169–77
    aromatic, with halibut fillet and soft herbs 110
    in Parmesan pastry 80
velouté sauce 109
venison
    saddle, with juniper and chocolate 162
    with star anise sauce and cornmeal orange
        dumplings 163
vinaigrettes *see* dressings
vinegar 22, 32
    with mixed livers and lentils 141

walnut
    chickpea and cumin salad 72
    and chickpea purée 170
    duck skin and orange salad 71
    sauce with poached chicken 139
watercress and almond soup 57
white cabbage cooked with sweet peppers and
    onions 171
wild mushrooms, artichokes and black pudding,
    with roast partridge 164

General Index

Abergavenny 1
   Food Festival 191
adrenalin, boosts staff performance 222
advertising, S.B.'s career in 2–3
air-handling units 90–1
ambience, restaurant 65
American cooking 12
Anderson, John 6
art, cooking as 15–16

banks, S.B.'s relations with 9, 56
Beeton, Mrs 134
Bemelmans, Ludwig 2
Bentham, Jon 200
Blanc, Georges 122
Blanc, Raymond 15
Blandford Street, S.B.'s restaurant, see Bull, Stephen,
      restaurants
Bon Appetit 200
bovine spongiform encephalopathy see BSE
British culinary tradition 12
BSE 217
buildings, adapting for restaurant use 90–2
Bull, Stephen
      advertising career 2–3
      childhood 1
      commis waiter at Odin's 3–5
      cooking philosophy 12–15
      culinary influences 1, 12
      daughter's coeliac disease 19
      favourite flavours 15, 218
      and horse racing 211–12
      learns to cook 5–6
      love-hate relationship with restaurants vi, 222–3
      restaurants
            Blandford Street 8, 10, 39, 40, 55, 91, 192, 211
            Fulham Road 9, 39, 40, 128–32
            Lichfield's 7–8, 29, 39, 67, 91, 99, 179–80
            Llanrwst 5–7, 39, 76, 178–9
            Lough Pool Inn 11
            St Martin's Lane 9–10, 91
            Smithfield 8–9, 10, 67–8, 90, 222–3
      son's intolerance of HVO 36–7
      tires of working in London 10
butchers 17

Caprice (restaurant) 90
celebrities in restaurants 66, 210
chairs, faulty 129–30
chefs
      S.B. speaks at conference of 192
      volatile 130–1, 132
chips, S.B.'s attitude to 6
clichés, foods which become 13
Complete Guide to the Art of Modern Cooking (Escoffier)
      26
Condon, Richard 2–3
Connaught (restaurant) 90
Conran, Terence 90
Conwy, River 39
cooking, art or science 15–16
Coq d'Or (restaurant) 90
Costa, Margaret 12
Crockfords (casino) 56
Cuisine Gourmande (Guérard) 23
culinary influences on S.B. 1, 12
customers
      bad behaviour by 209–10
      complaints 55, 209–10
      media influence on 13
      no-shows 167–8
      perception of quality 65

David, Elizabeth 12, 25, 99, 144, 188
design, restaurant 90–2, 131
Dordogne Gastronomique (Jones) 191
Down and Out in London and Paris (Orwell) 2, 178
drains, problems with 39–40

Empress (restaurant) 90
Escoffier 26, 59, 188
European culinary tradition 12, 14

fashions, food 13
Fine English Cooking (Smith) 63
fish
      buying and storing 17–18
      dwindling stocks of 101
fishmongers 17

flavours
    latitude and the successful blend of 14
    S.B.'s favourite 15, 218
food
    allergies 76
    fashions 13
    poisoning 76
    pronunciation of 209
Freeling, Nicholas 2
French cuisine
    influence on S.B. 12
    mystique of 26
French Provincial Cooking (David) 25, 188
fruit, how to select 18
Fulham Road, S.B.'s restaurant, *see* Bull, Stephen,
    restaurants
furnishings, restaurant 129–30, 131
fusion cooking 14

George, Mike 6
gluten-free recipes, S.B.'s interest in 19, 191
Good Food Guide 7, 67
Good Things (Grigson) 184
Gorman, Roger 164
Grigson, Jane 12, 184
Guérard, Michel 23

Haroutunian, Arto 134
Harvey, George 185, 190, 194, 217
Herefordshire 10–11, 223
horse racing, S.B.'s interest in 211–12
HVO *see* hydrogenated vegetable oil
hydrogenated vegetable oil 36–7, 217

ice cream, real 1
India, influence on British cooking 12
industrial tribunal, restaurant manager takes S. B. to
    132
ingredients 17–18
    quality of 13
    store cupboard 13
    symbiotic relationship 14
innovation, pressure for 13
Italian cuisine, influence on S.B. 12

Jones, Vicky 191
junk food, S.B.'s attitude to 37, 153
kitchen
    porters 178–80
    temperatures 91
    ventilation 90–1, 129
Kitchen Book (Freeling) 2
Kromberg, Peter 84

Ladenis, Nico 3
landlord, litigation with 211
Langan, Peter 3–5, 205
Langan's (restaurant) 90
L'Art Culinaire (Escoffier) 59
latitude, influence on successful blend of flavours 14
L'Ecu de France (restaurant) 90
Lewis, Danny 104
Lichfield's, S.B.'s restaurant, *see* Bull, Stephen,
    restaurants
Llanrwst, S.B.'s restaurant, *see* Bull, Stephen,
    restaurants
Locatelli, Giorgio 150
Lough Pool Inn, S.B.'s restaurant, *see* Bull, Stephen,
    restaurants

Ma Cuisine (Escoffier) 59
Ma Cuisine (restaurant) 91–2
McGee, Harold 25
Maison du Chocolat 196
Maschler, Fay 131
Mastering the Art of French Cooking 5, 12
Mayle, Peter 2
Mazère, Roland 15, 16
Meades, Jonathan 9, 128
measurements 19
meat, buying and storing 17–18
media influence on restaurant-going public 13
menu writing 208–9
    in French 8
mice 222–3
Michelin 8
    Red M 6–7
    stars 7, 130, 131
Milan, S.B. visits 2
Mirabelle (restaurant) 90
monosodium glutamate 36–7
Mr Poon 90
MSG *see* monosodium glutamate

naming restaurants 128–9
no-shows 167–8
Norman, Philip 4
nouvelle cuisine 8

Odin's (restaurant) 3, 4, 5, 205
Olivetti 2
On Food and Cooking (McGee) 25
Orwell, George 2, 178

Pacific Rim cuisine 12, 14
peasant food 13
Perry-Smith, George 134
planning permission for restaurant use 9
planning regulations 91
porters, kitchen 178–80
power cuts, S.B.'s problems with 40, 130
produce *see* ingredients
profit margins 130, 131, 167
pronunciation of foods and wines 209
Prunier (restaurant) 90

rats 223
restaurant staff
    benefits of adrenalin on 222
    chefs, volatile 130–1, 132
    effect of serving the 'boss' on 66–7
    kitchen porters 178–80
    S.B.'s dificulties with 130–2, 192
    shortages 99
restaurants
    ambience 65
    design 90–2, 131
    furnishings 129–30, 131
    naming 128–9
    planning permission for 9
    S.B.'s *see under* Bull, Stephen
    space allocation in 90–2
restaurateurs
    dining in their own restaurants 66–7
    rewards and problems of vi
risotto milanese, turning point in S.B.'s career 2
Roberts, Emrys 6
Roden, Claudia 134
Ronay, Egon 68

St Martin's Lane, S.B.'s restaurant, *see* Bull, Stephen,
    restaurants
science, cooking an inexact 15–16
scones (S.B.'s favourite food) 218
Scrutton, Marion 40
shopping 17–18
smells, bad 223
Smith, Frances 17
Smith, Michael 63
Smith, Peter Glynn 91
Smithfield, S.B.'s restaurant, *see* Bull, Stephen,
    restaurants
snails 76
soy sauce 13
space allocation and constraints, restaurant 90–2
spelling, on menus 208
spices, buying and storing 18
staff *see* restaurant staff
stock cubes 13, 36
store cupboard ingredients 13
supermarkets 17–18

tapénade 8
temperatures, kitchen 91
truffles, white 2
Turin, S.B. visits 2

vegetables, how to select 18
ventilation, kitchen 90–1, 129
Vergé, Roger 26
Virgile and Stone (designers) 10

Wallace Collection courtyard restaurant 10
water, S.B.'s disasters with 39–40, 99, 130, 223
White, Marco-Pierre 128
white truffles 2
Williams, Betty 178–9
wine cellar, flooded at Llanrwst 39
wine lists 209
wines, pronunciation of 209
Winner, Michael 129
Wolfert, Paula 134

Zafferano (restaurant) 150